Peace Comes Dropping Slow

By the Same Author

Earth and Water: Encounters in Viet Nam

Peace Comes Dropping Slow

Conversations in Northern Ireland

Edith Shillue

University of Massachusetts Press

Amherst and Boston

LC 2002010177
ISBN 1-55849-368-9

Designed by Dean Bornstein
Set in Fournier and Gill Sans by Graphic Composition, Inc.
Printed and bound by The Maple-Vail Book Manufacturing Group.

Library of Congress Cataloging-in-Publication Data

Shillue, Edith, 1963 –
   Peace comes dropping slow : conversations in Northern Ireland / Edith Shillue.
   p. cm.
   ISBN 1-55849-368-9 (alk. paper)
   1. Northern Ireland—Description and travel.   2. Shillue, Edith, 1963—
Journeys—Northern   Ireland.   3.   Northern   Ireland—Social   conditions.
4. Peace movements—Northern Ireland.   5. Social conflict—Northern Ireland.
I. Title.
   DA990.U46 S53 2003
   914.1604'824—dc21

                                                          2002010177

British Library Cataloguing in Publication data are available.

For Mother, who enjoyed a good laugh and on whom nothing was lost.

Contents

Forewarned

It was an idea that bordered on the comical, but I had it: Write about Northern Ireland but don't write about politics or "the Troubles." No doubt I'm not the first outsider to be curious about this place apart from its politics, its everyday life built amid the fury of civil war. Ireland, however, does not suffer fools gladly. So intertwined are daily life, politics, and violence that it is not fair to any reader to pull at a few colorful threads and leave the rest of the tapestry untouched. As a result, the immediate context of the Troubles is presented to the reader with an explanation (however limited my understanding), and the larger historical context is referred to as necessary. My own political views will become apparent, but like so many, I am weary of that talk and confess to happily, creatively, and, I hope, comically dodging the issue.

By way of warning, however, I ask the reader to remember that everything has its vocabulary. Northern Ireland is no different. In fact, it is famed for the debate over what words to use in reference to the place itself and what the use of those words reveals about one's allegiance.

In a land of poets, storytellers, and musicians, words and their sounds are everything. In Ireland, they are so powerful that to withhold them is an aggressive act or, as I think, a cruel weapon. The Irish are notorious both for the power of their words and the power of their silence. In Northern Ireland, words are especially powerful, and everyday language is layered with multiple meanings that the traveler can only glimpse. The double entendre is a complex art built by this wordy society, and an outsider writing about the population is invariably stepping on someone's toes when she dares pick up these tools and join in this rough game.

I've wandered through many a neighborhood in Northern Ireland and tripped like a fool on various references to the name of the place. When I first arrived, I wondered what "Ulster" was, as opposed to the "six counties" or "the North." I played with "N'orniron." I sat for a while with "occupied territory," tried "the province," returned to "Ulster," tried the neutral facade "the north of Ireland." For the longest time I simply wrote "NI" in my notebook, avoiding the debate altogether, then I added my own hair-splitting twist: northern (lowercase) Ireland vs. Northern (uppercase) Ireland. Each time I made a choice someone's face floated in front of me and asked me to choose sides in the conflict. Sectarian, set minds demanded my allegiance; their followers begged for my understanding.

On all my trips to Ireland I arrived at key moments: first, in August 1997, when peace talks were being discussed. I visited again in winter 1997–1998, just before the signing of the Good Friday Agreement, and then moved over in August 1998, at a time when many people in the world believed things were about to be settled. But "solutions" never really present themselves in neat packages. I remain confused about the official and unofficial status of this place, so in this text I use the terms "Ireland," "Northern Ireland," and "northern Ireland" interchangeably to refer to the counties Antrim, Armagh, Derry, Down, Fermanagh, and Tyrone. Those familiar with the subject matter know the writer's struggle. Those with any emotional or intellectual investment in Ireland as a partitioned island may be disconcerted. In addition, I use "the Irish" to refer to everyone in the population. Religion is referred to only in context, and family names are conspicuous by their absence. In addition, to respect personal privacy I have exercised poetic license in reference to names and places.

Myth and history—inextricable in a nation such as Ireland—are often merged in consciousness. Relying on text, talk, and picture, I attempt to explain what I refer to as the Ireland of the Imaginations, and, where appropriate, the myth is unfolded for the reader. The northern Irish people inhabit one of the prettiest corners of the world I have seen. The ghosts that haunt it and them do not leave the memory easily. Nor do the exquisite colors, sounds, and impressions found in cities, on farms, and along footpaths. It is those images that I strive to capture.

Finally, though acronyms have been the heart of many a journalist's work on this part of the world, you won't find many in this one. There are a few references to specific elements of the Troubles, but for purposes of reading this book one need know simply that IRA refers to the Provisional Irish Republican Army and RUC refers to the Royal Ulster Constabulary (also referred to as "the police")—they are the only paramilitary organizations I discuss. No one I know was or is in the IRA, INLA, CIRA, RIRA, UDA, LVF, UVF, UFF, or even in any of the political parties. You won't be bumping up against that hard-edged cryptogram, because this book isn't about them. It's about the others.

Peace Comes Dropping Slow

Chapter 1

Name Games / Good Craic / Surveying the Landscape

"Nosy git, in't she?" someone interrupted.

I turned around to see a man in a suit and tie gesturing toward me with his chin. He was good-looking, with curly, blond hair and the spooky, blue-gray eyes for which the Irish are famous.

"Yeah," the man next to me answered, unperturbed by the intrusion. Then he winked at me. I assumed this was invitation to a game, so I smiled at the rude stranger and awkwardly replied.

"Well, I've got some leeway, bein' a tourist, right?"

"Yeah," the older man agreed, sweetly. "She's a writer, from Boston— she's here for a few weeks."

"Yeah, I know. She was here four months ago," the handsome one answered.

I *had* been in Belfast four months earlier. His comment spooked me, but I couldn't let it show. Trying to act cool, I asked about his occupation: "What are you, a cop?"

This prompted the older man to laugh. Nice Eyes cracked a smile. I stared at him as I waited for an answer.

"Haven't you figured out that this place is just a village? Belfast, Northern Ireland, the whole island—it's just a village."

"Yeah, I've figured that out." I answered, then returned to sipping my glass of wine.

The older man, inebriated and leaning, was staring at me, and I had set my arms in a blatant defensive posture to ward off his unsteadiness. I was convinced he'd fall atop me if I didn't have my elbows pointed at him as if they were knitting needles.

What had prompted such a charming exchange was my usual conversation starter: "So what's your name?" This was my opening gambit throughout Ireland, and it was almost always followed by "Where ya from?" Innocent enough questions to me, but loaded with meaning here. I knew of this sensitivity beforehand, had read about the power of surnames in a society segregated for much of its history and fighting today over its very identity, but I'm often uncensored and curious and was no less so on the road in Ireland. Sometimes the response of listeners was understanding and polite in a way that suggested if I was tolerant of the ways of the place, the people would be tolerant of me. That very afternoon a man responded to my introduction—the usual spiel, my name, where I'm from, what I do—with a smile and a generous wave of his hand, as if to say, *It's okay, you don't have to do that, I'm probably going to like you regardless, you don't have to prove anything here.* It was a welcoming signal in a place where your family name defines your position in two warring tribes. The British journalist Tony Parker unwittingly tripped over this division in the early 1990s while trying to drop off film at a chemist's shop. When asked where they should send the film, he didn't know what to say. The assistant smiled and said, "They go either to Johnson and Hunter or Collins and Sullivan, which would you prefer?" The choice had a meaning (though he felt no malice from the shop assistant). When she made the choice for him, "it was obvious [which side she was on]."

I made no such blunders, at least none that stayed in my memory. I merely made the observation that people did not offer names readily, and, knowing my own name gave no clues, I offered it with stereotypical American openness. At any rate, I figured I was a goner—being from Boston. So, in the end, I yielded to the divide, rationalizing that it was best to "hide in plain sight."

I was in a bar negotiating conversation with these two men, whom I referred to as "Northern Ireland's kissing cousins *Banter* and *Slaggin'*." They stood out in the tony environment because they had none of the posturing of the cluster of Eurokids and Belfast yuppies who now live in the city. The bar was inside a trendy boutique hotel, Madison's, located on Botanic Avenue in the university district, just around the corner from where I was staying and in the heart of what tourist brochures call "the Golden Mile." It was conveniently located for me, and I liked its decor—warm rococo interior, modern abstract paintings, and a bar where I could sit and watch people around me. Ireland is one of the few places in the world today where there are no Irish theme pubs; this is great relief to both its citizens and its visitors.

On my first visit to the city in August 1997 (when the spooky-eyed stranger claimed he first saw me), Belfast left me unimpressed. It seemed a dreary, abandoned industrial city with elite sections that were laid out like

British suburbs, with heavy gates, high shrubs, manicured gardens, and security cameras at every turn. These areas contrasted sharply with the ragged but open working-class neighborhoods made up of housing projects and attached housing units that had small front gardens growing sad-looking rose bushes—and security cameras at every turn.

All travel begins in the imagination, so to arrive at a place long wondered about and discover its *un*remarkableness is to encounter a disappointment, like a lover long wished for who turns out to be nothing more than ordinary. Though the experience is the long-desired *realization* of a dream, it is also the end of the upward push of anticipation. Simultaneously, it is the beginning of something new: the journey to uncover the extraordinary within the ordinary. On this, my second, journey to Northern Ireland, I felt a desire to push back the tourist displays and banter, to avoid the hysteria and rumormongering of media commentary, to tear away the cloak of hard-edged insult, to find the center curve of Ireland's knotted history.

As a traveler, I liked Madison's precisely because it was a sort of meeting point for an Ireland on the threshold of change. I had arrived early in the evening, between "waves," as we used to say in the waitressing trade. I was sipping a glass of merlot, perched on one of the barstools, when I saw my newfound friend Banter. His sad-sack reflection smiled at me from the bar mirror. I had an ominous feeling, but my wine wasn't far enough gone for me to finish it and leave. He approached, a glass of Guinness in hand, and I muttered to myself a favorite line from Joyce: "The men that is now is only all palaver and what they can get out of you." As if to say, *C'mon, you know you're going to like me,* he proceeded to flatter and fawn over me, urging me to resist his charms. He was part of the five-to-seven crowd. Thus, by the time I arrived at eight, he was well into his cups, making his charms easily resistible. Mr. Nice Eyes—or Slaggin'—was a later, midevening prowler, a nonchalant nine–tennish guy. I had been arguing literature with Banter, who finally confessed his name was Frank, when Nice Eyes edged into our conversation. Frank claimed he had gone to school with the two poets Seamus Heaney and Ciaran Carson. I said I was enjoying Carson's latest work.

"He lives here!" Frank bellowed. "Call him up!" Then he smiled, "Tell him I sent you!"

He was spoofing, of course, since there are nearly ten years and two cities between the poets, but I acted politely convinced and promised I would. The illusion was nice; I had *a connection*. I was on my way to being an insider in a strange country.

We then began discussing the difference between essays and fiction. I reached into my memory for Americans—Ralph Waldo Emerson or, more recently, E. B. White, John McPhee, or Annie Dillard. Frank came back with classic British role models. America is going through a new renaissance of essays and nonfiction I told him, but my favorite essay is "Shooting an Elephant" by George Orwell.

"That's a short story," Frank exclaimed.

"It is not!" I answered.

In the mirror I could see Nice Eyes (for I was still at a loss for his name) looking around the room. He was scanning it for I-don't-know-what. (Younger Belfast men all seemed a bit like that—jittery and distracted, always watching their backs.) Frank continued with our conversation in a foolish but knowing way. At one point he pulled in Nice Eyes and told him to stay tight so we could avoid the arrival of an undesirable who had strayed in from the January cold. I was an insider by that point, so I acted knowing.

"I'm with ya, Frank. Now, why, precisely, is 'Shooting an Elephant' a short story? It is the consummate description of the nature of imperialism."

By now my elbows were down, since Frank was suddenly clear-eyed and focused. He explained Orwell, then went back to Ciaran Carson, friend, poet, author of *Belfast Confetti* and, of late, *The Star Factory,* a series of shaggy-dog prose pieces about the love of his life: Belfast. I wanted to meet Carson because I admired his literary voice.

"He's one of the greats," Frank assured me. "He's nice, too. Now, *that* man," he said, then paused for effect, "he has," he took a sip of Guinness, I leaned forward, "he has words you reach for."

His slow delivery was part of his verbal choreography. The *art* in Irish banter, it seems, is the swell of anticipation. I looked at him and envied the compliment; every writer harbors a secret wish for such praise. Frank called it "verbal certitude." I smiled at him and wondered about his sudden switch from clumsy drunk to clear-headed critic.

The foam from his Guinness lined the inside of the pint glass, gold tone against the brown remainder sitting warm and thick in the bottom half. Behind us, Nice Eyes pretended he wasn't listening to our pseudoliterary conversation. This is part of Northern Ireland's infamous "slaggin'," which is the hurling of verbal insult, followed by the further insult of silence. But this joker was pretending; after the debate was finished, he asked me what I was doing in Belfast again. I told him I was working on a travel book about Northern Ireland and I was back to do some more looking around.

"Why write about us? We're not nice people," he said with cold assertion. "This is not a nice place. People will pull the rug out from under you at every turn, any chance they can."

"Sounds familiar," I said.

When I travel, people are always warning me off their countries. They did so in Viet Nam, where I had last lived, and in China, where I lived before that. They told me I didn't know the real story, that people "behave" around visitors and I was naive to think they are being sincere. As a result of this and other bits of advice, I've grown circumspect around courtesy—distrusting it in excess. The headlines seemed to back up his bitter comment, too. It was January 1998, and the city was going through what has become known as the maintenance of "acceptable levels of violence." That is to say, the poor were getting it. Since Christmas, there had been a number of murders in Belfast and Derry, and in the bleak winter weather they created an ominous feel about the momentum of the peace talks already under way. I watched the talks and read the newspaper analyses with some interest, but citizens of the place seemed unimpressed. They had been down this road too often, and until solid changes came to the foreground, they would remain pessimistic.

For most of the evening Frank "chatted me up," moving deftly from Heaney, his classmate; to Orwell; back to me; to Carson, his friend; to the art of war as practiced by the great Chinese philosophers and/or the Celts. I'd look over to Frank, then turn to invite Nice Eyes to join in the conversation, but he'd refrain. Finally, I gave him my classic woman's look, hands forward, head shaking softly, the *well-are-you-going-to-say-something?* look.

"When I have something to say, I'll say it," he replied, lighting a cigarette with his butane lighter, then snapping it shut.

"Well," I said cheerily, "I'll have to remember to be there."

His stone face broke into a laugh. Nice Eyes was all bluster, with his smart remarks and unpleasant quips. Many Irish men challenged you that way, tested your nerve, tried to make you win their respect before you even knew them. It is an ancient form of saber rattling I am familiar with, since I was raised in an Irish American household. Of course, that doesn't mean I like it. I'd sooner retort with my mother's well-practiced reply, which is best explained as a smiling, calm "Yes, dear" and a tersely whispered "Knock it off." She was like her own mother with comebacks. In fact, as I thought about it, all the snappiest one-liners I had in my arsenal were from the women of my tribe.

Still, the battle of wits is perpetual in Ireland, and I admire the Irish for it.

Later, after Nice Eyes and I had broken the ice a little further, he told me that writing about Ireland was quite a formidable task: "I mean, I've seen places here so pretty they'd make a stone cry." I smiled, understanding already what he meant. A drive through the countryside, up the Antrim coast toward Giant's Causeway, where I had been during my summer trip, left me intimidated and nervous. Ireland has a landscape that renders both camera and pen useless. I could see the place unfold before me on each of my brief trips. It crinkled like a map being unrolled. In County Down, the mountains of Mourne looked as though they floated above the water of Carlingford Lough. The sun set late at night over village and city streets. Country roads unwound before me, twisting, turning, and merging dangerously. Outside the car, water ran in streams and rivers, winking at me from hillsides and seeming to move with the music I played on my radio. Often when I show slides from my first trips around the island to American friends, they "ooh" and "aah" while I sit in the back of the room puzzled.

"Oh, these pictures don't even come close to capturing what it looks like," I explain.

But why? That I couldn't say. The pictures appear flat and boring, and Ireland—well, sure it's something else, not flat.

Ireland is small, but it feels huge to a writer. Like other oral cultures, Ireland's historical and physical landscape is full of stories and myths (some dangerous, some charming), and everywhere you turn in your travels there's someone playing with words as if they're clay. Verbal arts run bone deep here, making up the heart of both celebration and daily life. After I first arrived, it seemed every conversation I had was a challenge to come up with something enjoyable to hear, be it the sound of the English or the content of the remark. Either or both of these things had to sparkle. The charm of it verged on stereotype, and I was always suspicious of being put on. But conversation in Ireland tugged at something inside you. As each sentence began, I could feel part of me planning my reply to work in a kind of musical harmony with it. That didn't mean agreement—in Northern Ireland there's little of that—it meant an exchange of sounds to create a short piece of music. It was, surely, the heart of "good craic."

❧ ☙

"Craic" (pronounced "crack") is an untouchable, unseeable element that fuels interactions in Ireland and keeps them moving forward. If a party was particularly fun—no fights, no excessive drunkenness, good food, good music, lots of interesting stories told with immensely exaggerated detail—the craic was referred to as "grand," as in, "Sure, last night at Annie's the craic was grand." In fact, often a visitor to Ireland will come across the following dialogue:

"How was your weekend in Donegal?"

"Och, great craic."

The end. No further explanation necessary. Anything else would be a sort of cruel tease. Something like: "So-and-so played music for hours, what's-his-name was there, your man told the funniest stories, he just kept going on all night, the beer was flowing, we showed up at the restaurant just as it was closing and stayed 'til three! The next day we sat around the kitchen eatin' Ulster fry and nursin' hangovers. Aw, you shoulda been there." Still, even that's not enough, so most people leave it at "Good craic" or "Great craic," and that's that. The rest is understood.

Irish craic is defined by a wide range of scholars, journalists, and ordinary people as "social exchange." It is also defined as "news or gossip, talk." This meaning applies only when the word is contained in the greeting: "Hey, what's the craic?" In the United States, it finds its equivalent in "What's up?" And, as in the States, an answer is not always expected. It is also possible, though I don't hear it as often, to describe someone as "good craic," as in, "Yeah, he's good craic, so he is."

Craic is the "atmosphere" the Irish Tourist Board tries so hard to describe in its brochures and media ads. A British friend who relocated to Cork touched on it as he tried to explain his move: "I love the passion here. I don't know about you, but I think . . . I think the Irish have great passion . . . " He stuttered on, trying to describe, within the confines of his Midlands restraint, the openness on the island that was such a relief to his system. I understood both the words and the pauses in his description and said, "Yeah, it's nice . . . there's no pretentiousness here . . . it's . . . yeah, I like it too." In the end, I shrug over the mystery of craic, because I'm too busy enjoying what it awakens in me.

If the essence of craic weren't so mysterious and elusive, the Irish wouldn't be searching for it all the time either. Sometimes as I walked out in the early evenings I would see men standing frozen in doorways, like dogs sniffing the air, and then they'd wander city and village streets like boats unmoored, trying to hook up with this thing no one can see or touch.

Craic is unique to Ireland, and, for my money, it's all about talk and story. It is impossible to record without painstaking adaptation to the limits of print, and even when recorded successfully, it succumbs to the rather frustrating feeling that "you had to be there." It is kept in the turn of phrase, the chat and the rhythm. Its accompaniment is live music, often but not always traditional Irish. It is based on complete and utter sincerity, and it results in a sense of coming together spontaneously and creating a shared moment. It is a laugh, mostly, but it's verbal music too.

Frank gestured to my wineglass with his hand. It was nearing the dangerously low, buy-you-a-drink level.

"Let me buy you a drink," he said earnestly, as if he was asking me a favor.

"No," I answered, "I'm set."

He replied with a dramatically sullen face, as if to tell me I had saddened him, invited tragedy to the table, brought up an unpleasant subject. He actually pouted and looked *hurt*. For me it was a point won, bait not taken.

"It's dangerous talking to the Irish," I said to a friend in the States one evening during dinner. "I mean, you'd better be ready to hold up your end of the conversation or they'll just hypnotize you."

She broke into loud laughter and speculated that it must be the accent. I said I wasn't convinced it was the accent so much as a deep love for words—something that was literally unquenchable. Liam O'Muirthile, a poet from Cork, commented that "deep down inside us there is a language inseparable from us." His reference was to the Irish language, but for me it was the Irish English I heard all over the island. Belfast was notorious for its indecipherable sound; the North in general was scorned for its heavy roll and turn, but I liked all of the island's accents. Irish itself sounded like molten rock to me, as if it was covered embers, unquenchable, never snuffed out. I could hear it and see it all over the nationalist sections of the North—it was flung in my face by people on the Falls Road, recited proudly by young schoolchildren, painted onto murals and store signs all over West Belfast, Derry, and other areas. During my trip, the Students' Union at Queen's University was embroiled in a scandal involving bilingual signs at student organization offices, with people complaining that posting signs with both Irish and English around campus was an empty political gesture meant to insult the majority population. Those in favor of the bilingual signs found the opposite to be true. I'm less interested in Irish than in what the Irish have done with English, but I've always been interested in language debates and the politics of language. In the United States, there is continual public complaint over what language is being spoken where. In Belfast, the fracas ended with the quiet removal of the bilingual signs during summer break. Language in Ireland was a battlefield as surely as it was a weapon. I had already learned that mere introductions could get you into trouble. Even "craic" itself was a debatable term, both in meaning and origin. For years it had been spelled as an English word—"crack"—but it was picked up at some point and turned into the Gaelic-looking "craic." Gaelic purists sneered their disdain and said, "Y'know, it's an English word. That spelling is just a pretense." But I'm from the United States, and we've been bastardizing languages for a few hundred years now. I prefer the Gaelicized version.

"Irish is filled with murmuring," O'Muirthile said. The same could be said of Irish English, with its many varieties. It is impossible for travelers not to strain forward as they first encounter Irish people, in country or out. As I traveled, I constantly found myself pulling forward and back from conversations, my long, thin neck craning out from skinny shoulders. The language was familiar, but the sounds and meaning were unclear. "Sorry? What did you say?" I asked politely. This perpetual request slowed the clip of conversations and marked me as an "outsider" (as if my vocabulary weren't enough). But clarity always seemed to elude me in Ireland. People and things changed in front of me, shifting and reshaping like quicksilver; rude monsters turned into sentimental giants, the seemingly untrustworthy made me laugh. Sure I was in trouble trying to keep up with the verbal competition of the place.

O'Muirthile found inspiration everywhere in Ireland, saying the earth gave him all that he needed to write. It's hard not to be moved by Ireland's landscape, but the slipperiness of the creative muse may have been fooling him. One of his poems begins with the words of a well digger: "I dig down deep for the place where the two streams meet. I dig for the dry September." He was out in the countryside digging into the ground for poems. In Belfast, Frank was wandering city streets reaching for the words of Heaney and Carson, but most of us who write of and about Ireland find the muse shifting around and slipping out through the mouths of its citizens.

As the winter evening waned, I sat perched comfortably on my stool. I was thinking about poets, interesting conversation, and "good craic." I was happy to have held my own in the challenge of conversations and I made a mental note to thank my female ancestors for my verbal inheritance. The bar was getting crowded with Eurokids at this point, and Frank wanted to say goodnight. He threw back the dregs of his Guinness and said I was welcome in Ireland.

"You've got a very charmin' accent, so you do, very charmin', Edie from Boston." And there it was—the compliment to make me blush, the laugh that disarmed me, the flattery stolen from my own scheming mind. Game. Set. Match.

～᠊ᡃᢃ ᡮᡃ~

The next morning, the thumping sound of helicopters woke me. I thought it was the traffic report, until I remembered I was in Belfast. On radio and television as well as in newspapers, people were being told that the peace process was on the "verge of collapse." Loyalist paramilitaries were picking off Catholic men as if they were in a mafia war. Taxi drivers and doormen had been shot in recent weeks, in what some claimed was a response to the recent prison murder of the terrorist leader Billy Wright—the originator of the phrase "The only good taig is a dead taig" ("taig" or "teague" being local slur for "Catholic").

I lay staring at the ceiling wondering about the jitteriness of the men I met, about Nice Eyes looking over his shoulder in the bar, about the police swaggering in and out of bars and pubs wearing their bulletproof vests. I calculated that the men thirty-five and over had all been raised in a state of emergency, one in which the government could lift them from their homes "on suspicion" and hold them for a number of days. But it was "better" now, people said. The peace negotiations were fractious (at best), but heavily watched and debated. The political wing of the Provisional Irish Republican Army, Sinn Fein, would now be included in the talks. The paramilitary organizations maintained their cease fire. I looked at these facts and felt optimistic.

Though the army patrols were light, practically nonexistent compared with ten or twenty years ago, they oppressed me on a physical level. The thumping of the helicopters was a distant buzz to most, but I could see them hovering over North and West Belfast and was reminded of the policing of south central Los Angeles and of the intimidation of populations in Viet Nam by the American government during the war.

The weather was gray and drizzly when I later stepped outdoors to walk into the city center and visit Linenhall Library. Across the street, inside a squat, red-brick terrace home, a woman was boxing up Christmas decorations. The curtains on her front bay window were drawn back, and the walls, painted deep red, caught my eye. She had beautiful gold tree ornaments lined up on the dining table. Her hands moved slowly, almost timidly, in and out of a box, as if she was reluctant to let go of the sparkle and color of the holiday. I lingered, looking over the hedge at the bright colors for an instant, mumbling some encouragement to leave the decorations out a little longer. We both stared down at the table briefly, then I moved on.

On my way to the library I stopped by Blue Cat Antiques, a shop on Bedford Street near the city's main shopping area. The windows were dressed like a magazine layout: two wooden roll-top desks were covered with Tiffany lamps, sets of English china, teapots, piles of mismatched saucers, a glass inkwell, and a large, rather ugly paperweight. Blue Cat is the kind of antique store without any dust or must, the kind you suspect may contain manufactured "antiques" to complement a newly purchased country home.

I moved around the room of organized clutter a bit nervously, hoping the pack on my back, small though it was, would not knock any of the overpriced knickknacks onto the floor. Just as my discomfort began to push me toward the door, a set of maps hanging in the corner caught my eye.

There I discovered that "Ancient Hibernia" was a fascination for eleventh-century Norman explorers and invaders, who created colorful red, blue, and green designs of both the northern province, Ulster, and the entire island. The coast jutted this way and that from behind the glass frame, and the paper grayed and darkened where there were mountains. The mystery of both the art of mapmaking and the island itself showed in the ornate symbols of the cartographer. I stared a bit, then was shocked awake by the price tag and decided to move on.

❧ ☙

When I walked into the library on that first winter day, the man at the front door asked me if he could be of some assistance. I must have looked confused, since I gestured to show him what was in my bag, but he gestured back that he wasn't interested. He was a balding man, with glasses and a friendly, welcoming smile. I wanted to laugh. I was certain I looked foolish.

"Are you a member?" he asked, gently.

"No, um, uh," I fumbled about for words, "I'm a foreigner, a visitor. Can I have a look around?"

"Oh? Where you from?" he asked with a smile.

"Boston, uh, America, the U.S." I stuttered.

"Oh, sure you're no foreigner! Go on."

Up the staircase, I discovered that talking wasn't the only hobby of the Irish. I had arrived embarrassed by the American obsession with Irish roots ("and the dirt around them," I joked) only to discover that genealogy was a veritable industry in Ireland. Indeed, it seemed a household wasn't complete without a book of surnames or a family shield. I initially disliked both of these household trappings, but later came to feel that these symbols and records blended history and personal stories. They placed you in time and told you whose footsteps you were following.

But looking at and listening to the past is a lot of work. In large glass cases on the second floor of the library there were dusty blue and black books that taught you how to research your family name or how to find other books that would help you research your family name, including dictionaries of the most common family names. Hostility provoked by the conversation starter "What's your name?" began to make sense to me then. But, in the library, all the pages on the oldest books seemed to be rotting under the weight of time. They were yellowed and dusty and, worse still, had a text that was punishingly boring. I'm happy to look up the historical origins of words, of languages from all over the world. I don't mind indulging in the details of language systems of obscure places, trying out the sounds and minutiae of grammars, but genealogy is not the least bit appealing to me.

Thumbing through these and other resources, I discovered that drawings and maps found all over the province begin as early as those exotic, colorful designs of the Norman invaders and continue as late as this century, with a 1931 map of a part of West Belfast known as "The Falls." This reprint includes an essay by the writer Ciaran Carson, who tells a tale of Irish people around the world telling tales of ghostly sounds in the streets and alleys of his old neighborhood, of the murder of a policeman on the corner of Balaclava Street in 1922, of a tin can that rattled down the street on its own, and of the way people shape history with their memory and ask it to serve them. I look at the details of the map, see the names listed on the back, and realize that the government had every house in The Falls recorded, including the owner's occupation. I wonder about the life of one Margaret Kelly, who lived near the intersection of Raglan and Cape Streets and was employed as a weaver. This kind of detail stuns me as much as the irony that the city actually has a street named Balaclava. The reference is to the Crimean War, but for me here at the end of the twentieth century, it means a terrorist hood.

At the center of the library's second-floor study were two long wooden tables. On any given day, students are hunched over them, thumbing through old books and rewriting them into their notebooks. Men in suits linger over old history books during their lunch hour; foreign exchange students, dressed in Aran sweaters and jeans, stare into piles of books, hoping to discover ideas, facts, and theories heretofore unknown by the scholars of hundreds of years who preceded them. Like me, they searched for a new take on the place, rustling through the piles of pictures, ideas, literature, and stories as though they were a jumble sale and we could transform yesterday's trash into tomorrow's novelty. I checked my watch; it was three-thirty. I would be meeting a contact at five o'clock. Before leaving Boston, I had called friends, colleagues, and friends of friends with a host of questions about how to write of daily life in contemporary Northern Ireland. The response was overwhelming, and I half decided I wouldn't talk to any "experts" but only to "regular" people, who had an expertise often left unrecorded. What I was really looking for, though, was good conversation and company, a feel for the place. I arranged to meet that evening with a couple from West Belfast named Dennis and Rene. They worked in community theater, wrote poetry and plays, and even published the work of others throughout the province. It promised to be an interesting, creative conversation.

In the meantime, I stared through the glass door on the first cabinet and felt overwhelmed, unable to choose even a single work to thumb through. My eye finally fell on a title that looked interesting, *Long Shadows Cast Before*, by C. E. B. Brett. It is a history of the family of Charles Brett, a solicitor and former member of the Northern Ireland Labour Party. I liked the title, so I pulled the book down and began reading. It is a lucid and warmhearted exploration of his family dating back to the seventeenth century. I considered him fortunate to know the stories, to have heard or read the tales that made up his family life and brought him to this small spot in the world, one he described as: "latitude 54 degrees 35' 49" 68N; its longitude: 05 degrees 55' 37" 53W; it is at a height of 29 feet above mean sea-level as defined by a mark near the base of the Poolbeg lighthouse."

To me, this introduction to his place in history is unpretentious, simple, and clearly free of bias in a territory constantly burdened with claim marks. Americans rarely have the luxury of going that far back into their history to see the hardware of their lives taking shape. Brett followed his family's businesses, education, marriages, travels, politics, and religion until he ended up in his own backyard in 1970s Belfast, listening to bombs go off inside the city. He described himself as having loyalties that are "strained and divided," and I breathed a sigh of relief, knowing I would not have to suss out any code words or clues that revealed his secret, hidden prejudices. Finally! I thought, someone who might be as confused and frustrated as I was over the mixture of violence, courage, creativity, and grace that makes up human history.

On the same set of shelves, mixed in with memoir, fiction, poetry, and genealogy, I found a long stream of white paperbacks. It was a multivolume publication of *Colby's Ordnance Survey*—a gargantuan project undertaken by the British Crown in 1837 to map every spot in Ireland. They spent enormous sums of money on cartographers and memorists who drew and described every stone and building on the island. Beginning outside Derry, the project went on and on and on, producing volumes of detail, enough so that at some point London stopped funding the project, and the remainder of the island was left incomplete.

Maps are abundant in Belfast, it appeared, but, as the *Ordnance Survey* notes, a place can only be advantageously recorded in a memoir to which the map serves as supplement. The "memoir" Colby's cartographers undertook was an attempt to capture in words all the elements that made up the physical world of the Irish. They tried to capture and explain the sound-smell-feel-touch of the place and then translate it. Topography, landscape, and genealogy are important to every ancient country, but the British and Irish obsession with straightening what is obviously a tangle fascinates me to no end. It is like the knots, crosses, and lines of the knitting and embroidery that dress so many people and homes around the island. The inspiration for all of it—both the art and the science—is a landscape split, divided, twisted, and turned by natural and man-made elements.

Still, though it was a "necessary" and interesting task, it must have been frustrating. Ireland strikes me as *un*recordable. The roads twist and turn on you as you traverse them, and direction has a way of changing before your very eyes. If you took the M1 outside Belfast up toward Derry, you began on a simple highway, then, as the lough became visible in the distance behind you, and the hills surrounding the city rose and fell, you got just a taste of what the countryside was like. You got the distinct impression that you were moving into what eighteenth-century world explorers would describe as "the interior."

Of course, Colby wasn't the first to try to get the island down on paper. I sat up straight when I came across the words of John Davies, appointed by the British Crown to explore Ireland in the sixteenth century: "Our cartographers do not forget the entertainment the Irish of Tyrconnell (Donegal) gave to a mapmaker (Bartlett) about the end of the late great rebellion (the Nine-Years War). When he came into Tyrconnell the inhabitants took off his head because they would not have their country discovered."

I put the books and maps aside, then left the library to meet my contacts, Dennis and Rene. Wandering across the street to the city hall gate, I looked for a white sedan.

"Are you Edie?" a plump, brown-haired woman asked.

"Yes. Rene? Hi," I answered.

"Hi, luv. C'mon over here," she gestured to their car. Dennis sat behind the wheel slouching and slightly resistant to his diplomatic obligation. His salt-and-pepper hair was combed back long against his neck, and he had a mustache. He growled "Hello" over his shoulder as I got into the back seat. We drove toward the south end of the city. Rene, with a soft face and green-gold eyes, turned toward me and politely inquired, "Now, how do we know you, pet?" My embarrassment rose quickly, and I could only answer with the truth.

"Umm . . . well, you're friendly with my hairdresser's friend's daughter, Karen."

"Oh," she said, satisfied.

⤝ ⤞

In Ireland today, it seems such distant connections are enough.

Chapter 2

Bad Timing / Cargoes / Proper Toast

"Excuse me, I don't mean to be rude, but what are you doing in our house?"
Lizzy stared at me with polite determination.

When I walked past her earlier, she was sitting on the hall stairs talking on
the phone to her classmate, twirling her hair, and tugging on the skirt of her
school uniform. When she got off the phone, I was "still there," but now I was
sitting in the front room, drinking tea, looking through the newspaper, and
talking with her sitter. She peered through the door, then closed it, picked up the
phone quickly as it rang, talked to another friend, then looked at me one more
time while I talked U.S.-Irish politics with a visiting neighbor. This was the first
she had seen of me and I was, without doubt, making myself at home. After her
polite question, I put my cup of tea down, smiled and laughed as I answered.

"I'm the new lodger."

This made sense to her, and she nodded, then answered, "Oh, okay . . .
well, new lodger, you have cool earrings," she said, then turned and left.

"Oh, thanks," I answered as she disappeared into the next room. I fingered
my ears awkwardly as she walked to the kitchen. Her sister, Aisling, then
walked into the room, looked at me warily, turned, and walked out without
saying a word.

After I arrived in Belfast again in late August 1998, a new acquaintance
had taken me in as lodger while I was waiting for my own flat to be vacated
by the leaseholder. Pauline—my temporary host—was a divorced mother
of two teenage girls and a social worker (in that order, but not without a
typically modern-day struggle between family devotion and social compassion). When Dennis and Rene took me to the Four in Hand pub on my previous visit, Pauline and I had met briefly, and she happened to be around
when I arrived again. Sitting in a café on the Lisburn Road, I mentioned that
I needed temporary lodgings before my long-term tenancy began. Without
so much as a pause for breath, she opened her door to me.

"Pauline," I said over coffee, "you're so nice to let me stay. I'm really in
quite a jam. My landlord said the house would be ready, but it's not going to
be for another few weeks."

She picked up her bag and said it was no problem, "But you'll have to take it as it is," she warned. I smiled.

"I'm not fussy, really."

We got up to leave together. Walking down the street, she pulled her dark red hair back into an elastic.

"Me and the girls are working on it, ya see." She continued about the house, "So it's a bit undone. But it's going to look great."

"No, really," I said, "I'd just rather not stay at a hostel; this is an enormous help."

My arrival in the neighborhood coincided with the end of a horrific summer. I departed Boston on August 15, 1998, just as a bomb went off in the town of Omagh, County Tyrone. It killed twenty-nine people and injured over two hundred. It was the worst calamity of the Troubles and came at the end of a painful, struggle-filled summer that also saw the death by arson of three boys in a town called Ballymoney. Each event was subsequently blamed on the opposing political movement: the bombing on Republicanism and the boys' deaths on Unionism. The Unionist community was divided and pained by the arson, a hate crime committed during rioting over the Orange Order's right to hold a parade in Portadown. The parade had been cut short by a government commission, which stopped it just outside of the Garvaghy Road, a neighborhood populated by Catholics. The Order stood firm in its belief that it must be allowed to walk down the street as part of its expression of "Protestant Culture." They condemned the death of the three boys and the rioting that accompanied their protest, but refused to move from the spot where they were stopped by the police and the British Army. Sinn Fein and the Republican movement were blamed for the Omagh blast, but they openly condemned it and stated that they were willing to cease violence permanently, that, in effect, "the war" was over. For me, it was impossible not to see a connection between violent events and political institutions.

News of the bombing was being broadcast at Logan Airport in Boston as I waited in the Aer Lingus departure area for my flight to Ireland. The report seemed strangely removed from reality, and I felt odd trying to suss things out from my lucky distance. At one of the airport bars, some men started singing Republican rebel songs. Such a gesture was enormously vulgar, but they seemed far too drunk to realize what was happening simultaneous to their Irish getaway. I sighed, depressed. It was late summer in Ireland. The sun would shine more often than not. Flowers were hanging heavy at the end of stems. Journalists were probably yawning at the boredom of a summer news day. Wasps would fly slow and heavy, drunk on the sunlight and heat caught in kitchen windows.

"This is the last thing people need," I muttered as I stood in line to board the plane.

Nonetheless, it seemed Ireland was at a turning point. The Good Friday Agreement, passed by an overwhelming majority of the population in April 1998, was a mandate for leaders and citizens to create a new society. A summer of torment would surely follow such a strong determination. I was reminded and reassured (though shaky in my faith) by the words of a Japanese sage, "Great events never have minor omens. When great evil occurs, great good follows." This was not something I said to people as they endured the grief and shock of the Omagh bombing, but I tried to reassure myself with those words. Journalists spoke in hushed tones and repeated the words "terrible tragedy" and "atrocity" over and over. But as I walked about during my first week in town, I realized that I could not interpret the grief of a society without shifting uncomfortably at the enormous arrogance of such an attempt. An outsider, even the most sympathetic and perceptive one, has no right to speak for people during such a tragedy, when the proper response is compassionate silence. Suffice it to say, a sense of enormous frustration and seemingly boundless despair came over the place.

It was strange to be in northern Ireland in those weeks after the bombing. I was uninitiated in such social traumas, but the Irish took bombings and burnouts in a type of stride I came to admire. I could see this acceptance and equanimity all around me as I walked around Belfast. Only a day after the explosion, buses ran on time and phones rang in offices. A man called in to an employment agency looking for work; there was a half-price sale in a shop on the city's main thoroughfare, Great Victoria Street. The local Boots was crowded at lunchtime as businesspeople bought sandwiches and orange crush before they hurried back to their desks. Outside Tesco, the grocery store, a woman was selling sport socks at three pairs for five pounds; her voice with its thick accent bellowed and rolled in my ear. I made a mental note as I wandered through the crowd to buy some household items, then had to jump back quickly, remembering the opposite traffic patterns and avoiding a bus as it went by, its diesel engine puttering loudly. As the bus paused, the door swung open for a frail, white-haired woman carrying a cloth bag. Behind me, a father scolded his wandering son: "What did I tell you?" he snapped over and over again to the toddler. "Don't you wander off!" It was too crowded for my usual urban pace, so I had to slow down. Nonetheless, I brushed up against a little girl with pale skin and fine, curly red hair. She drew close to her mother's leg as I apologized with my loud voice. It struck me then that contemplating—never mind *remembering*—the bombings and bomb scares so common to the 1970s was unnerving. And later, as I sat away from the crowds, drinking tea and looking over a grove of trees, I worried about the people in the Republican and Nationalist communities. They both sought an eventual united Ireland, but the former was radical in its approach, while the latter favored a more moderate campaign. All those seeking an end to division of the island would now be caught in a broad brush of condemnation. Foreign friends who claimed to be "in the know" about the Republican movement told me the bombing was a terrible shock, since Omagh was considered a "safe" town. I was dumbstruck by the contradiction.

Karl Marx noted that "history repeats itself; first as tragedy, then as farce." The absurdity of the crime and the fantastic reasoning of the criminals reached their apogee when the bombers—calling themselves the Real IRA—telephoned the media the day after the blast. They blamed the deaths and trauma on a local television station. "It was their fault," they claimed, like adolescents, "because they got the warning message wrong." The crime, then, in this most Republican of Ireland's counties, isn't the bomb itself laying waste to the heart of a beautiful town, but rather that people ran *into* its path and placed themselves at the heart of the blast. The group was classified as "dissident Republicans," but "dissident" is a generous term, since it was also applied to Gandhi when he was protesting British rule. The Real IRA was so hackneyed and ham-fisted, both in word and deed, that on the street they had earned themselves the disdainful moniker "The Coca-Colas."

"They won't listen to reason," a member of the Republican community said to me (without a trace of irony). "Everyone knows . . . " and it went on from there. "Everyone knows" was the initial phrase for explaining this rather warped turn of events: "Everyone knows who it is," "Everyone knows they're out of control," "Everyone knows the IRA helped them," "Everyone knows they're tools of British propaganda." The phrase is a flag for any alert listener, and what follows is a weak but still believable mix of street conspiracy theory and just plain gossip. Indeed, much of the political talk in such small environs took on the air of back-fence gossip. "They," "Some people," and "Everyone" were ubiquitous.

In response to the bombing, the British and Irish governments began an investigation and then hastily passed draconian anti-terror laws. The barbarism of internment was talked of as "a possible option" by both London and Dublin. I thought of friends in their forties who got edgy each time a manhunt took place and their memory of being "lifted" from their homes was resurrected. The British government already has the most comprehensive arrest and detention laws in response to terrorism of any democratic nation. Young men living through the seventies and eighties were haunted by the prospect of government agencies—be they police, military, or something known as "Special Branch"—placing them under arrest. For years, powers of arrest were so broad that you could be "lifted"—taken into detention, questioned, and held without charge for a number of days—with very little provocation. The laws were adopted, then adapted to changing circumstances, and were applied strictly to the province but not to other parts of Britain. They were expanded when unchallenged, modified when challenged, and over a twenty-year period, such politics had created a panoply of authority over the lives of individuals and communities. As the writer Paul Theroux noted during a visit to the area during the eighties, it was the future police state. After the police and the military, there was the IRA to worry about. Extensive bombing campaigns from the late eighties through the early nineties meant there was, essentially, nowhere to turn if you didn't want to pick up a gun.

Unionist and Conservative politicians said the Provisional IRA had trained the Omagh bombers, that, in fact, they had the arsenal for them and therefore were responsible. But I come from a country where weaponry is easily acquired, and I couldn't follow this reasoning. I just didn't believe people had the control others accused them of having. Some justified such actions with an old rationalization known as the "physical force tradition," but that had lost all intellectual currency long ago. To me, the bombing was an act that reflected violence as an object of worship, as a primitive muscle memory or an addiction. I dreaded the news of the next week, knowing it would be blanket coverage, complete with finger pointing, mourning, and commentary on the "collapse of the Good Friday Agreement." I looked at the newspaper coverage of funerals in mute shock. In Buncrana, County Donegal, political leaders and citizens walked together in a crowd beneath the smallest of child coffins, and it floated above their heads like a ghost. The majority of the dead were women and children. *Who else would be up the high street in a village town on a Saturday afternoon?* What's horrifying to realize, though, is that somewhere, sometime later, the bombing will claim other victims through either depression or addiction.

While I mused on these thoughts and observations, Pauline and her home, which was populated by the four of us humans, a cat, and a three-month-old puppy, offered a warm welcome to my fatigued traveler's spirit. A small, three-bedroom attached home on the far end of Adelaide Street, off the Lisburn Road, the house was in a state of transition. (For a traveler, that's not a term used with the faux politeness of diplomacy, nor was it an understatement for the likes of Pauline, who was adept at transition, having successfully worked her way up in a difficult business while raising the girls, and was now on her way from one job to another.) Each room seemed to be a work in progress—much like the house I grew up in—and as Pauline tried to apologize and explain what would be where when, I kept repeating, "No, it's okay, I'm used to this kind of thing."

The television room was, fortunately, uncarpeted and thus served as the evening play area for the hyperkinetic Jack Russell puppy, "Gizmo." His claws scratched against the cement as he raced around, jumping from floor to furniture to table to lap, then back to floor. The front living room was piled high with toys, chairs, and books, including *The Mysteries of the Baby-Sitter's Club, The Hardy Boys,* and *Nancy Drew,* alongside *Women's Bodies, Women's Wisdom,* two case studies on the lives of ex-prisoners in the community, and a thick green book with the words *Human Rights* scrawled across the binding. The kitchen, home to the pup each night, was often layered in newspaper and filled—at various points in the day—with laundry, school lunches, takeaways, and Pauline's purple bike, which was squeezed into the corner by the door, looking like a piece of modern art.

My room was on the second floor, above the living room. It doubled as a storage area for the toys that the girls, in their adolescence, were quickly leaving behind. My windowsill was full of kids' knickknacks: wee bears, empty picture frames trimmed with flowers, a rainbow Hacky Sack ball, ceramic cats, a dusty camera, two miniature jewelry boxes filled with toy necklaces. The corner next to my wardrobe was full of board games that no longer pleased the girls—Dr. Dreadful's House of Horror, Candyland, and a 3-D puzzle of a grayish pink Victorian home (with a collapsing roof). I looked around the house and then at the girls begging Pauline to let them stay up late. Lizzy and Aisling were astonishing to look at; they seemed to change daily and grow before my very eyes. The toys were a reminder of the pre-teen's rocket ride out of childhood and the sudden, severe abandonment of all the things that represented their earlier, innocent curiosity. The puzzle fell to pieces and gathered dust while Aisling marched about the house in high-heeled shoes and Lizzy talked about the braces she would be getting in a few months.

"I want them to be brightly colored!" she told me, as we watched television one night.

I tried to imagine a magenta smile breaking up her beautiful face and straight, blonde hair.

"That would be cool," I said diplomatically.

I hopped up from the chair and went into the kitchen, banging my elbow on the door frame along the way, then jumping back as Gizmo yelped.

"Well, get out of the way, Giz!" I said. He was undeterred, however, and began jumping up, a signal for me to hold him.

"Care for biscuits, Lizzy?" I called.

"No thanks."

As I fixed myself a cup of tea I examined the kitchen and thought of my own special designs for the house. (It was newly purchased. Pauline had plans for expanding and remodeling, but she often had to put them on hold as money made its roller-coaster ride in and out of her life.) I reached back into the cabinet behind me for a cup as the water began to boil.

Homes in Ireland seemed terribly small to my eye, and I was always mismeasuring distances in them, banging against a counter or tripping over "wee" steps, picking up things and then dropping them. My elbows remained slightly bruised for the first month after my arrival. The standard housing, "two up, two down," was a building that seemed cramped and shaky, and inside it people were always walking with a thundering heaviness. People pounded up and down narrow stairways, which rose up from front-door landings, and doors, swelled from the damp, were pushed and kicked open. And everything inside seemed the wrong size; kitchens had small, wobbly cookers with grills on top; microwaves were tiny and slow; small, spinning washers shook the counters they were tucked beneath. But I looked closer at these homes and watched as they came to life each day. Tilting windows opened like blinking eyes, doors clicked and swung back and forth as traffic passed through, small garden gates dragged slowly against patio tiles.

To grow up in an Irish American family is to cultivate an appreciation for the noisy household. Half asleep at Pauline's each morning, I tuned in to the music. I could hear her feet tramping around downstairs as she got up before the girls. Outside, a milk wagon zooms quietly along like an amusement park monorail. I can hear Pauline throw on her leather jacket and slip on her black shoes with their big, thick heels, then hear them banging against the cement floor in the TV room. Newspaper crinkles, and Gizmo is brought outside to his pen to do his duty. Chimes jangle as the kitchen door is opened and closed. I look at the clock and know Lizzy needs to get up shortly. She's older and will be off to school first. Her bedroom door creaks open, and she slips into the bathroom. The water runs. Pauline comes back inside the house and moves about the kitchen. I know she is throwing together both breakfast and lunch. Cutlery plinks and rings against plate and bowl. The pup begins to whine like a baby.

"Gizmooooo," Lizzy calls from the bathroom, as if that'll stop him.

Conversations are muted and brief with the early morning, but in my mind I can see Pauline, who has wild, red hair, high cheekbones, and beautiful legs shooting out from her short skirt. And I know Lizzy must have nervous imaginings about her school day; I see her running a comb through straight, silky blonde hair, then hear the comb fall against the enamel of the bathroom sink. She pushes through the door of her bedroom and pulls her gray school sweater over an ironed white shirt.

Downstairs, the dishes begin to pile up and rattle in the sink while Pauline's still gravelly voice gives firm orders. The kitchen door handle turns, the door is jammed and then released, the purple bike is dodged. Water runs again in the bathroom, Aisling rolls over on the bottom bunk of her bed. I can hear the duvet being slipped up over her head. The pup whines more and lets out a lonely yelp. It's spitting rain outside, and I'm sure his coat is covered with a beady film. I think about my greasy face and hair, smack my lips together to wake up my cottony mouth, and contemplate a cup of tea. Pauline pounds her way down the stairs and then up again,

"Aisling? Are ya up, darlin'?"

A bag is swung across shoulders, and a cabinet door slams shut. All the while a chilly mist soaks poor Gizmo in his pen.

"Listen to that," I mutter in a sleepy voice, "he wants to be inside with us beauty queens."

Another morning, as I was making my way out into the day, Lizzy came running in from her father's house, where she had stayed the previous night. She pushed the door open, the chimes jingled annoyingly, and Gizmo scampered across the kitchen floor, trying to get out; Lizzy stuck her feet out to stop him as if he was a soccer ball.

Breathless, holding her schoolbag and saying that she was late, Lizzy said, "Mummy, you remember I told you about that field trip? I need to give them money for the cost." Her kneesocks looked stretched to the limit, rising up out of the thick-soled black slip-ons the girls wore as part of their school uniforms. I sipped my tea and smiled. Pauline and I had just been discussing the struggle of keeping finances in reasonable order. She reached into her bag, pulled out a checkbook, and began to write.

"Tell him the check is postdated," she said to Lizzy.

Her face dropped, "Why?"

"Just tell him it's postdated, because it is."

"What's postdated?"

"It's dated for the future," she said with a sigh.

I laughed at the familiarity of the situation. Lizzy looked suspicious, but took the check, pausing before she left to show Pauline a drawing that had earned her great praise the day before. The dog whined by the door as Pauline marveled at her daughter's work, then Lizzy was off.

I didn't stay long with Pauline and the girls, a few weeks only, but I loved every minute and every dusty, cluttered inch of the house. Oftentimes when traveling, you're just happy to have a blanket. The musty, warm smell of furry pets doesn't deter me from relaxation or awaken the sneering consumer who would check out every inch of a five-star hotel to make sure it is "up to standard." "We'll be happy to make your stay as enjoyable as possible," the little leaflets inform the hoteled traveler, "please take a few moments to fill out this quality-control questionnaire." In contrast, the spare room at Pauline's house had a drawing taped to the wall for lodgers like me. It was drawn by one of the girls and across the top of the masterpiece was the phrase "Have a _____Day!" with a yellow smiley face in place of the word "nice." The eyes were enormous, the mouth a straight, thick black line against the bold yellow. This was followed by a tiny postscript: "This is actually quite scary, isn't it?" Teenage girls are hyperobservant and very amusing. I looked at the picture each day for a giggle. It always seemed that when the Irish stereotyped Americans, "Have a nice day!" was the turn of phrase they used.

In August and September, I watched the girls get up each morning, saw Pauline go to work each day to help people with things like housing, unemployment, access to the job market, and schooling. As I watched, any questions I could come up with about the bombing—but dared not utter—were answered. Before I knew it, I was swinging back and forth again, tangled between hope, realism, and determination.

~≈ ℘~

Then, I moved from Pauline's house to a nice attic flat off the Malone Road, also in South Belfast. There were eaves bending and curving every which way and large windows that let in sunlight at various points during the day. I could see Black Mountain, above West Belfast, from my front window, as well as the beautiful colors of the changing sky. Surrounding groves of trees gave haven to lapwings, magpies, and various other birds who darted in and out of them in the autumn weather. But old houses have their drawbacks: dust gathered quickly, spots in the walls revealed spreading damp, pigeons often nested in the eaves outside my bedroom window. I woke many days to their scratching crawl as they outmaneuvered the wire traps set for them by my landlord. (This was an amusing reminder of home, and on occasion I'd wander around half asleep, slightly giggly at the memory of a family joke. It was an imitation of the comedian Carol Burnett, dressed as a toothless old park visitor, mumbling "Here pidgy, pidgy, pidgy" as she threw crumbs on the ground. I banged on the windows, as I had at home, but the birds were dug in—particularly when it rained—and they ignored me.)

South Belfast is a tony neighborhood, complete with fancy gardens and overgrown hedges and neighbors who had to warm up to you. Kids played with hurling sticks, and parents drove Volvos, Vauxhalls, and BMWs. I walked each day along the nearby river Lagan, demonstrating the typical American fetish for health and exercise, my stringy legs shooting out in front of me in long strides, my arms swinging like I was cross-country skiing. I exercised each day to free my head of the clatter of history and the story/tale/poetry that filled it every time I wrote about and watched Ireland. It was physical exertion to balance my mental gymnastics and keep me from going crazy.

The landlords didn't seem really to own the house so much as care for it, the way one cares for an aging matriarch. A gracious couple, they had filled it with enough antiques and novelties—dishware, furniture, books, a collection of antique teddy bears—to engage you in a museum-type conversation every day for a year. A gorgeously neglected garden in the back had patio furniture that was turned upside down against the rain, but it hadn't been restored to its original position. The house was carpeted with dhurries and throws scattered on top of fading, old wall-to-wall. There were two large stained-glass windows in the style of the Scottish designer Charles Rennie Mackintosh. The other windows, long and plain but allowing in plenty of sun, were dusted and washed, their frames freshly painted at the end of the summer. An Electrolux vacuum cleaner lay in the second-floor hallway for days, its hose and nozzle sprawled out from the round base like an unsprung coil. It was all fabulously cluttered and casual. How long it takes to clutter up a Victorian house with ten-plus rooms and an attic apartment is an accomplishment I can't imagine.

The couple often rented rooms to opera singers, which was just another quirky detail about the place I admired. I kept waiting to bump into some huge European who'd refuse to speak to me in order to preserve his voice or a tall, fussy diva who spurned milk and wouldn't be seen without lipstick. I loved the casual nature of the place and the unpretentious attitude of the owners. I wanted only one thing to send it all over the top: an Irish wolfhound. It had to be something big, a dog who could rest his head on the windowsill from a lying position, something musty smelling and barking, something with an absurd name like "Scout." But a dog was not part of the decor, so I would have to settle for the silly scratch and claw of the pigeons in my eaves (though later a neighbor bought a Great Dane pup who grew enormously before my eyes; unable to control himself, he ran wild on occasion, jumping over the low plants in the front garden like a horse in a steeplechase and, on a certain dark evening, leaping like a mugger from behind a hedge as I returned quietly home).

As I settled in, I developed the morning habit of getting up and opening my windows onto the day. The sun came in through the living-room window. From the front window I looked across the yard at the distant hills and realized, with each glimpse, what motivated the Anglo-Irish to profess such loyalty to Ireland over the centuries, what made Lady Gregory write, with what I thought was purply prose, juvenile descriptions of a romanticized, nonexistent place. I felt that such emotional intimacy was bad taste in a nation where suffering has been forged into a steely exterior, where wordplay begins at insult.

But even on the grayest day in Belfast, even when I felt oppressed by the "Englishness" of my neighborhood (an unfair description, yes), I could see the hills that Jonathan Swift saw and referred to as a "sleeping giant," and I knew the Anglo struggle with cultural identity and loyalty. Sometimes you'd look into those hills and understand the poetry and sentiment that fell from the mouths of Irish citizens, and then you'd understand the huge loss forced upon everyone by political and institutional violence.

After getting up each morning, I would wander about the nearby neighborhoods and watch the Irish move forward into the day. They were single mums and unmarried women, businessmen and retirees, and couples with kids who carried hockey and hurling sticks to school in the early autumn weather. I watched girls reluctantly get out of family cars outside school gates, or arrive late from the stumble of an early-morning household fight over the bathroom, lingering in bed until something or someone pulled them from the warm and breathy darkness under the duvet.

On sunny days in summer and fall, I could feel sentiment well up in the community as it endured, in silence, yet another explosion. Blackberries ripened on the vine, Japanese lantern flowers hung like red lights against green hedges, and roses blossomed in yellow, peach, and red in public gardens. Rain fell, rainbows emerged and faded. I sniffed at the moist air, looked out at the blue sky, watched the black-and-white magpies, with their long tails, soar and dive. The regularity and quiet were deceptive. Omagh and many other bombings were etched deeply in people's lives. I called my mother at the end of one day. She shook out a comment, "Oh, honey, everyone here feels so terrible, it's so terrible."

My new friend Dennis, who'd endured such news for a long time, wrote eloquently of it in his poem titled "Fifteen Lines for Omagh":

> I shall not describe in pretty terms or metaphors
> our making love that morning.
> I shall not enumerate in rhyme or any verse
> events occurring miles away.
> I shall not mix children's faces in any palette,
> tally-up a shopping list
> or place a bet.
> I shall not chide advice by any voice
> nor poets' silences at times like these,
> not even talk or write about the weather.
> Romantic murder mocks
> and robs the pen of power.
> Today there are no terms or metaphors,
> no lexicon can call a single syllable to mind.
> I shall not describe.

As I watched schoolgirls go through gates and little old ladies walk into shops, I thought that on days like these every gesture is a prayer for the deceased.

Eventually, I landed a part-time job in a café near my apartment. It was a small, unpretentious shop with a tile interior and modern silver metallic tables and chairs. Its shelves were full of European and Irish foodstuffs.

There were oils and sauces, teas and chocolates, and a refrigerator full of sparkling water and fruit juice. Behind the deli counter were a selection of meats and cheeses, a cappuccino machine, and a sandwich bar. The owners, Radha and Mary, had bought the shop five years before and had kept the original name—Cargoes—which was also the title of a poem by the British poet laureate John Masefield:

> Quinquireme of Nineveh from distant Ophir
> Rowing home to haven in sunny Palestine,
> With a cargo of ivory,
> And apes and peacocks,
> Sandalwood, cedarwood, and sweet white wine.
>
> Stately Spanish galleon coming from the Isthmus,
> dipping through the Tropics by the palm-green shores
> With a cargo of diamonds,
> Emeralds, amethysts,
> Topazes, and cinnamon, and gold moidores.
>
> Dirty British coaster with a salt-caked smoke stack
> Butting through the Channel in the mad March days,
> With a cargo of Tyne coal,
> Road-rail, pig-lead,
> Firewood, iron-ware, and cheap tin trays.

I found the poem on a rainy day in the Linenhall Library, in a dusty collection of all of Masefield's work. It seemed largely unremarkable at first, but as I read it over, I came to appreciate its sneer at the false, grimy promise of the British Empire. "Cheap tin trays" reminded me of George Orwell and the socialist literature of Tressell and Shaw. Reading it in Belfast, I thought about factories and shipyards and brick piled upon brick.

꩜

On sunny days, I'd finish working and wander across the Stranmillis area along the Lagan River to Ormeau Park. One afternoon an American businessman who jogged his way through the footpaths, turned and said loudly to his companion, "That's a lovely old tree, isn't it." His voice was a blunt instrument in the grove. I passed by a rose garden and a bandstand, then strolled back through a set of gates to the street. I thought out a route through the local neighborhood, then into the Botanic Gardens, down to the Lisburn Road, and ending by Adelaide Street, where I would drop by and check in on Pauline and the girls. I made my way toward the Ormo bread bakery, a large factory on the Ormeau Road, and I passed on around it. Viewed from the back, it stood like a bleak monument to industry. The chimneys spewed out a brackish smoke that would be gloomy if it weren't coated with the vanilla aroma of white bread, and the scent stayed with me, even on the grayest days. The reassurance of this smell took the edge off the dark shadow cast by the brick building. Moving in the opposite direction from the park was a series of shops and pubs, some newly renovated and refurbished (part of what a friend called the "current bar wars"), and an old movie theater, the Curzon. Brick houses were lined up in neat, if monotonous, rows; trash bins (collected each Tuesday morning) lay about the sidewalk like bowling pins knocked over in a match. I passed through the serpentine maze of a small neighborhood just as Holy Rosary primary school was letting out. Parents brought young ones home by the hand, while a crowd of children remained behind and tried to see who could yell the loudest (at least that's what it seemed they were doing), and cars pulled away slowly, among them a wagonful of teachers who huddled together reassuring each other with back patting and cigarettes.

I picked up my pace and walked down Sunnyside Drive and through the city's Botanic Gardens, where a teenage boy heckled me with, "Hey, Lady, ye fergaht yer ski powls!" to the brittle amusement of his pals. I stifled a laugh, then made my way through the gates and down another block to Lisburn Road. Traffic was thickening, and the sidewalks filled again with students as Methody College emptied out, like a bucket spilling blue water. I stopped and started for a few blocks before making my way to Pauline's house, where, per usual, the door was open. In the late afternoon light, a very serious discussion was taking place. Pauline smiled and waved to me. I waved a quiet hello, then moved across the floor to listen in:

"You know who makes the best, proper toast is Grammy O'Kane," Lizzy said.

"Aye," Pauline agreed, leaning on the counter, "she does."

"With the grill."

"Hi, Edie, . . . yeah," Aisling said, "she makes proper toast, Grammy O'Kane."

Lizzy dipped a bit of bread into a cup of soup she held in her hand, popped the soggy end into her mouth, and mumbled a crumbly greeting. The bell on the microwave rang. Aisling opened the door and took out her own tomato soup. She continued on with her theory: "You have to be careful with the toaster because sometimes it comes out too dry." Lizzy reached across me and pushed the button on the toaster to give her gold-speckled bread another go round.

"Of course, girls," I said, by way of teasing Pauline, "your mom here remembers the days when toast was made on an open flame." Pauline smothered a laugh.

"You took the words right out of my mouth."

"We cooked over an open flame once," Aisling added.

"It was marshmallows!" Lizzy said, rolling her eyes.

"Sausages," Aisling corrected. She dipped her toast in the soup, then bit into the corner.

"I love toast," Lizzy went on.

"There is an art to it," I said, tempted by the smell of the bread and the soft orangy red of the soup.

"It has to be soft," Aisling said. Butter was dripping down the crust of Lizzy's bread. She licked it off the side of her finger; soup stained the corner of her mouth.

"You can cook it on the stove grill," Aisling said.

I had grown up using only toasters, so the art of toasting bread on a flame grill was unknown to me.

"You have to stand the bread the right way," Aisling added.

"It has to be separated, spread out right," Lizzy said.

"And it has to be buttered properly," I said.

"It has to melt," Lizzy added.

"Grammy O'Kane does it the best."

Good toast was kin to the right cup of tea, I thought. Ireland's many Grammy artists never acknowledged their secrets, but instead dismissed their great timing and gentle touch as common sense. You used just enough sugar in a cup, the right amount of butter or flour in bread; you found a way to keep yourself occupied so you weren't forced into watching the bread transform, the kettle boil, the water change to a rich, deep black-brown before it was poured in the cup.

The bread popped up from the toaster. "Just right," I said, looking at the beige color, knowing it would fold neatly and be dipped into the thick, red soup. Lizzy smeared some butter across both slices and gave one to her sister.

Aisling stood near the doorway between the kitchen and the sitting room. I could see sunlight fall through the window and across her face. Her long hair was pulled out of the barrette, and I could see the last traces of "little girl" as she stood half in light, half in shadow. There were freckles across the bridge of her nose, and her teeth rested softly on her lower lip as she thought about things. She had a voice that questioned quietly but curiously. She would move next year from elementary school to secondary school; this winter would bring with it the dreaded eleven-plus exams that would determine her placement.

"Well," Pauline said, moving from the counter to place a few groceries in the refrigerator, "whataboutche? What's your craic?"

"Stayin' out of trouble," I answered.

Aisling walked up to me quietly after she finished her soup and began fiddling with my earring. Her fingers were warm against my chilled lobe.

"You wear really pretty earrings."

"Thanks," I said, smiling at the memory of my own adolescent longing for earrings.

"When you're sixteen," Pauline said, reading her mind. "How was your day today?" she asked, looking at me.

"Oh," I answered, "you know . . . nothing special."

That was the best response, but it wasn't true. In August, September, and October, I stood in a lot of city and country doorways in Ireland. I leaned against a lot of walls, casually watching grandparents, parents, and their kids, and I felt overcome by a strange mixture of grief and hope. I smiled awkwardly at Pauline's question, remembering one customer that day, a dark-haired woman chatting with a colleague. I had cleared away her empty dishes and turned to walk toward the kitchen. Still within earshot, I heard her say her good-byes in a way only heard in these parts:

"That's me, Trish, I'm away. It's off to Derry. They've asked me to take testimony for the inquiry into Bloody Sunday. Then I've got to be back in time to pick up the kids from their father's."

Taken aback, I dropped a spoon, then rattled the cups together as I tried to prevent them from falling. The women looked at me.

"Uh, . . . sorry," I said, awkwardly.

"Ach, you're all right," one woman said, reaching out for the spoon and giving it back to me.

The Bloody Sunday inquiry was an examination of the 1972 military shooting on a Catholic civil rights demonstration in Derry. Officially, this was an inquiry into an accident of sorts, for, according to the British government, no one could really say what had happened. Of course, in the United States and Europe, it's not really possible to talk of such events as human rights violations. We haven't the vocabulary for it. Those words, we are taught, apply to the other countries of the world. For an instant I pictured the woman's kitchen table at home, covered in work notes, coffee cups, and cigarette ends. Inside these houses that I found too small, people's lives were like that: tea and lunch, dogs, laundry, and plans for dinner. I knew the conversations ran along the lines of *Oh, and don't forget to attend the inquiry*. Or *Remember to forward information to the committee to reform the police force. Remember to get to the meeting of Survivors of Trauma*. Politicians and panels made the news, even won the peace prizes, but the real work in Ireland was done over mountains of cigarettes and rivers of tea in council flats and mortgaged homes. As the woman's shoes clicked against the floor on her way out of the shop, I put the dirty dishes on the counter and wiped the damp from my hands.

The world is propelled on its axis by the deeply personal experience of everyday life, but the cargo of "history" is the burdening weight of major disasters. It seemed to me that Ireland was a ship guided by an inadequate, ancient map people were calling "tradition." But the struggle to move forward from the past, to move away from what the Good Friday Agreement eloquently referred to as "a deep and profoundly regrettable legacy of suffering" was difficult. "History" leaves infinite traces on those of us passing through it. Everything that has come before leaves its mark on us, less on the physical world than on the spiritual. The Good Friday Agreement was passed, but would the government be formed and the terms be implemented? Sometimes—on the ground—it seemed irrelevant. People would keep moving, keep demanding, keep surviving.

Working with and moving among the Irish, I felt myself in a strange sort of time warp. It was as if I were walking toward the future, but being forced to do it backward, while facing the past. One moment I would be fixing a cappuccino in the café, flicking switches on machines and looking at a crowd of people talking about the future. Then, as had happened that day, I looked out the window and the Ireland of the Imaginations reared its eternal head. A cloud passed from in front of the sun and the light fell just so over a large tree, spotlighting an old man in a tweed suit and a flat cap who stared nervously at traffic on the Lisburn Road. His face was a bundle of pink wrinkles, and he was so much a stereotype, so much something out of a book, that I thought I was staring across eons of time. BMWs zipped by, trucks and Volvos trundled along, a woman walked a pram past him to the nearby greengrocer. In the middle of it all, I could hear my colleague Annie talking to me:

"Y'all right, Edie?"

I turned. Her hair is a shock of bleached white, cut in a male fashion. She has a silver stud pierced in her nose and two hoops on her left ear. She's beautiful, young, athletic. She floats around the shop like a bird moving from tree to tree. She's something I can relate to.

"Yeah, I'm fine," I answered.

The other young women working in the café talk about nightclubbing and fashion, soccer matches and trips to Europe. The radio announces hi-tech companies opening offices in the city, European Union grants, and job-training programs. The old duffer edges into the fray, and with one of the customers, I wait for his safe crossing.

Chapter 3

Passing the Time / Oral History / Derry's British, Y'know

In my wanderings around cities and towns, I came to realize that the barside comment "This place is just a village" was true. Even in Belfast the coziness of daily life appealed to the small-town part of me. I found comfort in familiar faces turning up in different parts of town; I enjoyed the sleepy nature of weekend days, the banter about the weather. I liked the local focus of news reports. I listened early each Saturday to a radio program called "You and Yours" and heard about community groups gathering together to raise money for such far-off places as Honduras or reading piles of books to give the proceeds to cancer research groups. In Belfast one afternoon, a teen group raised money for the organization Age Concern by rappelling from the roof down the side of the Europa Hotel (until the siege of Sarajevo, the Europa had the dubious honor of being the most bombed hotel in Europe). One weekend a local historian was telling us about a town called Warrenpoint; on another, a Fermanagh landowner claimed that a mysterious "big cat" had shown up on his property in the dark of night, but after a struggle with the farmer, it "made off into the darkness."

I also liked the gossip at the café during the week. I walked in one Monday morning to hear whispering about how Annie broke up a bar brawl on Saturday night. University students complained about professors, parents of schoolchildren worried about upcoming school exams. I wiped down the counter while the girls chatted. A BBC cameraman was back from abroad and said to be working on a documentary—*but is he married or single?* the part-timers wondered. An Internet entrepreneur favored cappuccino in the morning—*but he's here so often, does he ever do any work?* Gillian, a full-timer, observed dryly. I smiled at her as I folded the cloth and looked about for customers.

"Hello, Joan," Gillian said, as a red-headed woman entered the shop. The woman didn't answer but walked up to the end of the counter and spoke with Annie, then turned and left. She walked with a cane and dragged one of her legs with a degree of grace I'm not sure I could muster.

"Not very friendly, is she?" I muttered. Gillian sighed softly and walked away in reply. It would take me some more time to understand her meaning.

In a village, history is told in terms of people known at reported events. The events, then, become secondary to people's response to them or the act of witnessing them. Henry Glassie, an American folklorist from Indiana University, recorded the art of history and storytelling in Ireland in painfully exhaustive detail in a study titled *Passing the Time in Ballymenone*. The eight-hundred-page volume is largely a text of recorded conversations, storytelling, and interpretation of how history is recorded in oral cultures. Glassie wrote deeply of Ireland and of this spot in Fermanagh. He loved his subject matter. And he makes an important point about how a town regarded its keeping of history. In this oral culture, literacy is a marginal convenience; print is not the final word: "Their world is ordered orally. When the song is sung, the ballat is absent. Matters of history, genealogy and land tenure, cooperative arrangements between farmers, rental agreements, sales at marts, the 'fireside law' governing land use, routes across private property and access to water, and most profoundly, the rules of the church—all are held in the memory and expressed face on, intimately, in words." It's an undeniably romantic world, and it's full of fodder for argument, dispute, and hatred. In such a world, whose history is true and whose untrue? The books I read in the library had a permanence I found difficult to swallow. But, often, my experience with people turned out to be no less frustrating.

Stories that were told to me in the casual form of pub and café conversation were the single element that pulled Ireland's many strands together and helped me see it as a whole. I could not explain political life in Northern Ireland to people I talked with back in the States, and I dared not conjecture with people in country for fear of mutual insult. I learned the rules of that verbal game by breaking them. I once let slip the word "Londonderry" in conversation with a Republican friend. She replied by giving me a withering stare and saying, "Or do you mean Derry?" Later, I overheard another slip by a friend from Dublin, who said "over the border," in reference to the Republic. Conversation stopped again, and someone said, with steely politeness, "There is no border." How is one to reply? Even after I knew of the survivors around me, what should I do? Walk up to them and say, "So, tell me about the day of the blast?" Or "How do you keep your spirits up?" The media were bad enough with their constant query: "Do you think the peace will hold?"

I often did not know how to talk about the gritty things that made up political life, and it was difficult for me to ask questions about these issues. Even among friends, I felt my ignorance was being held up as a measure of wavering support for the Republican movement or, conversely, as a reflection of naive indoctrination into Republican propaganda (after all, I was from Boston, a sanctuary for IRA gunmen). Either way, I lost.

One afternoon during a weekend in Derry, I found history slipping and switching, as it is wont to do, in a discussion of recent events. I was sitting with two friends in a hostel run by a man from Edinburgh named Steve. Neil was Australian; Uta, German; and then there was me, the American. All of us were puzzled and fascinated by the history of the city. Uta and Neil had been living there since the previous summer and had witnessed a set of riots following a march through the Diamond (the city center). The parade was scheduled, as it is every year, to commemorate the closing of the gates by the Apprentice Boys and the beginning of the infamous 1689 Siege of Derry. In December 1997 there was a protest, name-calling, and after that . . . well, a riot. It lasted a few hours—"until about teatime," a neighbor explained, "but they'll be back after they've eaten"—and sure enough they were.

The original siege lasted 105 days, well into the spring of 1690, forcing Derry's inhabitants to battle against the forces of James II until, by the account of George Walker, they "reckoned upon 2 days of life . . . of 7500 men regimented, we had now alive but about 4300. . . ." Military relief eventually arrived via the Foyle River, but within the walls there must have been such brutal exhaustion and such extraordinary determination. Uta, Neil, and I were trying to remember what British king did what when. We had all been to the Tower Museum inside the walled city and had come away quite impressed. I was especially taken with the events of the Siege of Derry, the exhibit on St. Columba, and the once ubiquitous presence of oak trees on the Irish landscape.

"But you know what really sticks in my memory," I said, "is that the Apprentice Boys were orphans."

Neil nodded his head in agreement.

"You know," I said, "I just pictured these raggedy-assed boys, these Dickensian castoffs from England getting dumped over here. Poor things."

"Yeah, it's true," Neil said, "so many people were sort of placed here."

But we couldn't get the order of things right. Derry alone is rich in the history of Ulster, England, even of Catholicism. Uta asked if it was Cromwell who had paid people in England with land he'd seized from Catholics in the Irish colony. He had. And those Catholics he didn't kill, he shipped out to the Caribbean and elsewhere, creating a new shade of meaning for the term "diaspora." But the indigenous Irish of the sixteenth and seventeenth centuries had not created a halcyon world, either; their battles were riotous and brutal. But—as a ten-year-old girl said in 1998—"It's not about religion, it's about land." This is true. The historian Roy Foster noted that those taking refuge inside Londonderry's walls identified their attackers, "quite erroneously, as representatives of that Gaelic uprising they had been bred to fear . . ." Ireland's Protestant planters had been given land and a political indoctrination that reminded them they were lucky to have it. They would, of course, have to beware the barbarians who inhabited the place. I said it reminded me of the conquest of North America.

"And Australia," Neil added.

I smiled at history's turns. They are both nations with significant Irish immigration.

"Wasn't the pope at that time supporting William?" Uta ventured.

"He was?" I said, shocked.

"Yeah, and I think William was even married to a Catholic woman," she said.

We all started laughing.

"And you know," Neil said, "the Loyalists make a big fuss over the Apprentice Boys closing the city gate every year. Well, if you were just a wee thing, a band of raggedy kids, and you saw all these soldiers approaching, what would you do? It wasn't heroic, it was sheer terror!"

"Well," I pondered, "action in the face of terror is heroism, isn't it?"

"Mmh," Neil answered softly.

"Well, I'm going to go back into town," I said, picking up my bag.

"Do you know the way?" Steve asked.

"Yes, I just walk down Creggan Street, past the church there."

"It's quicker the other way," he explained.

"Through the Bogside?" I asked. "I thought so."

"Here, let me show you," Steve said, turning off the cooker.

After walking to the end of the street, we stood together at the top of a set of stairs, looking over the Bogside. The sun was painting the sky a dramatic pink and blue, and it made even the gray wall of the city look beautiful. A chilly breeze blew past, and Steve explained the way back to Butcher's Gate. When he had finished giving me his directions, I pointed to the camera tower at the end of the city wall.

"Can I ask a stupid question?" I said, looking him in the eye. Before I even asked, his face softened into a smile to reassure me that what I saw was real. Still, I wanted to make sure I wasn't crazy.

"What the fuck is *that?*" I asked, raising my voice, "I mean, is that what I think it is?"

"It's a camera tower," he said, nodding.

"They're all pointed this way," I said, stating the obvious.

"Yes," he answered calmly.

"They're watching the Bogside," I said.

"They're watching the Bogside," he repeated, "a Catholic community," he finished.

"I mean, there must be twenty cameras on that thing."

He smiled, since there was nothing else to say. The camera tower is enormously offensive. Further behind it is a housing project populated exclusively by Protestants known as "the Fountain." And if you went further along the city wall and came to the Foyle River, you'd see across it to a community called Waterside, also exclusively Protestant. The city was cleanly and clearly segregated.

Steve spotted me, rightly or wrongly, as a lingerer on Northern Ireland, a late arrival, perhaps, in the debate about her future. I imagined him to be a romantic, misinformed Republican lover, a UK liberal out to witness the oppression of the Empire. This "sussing" passes between travelers on the road. We have conversations composed of innuendo and casual inquiry. How long were you in this place? Did you like that one? What were you doing *there?* From there we decide to linger together or move on.

I walked down the hill toward the projects and the Bogside Inn, Republican Derry's most famous stronghold. The streets were quiet, and as I looked down the alleys behind the rows of houses I wished I had my own camera with me. Backyards were fenced in with wood-panel walls and gates, some painted pretty pastel colors, some gray and peeling. The doors fell this way and that and were propped left or right by bricks or stones or sometimes simply hung ajar. The symmetry appealed to my eye. To my left, on the steep hill of Creggan Street, was St. Eugene's Cathedral, an enormous gray stone church which towered over the surrounding homes and tolled "Pinus Angelicus" each morning, a pleasant, if parochial, alarm bell. At the foot of the street was the infamous Bogside Inn, temporarily closed, looking as if it, too, were weary of the Troubles. I crossed Rossville Street and peered nervously down the street into the Brandywell neighborhood. A highway ramp overshadowed housing on Fahan and Rossville Streets. Combined with the painted curbstones and the weight of recent history, the effect was enough to get me to turn on my heels. I walked past another housing project and crossed in front of the FREE DERRY mural (a large white wall on which the words "You are now entering Free Derry" are painted) and the Bloody Sunday memorial (a painted replica of the famous newspaper photos taken on Bloody Sunday in 1972). Some German tourists were taking pictures of the murals, and I crossed quickly out of their way. I remembered that the wall the FREE DERRY mural is painted on was once the supporting wall of a house and thought about the layout of the area in the 1970s, then found myself stopping short as I imagined the sounds of Operation Motormen, when the British government knocked down the paramilitary barricades, gathered up hundreds of young men, and interned them.

A young boy walked boldly up to me as I made my way down the street toward Waterloo Place and Sorrow Square.

"Give me twenty P!" he sneered.

"I'm not gonna give you twenty P, kid," I answered, still moving.

His freckled face and short red-brown hair would have struck me as cute in another context. His mates came running up to him, daring him to pester me further. Their voices sounded like the rattle of tin cans thrown together in a plastic bag. Near a roundabout that led into the mall area I stared up at a mural demanding the release of political prisoners. Just around the corner was Sorrow Square, a main departure point for the diaspora, now a pedestrian shopping area with a bronze memorial to Irish immigration as its centerpiece. The stores surrounding the spot were closed, one or two were burned out, and up a small hill were a handful of pubs filling with young people. The bronze cast of crying women stood in the gray light as young people huddled together and moved from pub to pub, looking for a soccer game, some good live music, and their "mates." In the shuffle and query, you could hear the seeds of "good craic." Young girls wobbled in their platform shoes and high heels, getting tripped up by the cobblestones and bricks. Back at the corner of Waterloo Street an old woman stood with a full grocery bag, waiting for a taxi up the hill.

In a single glance around a mall in Derry, I could capture pieces of two centuries in Ireland. Traveling to places like Northern Ireland at the end of the twentieth century often makes you feel like you're one of those investigators who arrive on the scene after air crashes. We look around at the survivors and the detritus and, to stay sane, we reason through the events from our lucky distance. Along the way, during the time we linger, the places, crashes, and disasters become populated by familiar characters; history becomes the thing lived by people we know. Maybe there's a woman with a limp somewhere in your landscape, or a quiet, friendly man who appears to be a bit of a loner.

I wandered through the city gate, past the Tower Museum, into a small tourist shopping mall with arts-and-crafts stores. Silversmiths hammered out bracelets and earrings in old Celtic designs, then gave them a modern twist. Knitters and weavers pulled together gorgeous strands of blue, pink, and navy threaded with gold or silver. I fingered some of the wraps in a designers' shop, envious of the patience, skill, and vision entailed in creating them. Designs were new, and the shop owners were young and inspiring. They weren't the Ireland I was expecting, all kitsch and blarney. I wandered away from the jewelry stores, tripping (like the girls I had eyed before) on the cobblestones that so many people find quaint, and into the textile shops. I was looking for a sweater, and because I woke that morning from a dream of green, it had to be a *green* Aran fisherman's sweater. Traditionally, the Aran is always white, but on this I knew I could find compromise. Tourist demand had created wide variation in the sweater, and I was confident I would find one that pleased my eye. A small, messy wool shop on the corner of the mall had what I needed. I wandered in. A bell rang on the door as I entered, and a white-haired man said hello and continued about his work sorting yarns.

I'd like to say the sweater I wanted was a hand-knit, cottage-produced, "authentic" Aran sweater, but it wasn't. It was a thick, warm, machine-knit fisherman's with a traditional cable design on the front, and it was forest green, speckled with gold, brown, and rust. Traditional sweaters were designed with family and village in mind for the most pragmatic reasons: A body washed overboard by the freezing waters of the north Atlantic was easier found if wearing white, and the man (by then rendered unrecognizable by the water), identified by cable stitch. There is little chance of contemporary fashion hounds like me washing up on Ireland's shore, and since I was hungry for the colors of the countryside, green it was.

I pointed out the sweater I wanted in the window and asked if I could look at it.

"Why, surely," the man answered, putting down a ball of wool and walking to the display. He had a thin frame, which made him appear elderly, but he was not frail. He wore glasses and spoke in the friendly way the Irish seemed to have with me when I was traveling. It was curiosity and welcome combined, and it often made me laugh, since it was usually peppered with a corny joke or comment.

"Have you relatives here?" he asked.

"Not that I know of," I said, telling the truth, "but my folk come from Galway; my grandmother was born there."

"Oh, you're Irish," he said with a smile.

He handled the sweater with care, taking it off the hanger and preparing to wrap it for me.

"That's okay," I interrupted, "I'd like to wear it."

"Oh, very well then."

"Do you live here in Derry?" I asked.

"Yes, I'm from these parts," he answered, then laughed, "my folk came over here from Scotland; I guess they were sheep stealers! And look at me— still in the sheep business!"

I laughed as we completed the transaction. Scottish planters had settled in Ireland during the reign of the British King James I in the seventeenth century, after some vicious uprisings by Ireland's chieftains in the sixteenth century. With the "Flight of the Earls" (the desperate exit of the chieftains), the building of trade and the exploitation of natural resources made the northwest a small but important jewel for the British Crown. It was also a cultural laboratory of sorts. Some serving the British Crown sought to cultivate land and "Anglicize" this area of the island through the planting of communities on confiscated land available after the chieftains' exit. Others serving the crown sought to "colonize" the area, ripping traditional Gaelic culture out by the roots and "civilizing" the domestic population. The competition of ideas and administrative models led to an application of the plantation model that had little room for the mingling of "natives" and "foreigners." Scottish planters were in a struggle with Irish natives for available land, and they both had to keep the English "country gentleman" at bay.

I left the shop, threw the sweater over my shoulder, and left behind the chuckling sheep-stealer's great-grandson. The wool kept me warm against the quick burst of chill wind I often felt in Ireland. I walked up Shipquay Street to meet Dennis and Rene. I thought I'd mention the confused conversation we foreigners had held. Perhaps they could clarify things. They sat parked by the World War I memorial, eating a takeout dinner before their evening workshop with a local community theater group. I climbed in, and as we made small talk, I mentioned the confusing conversation I had had with the others over the city's history.

"The Apprentice Boys weren't orphans!" Rene said to me with scorn.

"Oh?" I said, embarrassed. "That's the way they were presented," I added, a bit defensively.

"Of course they were," she said, with a roll of her eyes.

I was not yet informed as to the specific cultural politics of the city and its influence on framing Irish stories, but I could tell I had inadvertently stepped on a land mine with this observation.

"Parents in this city would have saved large sums of money to have their kids apprenticed to learn a trade. They weren't *orphans*, cast over here like garbage! Orphans would have had to learn a trade in the workhouse system. No one would have wasted money on them—apprenticing was expensive."

"Perhaps I made poor notes at the museum."

"Maybe," Dennis said politely, "but y'know, this is a bigoted city, Edie."

What could I say to that? I had heard the same of Belfast—delivered with equal conviction. At any rate, the segregation of the communities was testimony to . . . *something*. It was locally known as "the divide"—an unsatisfying term. I resisted the urge to express a tourist's "shock" and sympathy over the tension. Could any American city claim full integration of racial and ethnic communities? Boston certainly couldn't.

"Look," Dennis went on to explain, "James II believed he was godlike— that the British king had divine rights. He used to write Sunday sermons and demand that *all* Christian churches deliver them."

"That's right," Rene continued, "and all Christian leaders appealed to the pope to displace him."

"So that explains the reference to papal support for William," I said, remembering Uta's comment. Both of them began to speak with a degree of frustration—*Was I buying Republican propaganda, I wondered?*

"This is all in history books!" Dennis exclaimed angrily.

Which books? I thought. I mean, it's all well and good that apprenticeships had prestige, but who had access to those positions? Who has access to their modern-day equivalents? Change religion to class and the picture changes and stays the same. Rene was right. Apprenticeships entailed sacrifice. But departure was sacrifice, too. Couldn't someone hold a parade for that? Looked at from the perspective of the twentieth century, the entire history of the island became a tapestry for me. It was complicated and riddled with knots, creases, and holes. Stone city walls competed with hedges and thick undergrowth in the pattern, both speckled with the hard hats of soldiers. Roads spun around like the circular torcs found at ancient Celtic forts, and people spoke in waves of contradiction.

~❧ ❧~

Glassie's exploration of Ireland through oral culture fascinated me, since it was so deeply grounded in daily experience; it painted pictures where history listed "facts." Ireland was perfect for such a tradition. It is one of the few places I've been where the everyday is endowed with the otherworldly and where history, even that recorded on the back of grocery store slips and inside the paper used to wrap fish, is celebrated. Indeed, this record of history, this retelling, is courageous—it is a way of refusing to allow the past to be "disappeared" by the outlawing of language, song, or symbol, all of which Great Britain had tried at one time or another, only to be foiled by the ethnic Irish community of scribes, balladeers, and teachers.

But on the ground, as a traveler, as a woman looking forward to the twenty-first century, and as an Irish American digging around at her roots, I found myself agreeing with young Irish people who found celebration of the past burdensome and embarrassing. In Viet Nam and China, I had experienced the same puzzle. Songs celebrating the ancient were, to me, overly romantic—particularly if the images contained therein kept people in positions of defeat or left your vocal chords quivering about martyrdom and suffering. In short, they were something I couldn't relate to. Thus, I find myself in disagreement with many interpreters of the storytelling ritual. But I am also enamored of Ireland's oral traditions when I encounter them. This contradiction is acceptable, I think. What entertains in the pub, what spills out over café coffee or kitchen-table tea, doesn't fit in print, where mere letters are a boundary that hems in sound and steals its glory. Tales set loose in taxi rides are limp on the page; they are burdensome to a writer. I was always trying, but falling flat in my efforts, to bring forward the rhythm of Ireland's many conversational moments as they pushed against me. Occasionally in America, I can retell one of the many stories and dialogues I heard, but it is mere mimicry.

The pub story or the party tale told over and over is meant only for vocal delivery; it fails on the page. Too many intangibles are missing: the giggle as an ending is anticipated; the slow, deliberate placement of the pint glass on the wooden bar; and the muttering of a spoiler who wants to tell the punch line before it arrives. These are the layers of ritual, color, and "tradition" peeled away by our twentieth-century analysis. In doing this, of course, we rip the heart from the creature, pluck the bud from the vine. More than anything, Ireland taught me how to sit back and let a moment unfold between people, as if I were privy to a flower's slow blossoming.

It wasn't until I was in Ireland that I could see the central role that storytelling and songs had played in keeping the Irish alive through so many years. If we see the Irish storyteller in a pub as a stereotype ("professional

Irishman" was the cynical phrase used by an American travel writer), then we have overlooked the key element of rhythm or musicality in language—banter or story is music from one person leading to response (often laughter) from another. More important is the rhythm found in the telling—it is a drug released only in talk (unbound by the borders of text), and it gives the listener a contact high.

I was searching for just such a rhythm that weekend in Derry. Trying to explain it to my friend Steve as we walked past St. Eugene's Cathedral one evening, I said I was in search of stereotypes: "I want to see something very Irish," I said. Neil was walking quietly behind us and muttered something like, "Oh, God."

"We could go to the Dungloe," Steve suggested.

"The Gweedore?" Neil added.

"We have to go to Peadar O'Donnell's," I said, referring to a pub on Waterloo Street.

This is a recently opened pub designed in an old style, with wood flooring, a mahogany bar, live music, and some very tough-looking guys working a very small door. Walking into a set of traditional music and loud conversation, I spotted a few seats at the bar and happily took them for the three of us. After settling in, I set my eyes on an older man sitting next to Neil. He rolled a cigarette on the bar, twisted the ends, and placed it between his wrinkled lips. He had a long nose and an even longer chin, which hooked up slightly. As he struck a match and lit the whisper of a cigarette, the flame tickled his nose. I liked him.

He turned to Neil and said, "Wanna hear a story about Australia?" The three of us stared at him for a moment in disbelief. That he had sussed that Neil was from Australia was enough to pique my interest still further. We sat down.

"The name's Malcolm," he said to Neil, "I'm from over in Moville. I was standing at the taxi stand round the corner there and I thought, "Now will I use this money to take a cab home, or will I go for a pint?" He took a pile of coins out of his pocket, "I've enough for one more drink and a cab ride home. I'm not from around here, y'know." He spoke the last bit a little loudly and looked over his shoulder, then he took a sip of his Guinness.

"It's only a short story," he continued, referring to his rigamarole about Oz. For some reason, he then felt it necessary to recite the geography of Australia, and upon reaching Queensland ("the deep North"), he added, "after that, it's Indonesia, right?"

I quietly hazarded a guess to Steve that he was in his seventies.

"Have you been to Indonesia?" Neil asked.

"Not yet," he answered.

This answer triggered a loud laugh from me. Malcolm looked over slyly, as if to say, *I'll get to you in a minute.*

Steve turned to me and asked, "Is this what you were looking for?"

The evening was damp, and the streets had that gritty feel to them I noticed about Derry—as if there were always a film of sand to be washed away. Behind me some musicians were reluctantly finishing up a session. I tapped my fingers on the bar to release the cold that had settled into my fingertips, then snapped them in rhythm to the music. As I listened to the musicians with one ear, I stared awkwardly at the ceiling and behind the bar and tried to eavesdrop on Malcolm and Neil. They were discussing the rights of Aboriginals, English socialism, and whether or not to have another drink.

"You tell your lads I am with them all the way!" Malcolm said to Neil, referring to the rights of Aborigines to land stolen by the Australian government. Then he turned to me suddenly, looked me in the eye, and said, "Wanna hear a story about Americans?"

I smiled. I had said next to nothing since we got in. What had betrayed me? I didn't register my surprise at his perceptiveness, but instead said—out of the side of my mouth—"I suppose."

He cackled, then reached into his pocket and pulled out a pile of coins and bills (it was the first time I had seen a man reach into his pocket repeatedly in a bar and come up with *more* money each time). He placed them on the bar, counted them out, then gestured to the bartender for another drink.

"I'll never forget it," he said, "it was after the Second World War. I'm British, see," he said, a little too loudly, then looked around, "from over in Moville. I haven't been to Derry in some time." He eyed the people around him (who were all, it must be said, taking no notice of him whatsoever). "I was working one of them minesweepers, y'know, during the war. I was in the British Army!"

I was thinking he was about to tell a story of the war, but he took a turn and brought us instead to a pub in Donegal.

"Oh, it was late one night, raining and windy, and we were all gathered together at the pub, drinking away and having good craic, when the door opens and there's two guys standing there . . . (he sipped). I'll never forget 'em." He held his hand up as he spoke, "One was tall, one was short; they're both wearing these trench coats with the collars up (and he gestures with his hands to draw us a portrait of someone like Bogart). We all stopped talking, of course, and just looked at them. They walk over to the barkeep and say (here his voice drops to a deep, dramatic version of an American accent): 'WE NEED A PHONE.' Well, we're all dead silent and staring away at'em. Paddy, behind the bar, says, 'Sure, there's one there in the back,' and waves them on . . . well, they go in the back and sure enough—they don't come out. They're GONE! . . . After some time I go to the back, then come out and turn to my mates and say, 'Lads, those were no visitors, that was the C-I-A!'"

At this point he fell into a fit of hysterical and loud laughter, then sipped his Guinness.

I love that story, especially since it was delivered for my benefit. I love the rain and wind, the tall and short, the trenches, the CIA agents before the CIA was established, and—especially—the phone conveniently located in a back room from which two dodgy characters can slip away. I wanted him to go on. And he knew it.

"I'll tell you a story, pet, can I tell you a short story?"

"Yeah, sure," I answer.

"Over in Moville I bought myself a trawler—this was a while back. This is only a short story, love." He sips his drink again and then begins to roll a cigarette.

"It was moored right in the harbor there . . . Well, the British army . . . ," the rolling paper crinkled . . . , "the British army, in its infinite wisdom . . ." He put the cigarette in his mouth and lit it. Again, the flame tickled his nose. "They decided they were putting metal fencing up around the pier." ("To stop smugglin'," he adds, a footnote revealing the "wisdom" to which he referred.) "In the winter comes a storm while my trawler, she's in dock, right?" He paused. Here I was to answer him.

"Yeah," I said.

"Oh, it was a terrible storm, right?"

"Yeah."

"But there was nothing you could do, right?" He sips his drink. "This is only a short story, pet." He drags on the cigarette and exhales . . . "So, my trawler, the metal pole—the tall thing, what is that? the metal pole?"

"The mast?" I ventured (I don't know or care if trawlers have masts, but I don't want to break his rhythm).

"The mast!" he says with a smile and the start of a laugh, because obviously I'm cooperating with the ritual. "My trawler is knocked about by this storm, right?"

"Yeah."

"And the mast goes flying, knocks down the fencing!" (I made a surprised and shocked face.)

"Yes," he continues, "Oh, there was nothing I could do, right? It was a storm, right?"

"Yeah," I said.

"Now, here's the craic, pet . . . I told you it's only a short story . . . here's the craic. I'm in pub come a week, right?"

I waited.

"Right?" he repeated.

"Yeah," I snap to, my head spinning with his rhythms and laughter. Then I giggle. This tickles him and he asks, rhetorically, "What're you laughin' for? We're not there yet." He sips the Guinness again and licks his lips.

"Come a week I go into the pub, and your man Paddy's working behind the bar, says to me, he says, 'G'day, Malcolm, can I buy you a pint?' I says, 'I'll let ya,' and I sit down. 'Why is that, sir?' I ask. 'Well,' he says, pouring my pint, 'I wouldn't . . . ,' (then there is that lovely *pause;* I lean in) 'but the I-R-A wants to buy you a Christmas present!'"

He threw his head back and broke into loud laughter, shaking his wrinkles and blowing smoke, then bringing his finger to his lips and saying, "Sssshhh."

I nodded my agreement.

"Do you like my sense of humor, pet?" he asks, gently.

"Yes," I said.

He exhaled from his cigarette. "There's a woman in Killybegs, when I ask her that, says, 'I think you're the funniest *bastard* I ever met!'"

I laughed loudly and said, "She's right."

"ssshhh . . . " he said again, dramatically, breaking his rhythm with laughter. "ssshhh."

He took his hand from his pocket and began counting his coins again. By this point, I was drunk on both the Guinness and the language. I stared at him as he rolled another thin cigarette.

"Pet, let me give you some good advice."

"Yeah?"

"Don't ever go muckin' about in Buncrana."

It takes me a second, but I remember that Buncrana is a town, not a thing or a state of mind.

"Yeah?"

"Red hot with Republicans. You meet a guy and he tells you he's from Buncrana, you hightail it out of there!"

"Oh? I thought it was Omeath?"

He stopped dead for a minute, looked at me, then broke out into another loud cackle. He brought his finger dramatically to his lips, widened his eyes, and said, "ssshhh," then continued, "but you didn't hear it from me! ssshhh." Then he looked again over his shoulder. "Derry's a good place," he announced, as if he'd never been across the border. "I work for no one," he adds.

I sat staring into the mirror for a minute, catching my breath and trying to come down to earth. Malcolm took the pause as opportunity: "So how long you been home?" I did a double take, then a fight broke out behind me. A table and two chairs fell over, and I turned away for a minute to look at two pigheaded young men getting into a fistfight.

Then, as sometimes happens in Ireland, I turned back and Malcolm was gone. I was looking into the eyes of a dark-haired Irish woman smoking a cigarette and wearing my own face. The hour was late, and the pub was closing. She shoved a tin can in front of me.

"Prisoner's Defense Fund!"

It was a splash of cold water. I sobered up and walked away.

~⋇~

The next day I headed for Buncrana. Moving like a pigeon on her way home, I drove through the "Inishowen 100" and almost crashed a few times while looking out at the view of Lough Swilly. On the way back, I felt the pull of the sweater factory Crana Knits, manufacturers of hand-knit Irish sweaters. It is a large, plain building across from a golf course. I saw it, and my wallet burned in my bag.

Inside the factory was a nondescript storeroom with one corner laid out as a small retail unit. Most of the clothing for sale was done by local knitters working out of their homes in nearby towns. This time I thought of buying a pullover in a more traditional white. I held one up against me and looked in the mirror. It was speckled yarn, creamy white, with the brown and black of peat. The moss stitch, representing wealth to the fisherman, ran along the edge; the honeycomb stitch ran up the front and along the sleeves.

"Oh, that's an odd one," someone behind me said.

I turned around to find a slight, dark-haired saleswoman watching me.

"Is there something wrong with it?" I asked.

"Oh, no dear, I just mean there's only one, there's not a lot of them, we've no more like it."

"Well, I'll take it. The odd one, that'll be the one for me."

I put it on the counter and continued to look around the showroom. I looked through the piles of kids' cardigans, with blue-in-green speckled with red, yellow, sky blue, and pink. Buttons hung like small candies on the edging.

"Well hello, Mrs. Duggan," the saleswoman said to a knitter who entered the building. The woman smiled and placed a pile of men's sweaters on the counter; two fell off the top, their long arms unfolding and hanging down like branches.

"She's in the back, dear," the woman continued, referring to the manager.

I had mentioned, a few moments earlier and to another saleswoman, that I was from Boston, and, as if picking up a conversation midstream, the dark-haired woman turned to me and began talking. Her language hypnotized me, too, and I began to search my mind for a way to describe it, only to end up at Joyce's still apt flowing-water analogy. Her voice was like water moving down a hillside over rock. It was just conversation, but the sound bordered on music.

"My daughter, she's a nurse, y'know, she loves it over there in Boston. She's bought a house with her husband; it's somewhere, now where is it? And they want to rent it, dear, one of the apartments—it's two or three houses in one, what are they?"

"A triple decker," I said.

"Yes!" she pointed, "and now she's got her license to practice—is it a license you get there, dear? She goes for the interviews at those hospitals, and all the time they say, 'You keep that accent of yours and you'll do fine,' and she's just got a job finally. Where is it? The women's hospital, I think?"

"Brigham and Women's?" I ventured.

"That's it! That's the one! And their house, now I remember, it's in Dorchester. Is that a nice place, dear?"

"Yes," I answered, "it's right near where I work. In fact, I'll be needing an apartment when I return next summer, too!"

"Will you!? Well, I'll be sure to tell her, and you're a teacher, did you say? Here, write down your name and address, and I'll give it to her, and have you got any family here, dear?"

I paused for a moment, wondering if that was a prerequisite to getting the apartment or a hazard.

"Not *here* here," I said, "but my folk come from Galway."

"Oh, my, isn't Galway nice, and where are you staying while you're home here, dear?"

"I'm visiting a friend in Derry," I explained.

"Oh, yes, Derry's lovely." She paused.

We turned to look outside, as if we'd be able to see the border as a physical object, with "wee Derry" behind it. For a minute I felt like a kid, my hands pressed against the window of a candy store.

"And, of course, Derry's British, y'know."

"Is it?" I asked.

"Yes," she answered, smiling, "and aren't they lovely people?"

Chapter 4

Myths and Legends /
Postcards from Belfast / Drinks and Stories

All travel begins in the imagination. In country, in the moment, we are burdened by an overload of sensory experience. When traveling, I think we carry
with us an understanding of places that leans heavily on the past. Informed by
a blue-gray fog of longing and sentiment, we see everyday events as echoes of
those stories and images. My first foray into the history of my own family was
a brief story from my father's older sister. Clare ("as in the county," she explained) had a lovely memory she passed on to me one holiday over dessert
and coffee. She showed me an old box of family photos from the 1920s.

"Your great-grandfather," she began, between bites of chocolate cake,
"served in the United States military in Mexico."

"The San Patricios?" I asked, excited at the prospect.

"The what?" she answered, slightly annoyed.

She put a piece of cake delicately into her mouth as I explained, "The San
Patricios—they're an Irish regiment that switched sides during the Mexican-
American War. They're heroes down in Mexico, y'know."

"No," Clare said, a bit put off, "I'm sure he didn't serve with them. But,
he *was* discharged in San Francisco," she took in another piece of cake and
sipped her coffee. "I don't remember when."

I prompted her with my eyes. She continued, "He made his way across
America to meet his bride." Another piece of cake, another sip, another
prompting, "That was quite an accomplishment in those days, you know,"
the chocolate crumbs were piled into a neat line, "they didn't have the trains
and planes we do." She put her fork down, licked her lips, and said, "Well!
That was delicious."

Patrick Shillue, my great-grandfather—County Clare man and newly
committed American—found himself discharged from the army in California after fighting an invasive war that caused many Irish Catholic men
to switch sides midbattle. Maybe. Clare saw him as a heroic immigrant in a
battle of a different sort. Perhaps she saw him as part of something referred

to by some in California as "settlement." Either way, he fought, struggled, suffered, and lived to tell about it.

"He came to meet his bride in Boston," Clare said, full of admiration for his journey across North America.

For weeks after I heard that comment, I saw Patrick as a giant stepping across the continent to meet a woman in a black cloche standing outside a brownstone. In the three-dimensional pictures that float around in my imagination, he's *huge,* a long, thin, wiry man with big hands and a gruff personality. The bride—Elizabeth O'Brien—is sad, stout, and dour looking. She's nervous. To my modern sensibility, this makes sense; obviously she had been bought. What else brought women across oceans alone to "husbands"?

Great-grandfather was one of the newer figures in my imagination. Up until that time it was all women: Elizabeth O'Brien, Anna Shillue, Nora Kilcoyne, Lil Clifford. After Clare's story, Elizabeth came to life, too; she rolled out in my imagination like a character in an old film. She stood rather solidly outside a brownstone on Beacon Hill, waiting. She would live, perhaps, in the areas where Ireland's diaspora settled: Boston's North End, not the best part of the city, mind you, but an overcrowded ghetto housing the unemployed. Or she may have ended up in what is today unromantically called "Southie," or South Boston, a politically contentious slip of land on Boston harbor. Or (here we are closer to the mark) she lived in Quincy, a small city south of Boston proper, or Hyde Park, one of Boston's inner suburbs. She would marry Patrick in Roxbury, part of Boston proper. In Clare's photographs—a veritable archive—Elizabeth wears thick-soled black shoes, which remind me of nun's shoes, flashing out from underneath swaying fabric, laces tied in a firm knot. I look down on her shoes, look down on her thick ankles and big hands. She's a workhorse, she has a sharp tongue, but sad, sad eyes.

Clare stood and lifted her plate from the table. "Are you finished?" she gestured toward my plate and cake.

"No," I said, "I'll stay here a minute."

"Okay," she said, then wandered into the kitchen to do the washing up.

I never see any of these Irish women as ambitious or romantic; they are all solid, pragmatic, even stern. Elizabeth migrated in the early part of the twentieth century, and in my mind that meant she was to be gotten rid of by the Irish and handled by the likes of Patrick, who walked across America with huge strides (and who still strikes me as frighteningly rugged). Elizabeth waits without considering that she might have other options. In fact, in early twentieth-century America, she didn't; it wasn't even conceivable that women ever would.

My imagined history rambles onward from that first image . . . working in Beacon Hill, through all the Irish enclaves and ghettos, to Hyde Park to Jamaica Plain to Dorchester to South Boston, and one afternoon, *my* Clare stands near Elizabeth. They are in the kitchen, and Clare's wee body can't quite reach the counter. Great-grandfather is still a giant sitting in a giant's house. He feeds a giant furnace in a building in downtown Boston (I can hear the door of it groan open, feel the wall of heat shoot out at him, and watch him tame it before he closes the door again with a heavy shove).

As I sat imagining all this at the dining room table, my thoughts were interrupted by Beth, one of my four sisters, who was offering to help Clare at the kitchen sink.

"No, no," she answered, "I'll do it."

Beth walks into the dining room, gives me a gentle push on the shoulder, and tells me I really ought to be helping Aunt Clare.

The story fades; I finish my cake and turn to enter the kitchen. Seeing Clare's back as she washes dishes, I remember another story she once told about Great-grandmother. Clare was a little girl standing in Elizabeth's kitchen one day, trying to figure out the world of these adults. She is only as tall as the sink, and looking over its edge, she stares at Elizabeth, her grandmother. The dishes wobble and clink in the water. Elizabeth's hands move in and out (I can even see them, swollen and red), handing Clare plates to dry. As Clare peers into a bowl or cup, she looks over her shoulder to see if Grandfather is nearby. The sun hits the window, and Clare takes a breath before forming her comment. She wants to be casual about the giant; she wants to dismiss his severity, his power; his face with its thick handlebar mustache looms in her imagination.

"Oh, Grandmother," she says, "how can you kiss Grandfather with that awful mustache?"

The hands rest on the edge of the sink, then Elizabeth looks down at little Clare.

"Kissing a man without a mustache is like eatin' an egg without salt."

What a shock! Out flies the spark, the passion, the secret giggle in the dark, the bawdy laugh in the face of parochialism. In the 1990s, Clare and I laugh along with it across six decades. Great-grandfather shrinks down to man size at the end of this story. His giant steps are cut short by the large, red hands of a bawdy woman. The furnace fire is cool compared with our Elizabeth.

By the end of the twentieth century, the names O'Brien and Shillue are part of some dry record somewhere, part of an extensive list of people who were born in Ireland but left it, part of the community of people recorded by British soldiers and memorists trying to keep track of a land where things change right before you. If I wanted to undertake a paper search, I could piece Elizabeth's life together. I could piece the lives of many people together via the slips of seemingly innocuous information put down by government surveyors in both Ireland and the United States.

I have no interest in doing that. Elizabeth finally exists in my life because I know a story about her and I can become her when I retell it. I do this all the time at parties all over the United States. It is a notoriously unreliable form of record, but one I participate in readily. I love its drama. Through the story, I can claim my inheritance of brash comebacks, tough wit, and the dismissal of fools. It all trickles down to me through time, and I barely recognize it as our Irish family tradition, as my inheritance of sorts. Most of the time I feel—and here I am "so American"—that the world is all brand-new and forward facing.

❧ ☙

In northern Ireland, amid books and maps and museum showcases, I wonder what Elizabeth O'Brien Shillue thought and felt as her son, Dennis, went off to fight in World War I. Did anyone imagine it was as the Irish poet T. M. Kettle described:

> So here, while the mad guns curse overhead
> and tired men sigh, with mud for couch and floor
> know that we fools, now with the foolish dead
> Died not for flags, nor King, nor emperors
> But for a dream born in a herdsman's head
> and for the secret Scripture of the poor.

I wonder what Dennis thought and felt when he dragged himself around southern France and encountered Irish soldiers in English uniforms.

"*Sure the American-born are different,*" I can hear the Irish mumble from across time. Dennis came home with a bullet in his leg that came out twisted like a piece of tree root, and it rolled around Elizabeth's palm, mingling with her relief that it was this that brought him home, not death. Clare showed me the bullet one wintry Sunday. I was sitting in an armchair in her front room. Outside the light was fading, and the wind threatened to keep the season with us eternally. She turned on a lamp and began rustling through papers and a box of family paraphernalia.

"Here it is!" she said, reaching into the clutter. She walked across the room and handed me a small, twisted piece of lead.

"It's so small," I marveled. It was curved in parts from the firing, and I tried to imagine how it could cause so much pain and yet be the lucky thing it was, bringing him home.

"He was very worried about the direction the country was going," Clare tells me, referring to Grandfather's postwar tensions. This says conservatism to my liberal ear, but I may be imagining it. "He had terrible tension and stomach troubles," Clare continued.

"Oh," I said, "PTSD?"

"Well, I don't know what it was," she answered.

No one did. It must have been that, I reasoned, otherwise why did he look so harsh? I had never met Dennis, but my strongest memory of him is a picture of him with his wife, Anna, who was an immigrant from Galway. Dennis's hands are on his hips—he looks tall and mean.

"Look," Clare said, handling another picture, "here's a picture of Mom with her sisters Mary and Nora." She handed me a photo of three tall, muscular women.

"They used to get together on weekends, y'know, and speak Irish all day in the kitchen."

"Could you speak it?" I asked.

"No, no, of course not—they wouldn't teach us—but I always used to stand outside the room and listen," she said, with a twinkle in her eye.

I reached into another shoebox and pulled out the very photo I remembered of Dennis and Anna. Clare dissuaded me of the opinion that he was bad-tempered.

"Oh, goodness, no," she said, "he could be *so* charming. Now look at this one; it was taken when they were first married." She picked up a large silver frame from a corner of her bookshelf and handed it to me. It is Dennis and Anna in black and white, but as I look at it, his eyes are so *blue* they almost scare me with their blueness.

When I was young, I once asked my father if he knew when exactly his mother, Anna, arrived and why she came over.

"Oh, I don't know, honey," he said, trying to dismiss my curiosity (which was intruding on his newspaper reading).

"Could you guess?"

"Sometime after the Troubles."

This was a most dissatisfying answer.

"Dad, you do know she came from Ireland, right?"

The paper snaps down, and he looks at me over his glasses. "Of course!"

"I just mean when weren't there troubles in Ireland? What troubles are you talking about?"

He folds the paper back up, "I don't know." Then a memory tugs at him, and he puts the paper down again, "But I do remember her telling a story once about hiding behind a wall, dodging bullets fired by the police."

"The Black and Tans?" I asked, referring to the mercenary police force.

"I suppose . . . " The paper went back up. That was the end of it.

I like that story. It gives me a host of images: Anna, my grandmother, a tall immigrant woman with a brogue, Galway folk, *bullet dodger*. By the time she arrived, there were droves of Irish in Boston and there had been for close on a century. Like other immigrants from Europe, they huddled together in ghettos, suffered from various diseases encouraged by poverty and poor housing, longed for education and wealth, settled for hard work and what they could get. In New York, Ellis Island had been established, and, naturally, an Irish girl was the first to cross its threshold. Annie Moore, fifteen years old, survived the journey across the Atlantic, after a farewell from Sorrow Square in Derry. I sometimes think about the feel of those waters and am stunned into admiration for the early immigrants. Did Annie realize what it would be like? Could she even imagine waters so big? Space and sky going on so far that you could feel yourself shrink in the face of it? The poet Eavan Boland writes of these immigrants and many others: "What they survived we could not even live."

Oh, what they wouldn't do for a bit of home, a symbol, a remnant of the place, something to hold on to, to keep them connected to where they came from so they could always know who they are. The trauma of departure from the homeland was captured well by Fintan O'Toole, a Dublin journalist who followed the paper trail I rejected. He went through newspaper archives in the United States to find a Fermanagh woman at an Irish fair in the Grand Central Palace of 1897 New York City. She was kneeling, weeping and praying over a giant topographical map of Ireland, complete with "the veritable Irish soil of each county . . . duly attested as truly genuine. . . . When she finally stepped off the map's Irish soil, she sighed sadly and clung to the fence, still gazing at 'Old Ireland.' She kept looking backward as she walked away, as if bidding a long farewell." He notes the scene's prescience for the end of our century: "A country has become a heritage attraction long before such an idea ought to have gained currency."

And yet, strangely enough, some time later, well into the twentieth century, my father, a second-generation American, "professional" son of an American veteran and an Irish immigrant, insisted that the Irish flag, the symbol of our ethnic "homeland," *not* be waved.

"Those who wave it are the least Irish," he muttered.

Indeed, this very statement is the source of much sociopolitical debate on both sides of the Atlantic. Who's coming, who's going, and *who's Irish* continue to be the subjects of coded, closed discourse in Ireland, the United States, and Great Britain. The poet Eavan Boland writes in her memoir *Object Lessons:* "What is this thing—a nation—that is so powerful it can make songs, attract sacrifice and so exclusive it drives into hiding the complex and skeptical ideas which would serve it best?" Boland expressed frustration with the entire literature of her nation, with its inadequacy and paternalism, its neglect of the complex lives of women. She explored her experience in dusky evenings in a Dublin suburb, on drives through hills that spoke to her, on islands she escaped to. But for me it was impossible to view Ireland without seeing it as a place fled in shame, anger, and tears. I had no landscape such as Boland's with which to imagine my ancestors' early lives and, unlike Brett in Belfast, no reliable record. I have only mismatched snippets of history unreliably reported from Anna's children. When asked about the shooting in Galway, Clare claimed ignorance. Her older sister Barbara remembered a shooting, but said it was Nora who had a bullet "whistling past her ear." Who's to be believed? I deferred to my father's reluctant historiography, but included Clare's overheard dialogues. In my version, Anna, speaking Irish with Nora in Boston, tells of hiding from the Black and Tans behind one of Galway's many rock walls. Nora does her one better, coming out with, *"Hide? Those bastards shot at me!"* In the end, I don't know what it is that makes *me* "Irish"—the language or the bullet?

If Eavan Boland talks of desiring to take apart the false idea of the Irish nation as one without women, to reexamine the very idea of the nation itself, the Belfast literary critic Edna Longley does just that. With a scolding voice, she tears down spiritually debilitating notions of identity that deny both gender and cultural diversity. She writes of a debt to British literary traditions, not of a burdensome historical conflict, and in addressing both gender and culture issues, she takes no prisoners. She scorns "starry-eyed lit crit" imported from the United States and the "Brit guilt" that feeds unhealthy mythologies. Latching on to the *Who's Irish?* question, she notes a 1989 comment by Irish Cardinal O'Fiaich: "'Many Protestants,' he said, 'love Ireland as devoutly as *any* Catholic does.' He then recited the litany of Patriot Prods (Tone, Emmet, etc.) usually produced in support of such statements. It sometimes seems as if Protestants have to die for Ireland before being allowed to live here."

Coming from the United States, I found both authors convincing. But this is symptomatic of my trips overall—they were plagued by emotional ambivalence tamed by a ceaseless intellectual curiosity. Though I've explored my father's family, my own ethnic identity is something about which I am ambivalent. This is not uncommon in Irish America, I think, at least among my own Irish American friends. Many of the attributes associated with the Irish personality came to flower outside the island, but a diaspora is a conglomeration of all that is both beautiful and ugly about a people. Irish American racism and parochialism are not banners I wave proudly, and though political clout represents a rise from discriminatory oppression and gross poverty, it is often manifest in vulgar displays of cronyism. Longley referred to Ulster Irishness and Britishness as socially constructed identities. So it is in the United States. What is this thing I'm supposed to be willing to kill and die for?

The things that are said to bind the people of Ireland—that is, its "culture"—will always have a powerful hold over me. They are music, literature, the ability to deflate arrogance with a cleverly delivered word or two, and a degree of endurance (what I call the "fight" in "fighting Irish") that leaves me speechless. Having struggled so much with the negative aspects of my ethnic inheritance, I speak confidently today of what I love about the Irish personality: We're argumentative when we want to be, manipulative when we need to be, good company when you're feeling low, loyal to a fault, and one hell of an ally in a fight. Add music that makes your head spin and your heart bleed, literature that (I think) is unrivaled in the English-speaking world, an island so pretty in spots you'd swear it really is "God's country," and you have a pretty interesting subject matter. The North (or northern Ireland, depending on what part of the political landscape I was standing in) appealed to me less because of my ethnic identity than because it was "troubled," and its intractability was the only thing about which outsiders ever talked.

～❧ ❧～

My fascination with immigrants is fed no less in northern Ireland, where the migration to America included a woman named Adele, whose postcard I found in an antique shop on Donegall Pass. On the front is a picture of Queen's Bridge and the steamers that dotted Belfast's waterfront; on the back is the comment "This is the place where I will be leaving when I am going to America. I hope it will not be long." The date is 1905, which means she may have arrived around the same time as Elizabeth, perhaps before. She may have migrated to Pennsylvania, or down south to one of the Carolinas. Or she may have been what my maternal grandmother, Lillian Clifford, referred to as "half-fares"—those who could get passage only to Canada.

In Ireland she was probably a factory worker. She could have sorted flax for Belfast's linen makers or worked barefoot as a washer in McCartney's rope mill. She may have been one of the women I saw in the extensive photo collections that define the grimy promise of the industrial revolution that made northern Ireland valuable to Great Britain. It's likely that each time she reached bravely into the monstrous looms that made fabric for the empire's couture her hands untangled threads with quick skill. The photos of all these women unnerve me. They have long hair, pulled back but loose, and they wear long dresses with petticoats. I shudder to think of that fabric getting caught in machinery.

Adele was longing for America, but Elizabeth was being encouraged to leave County Clare because the family was too big and she was the oldest. It was her responsibility to go, surely she could understand that? At least that's what I think. As a woman, Adele was no more fortunate than Elizabeth; instead, she was most likely brought to a factory where the noise was so loud that she couldn't speak to her mates, where she had to learn a new sign language just to communicate to the woman across from her, and where her body may have been strained beyond endurance—and thus she kept thinking, again and again, *I hope it will not be long*.

Factory worker or society girl, I'm not sure which Adele was. Nor am I certain who Elizabeth was, but once, curious to explore Elizabeth's arrival in Boston further, I asked Clare bluntly, "Do you think she was . . . you know . . . bought?"

Clare scowled a bit, but had a ready reply: "No. I think it was something else. Patrick and she were from the same village; I think she had her eye on him."

I smile at the idea. How does one keep a record of *that?*

When we're informed by the blue-gray mist of longing and sentiment, then everything we encounter in Ireland echoes these true-false stories.

In the same pile of postcards where I found Adele's is another one that tells a different story. This one is posted July 15, 1921, and was sent via local mail from Belfast to Whiteabbey: "Dear Jennie, I could not get down Thursday as there is very heavy fighting in Farnham St. They have been at it all week. We will try and get a run down the week end if there is no disturbance. From Maggie."

The "fighting" was keeping Maggie and Jennie apart. I read this in the shop and considered it akin to what is now the phone message or the e-mail correspondence. It's dressed up as polite information about a visit, but it really lets Jennie know that Maggie's all right, doesn't it? The month of July is known among journalists and leaders as northern Ireland's "flashpoint." It's the heart of the parade season, the bitter core of the debate over what gets celebrated as "culture" in Ireland. But the year on this card is also 1921—the middle of Ireland's civil war. Let's assume that Jennie breathed a sigh of relief knowing Maggie was safe, but that it was mingled with the grief and frustration generated by war. Imagine longing for America from Donegal or Belfast, then imagine being homesick for Ireland in America.

What happened to Elizabeth O'Brien in County Clare may have happened to countless others around the island; she was "encouraged" to leave because of the poverty or because of the war. Elizabeth was born after the nineteenth-century famine, but she inevitably must have listened to stories of its horror, stories that may have haunted her, just as this one gathered by the Irish Folklore Commission haunts me: "In the same yard as the O'Neill brothers lived a family of Danaghers, in the townland of Cratloe. The household consisted of the widow and four children. All were stricken with fever, the mother having the two younger ones beside her. When she got a 'cool,' as Con O'Neill put it, she discovered one of the children dead, evidently for some days. Unable to rise she used to put the hand over to the other child to feel if it were still alive; the second child died also. The other two survived and were later well known to the O'Neills." I'm haunted by this story because I can remember the feeling of reaching out for a loved one in the fever of sleep. I can remember wanting to know that they are there and that they're okay.

In this ghost-filled place, and as the oldest, Elizabeth could understand the burdens all the children placed on her mother and father. Surely she would do the right thing? But my Aunt Clare may also be right: a woman who has cast her eye on a man would easily cross an ocean to be with him. Nonetheless, we all concede that Elizabeth would somehow *have to leave*. In these circumstances, America stands as a mixed blessing. One is *forced* to leave home, but the rumor in the villages is that America is grand, absolutely grand, and you won't miss this poor old place a bit. *Why, Molly Boress claimed she heard from another that you could actually pick up money on the side of the street there was so much of it. Sure it's really the best thing, y'know.* And so she would not stay behind to hear again and again the stories of the dreadful visitation. But her listening made her kin to Joe McConaghy in Ballycastle, County Antrim, whose mother talked of people in comas being mistaken for the dead: "They would be waking them and they wouldn't be dead at all. She talked of some man from Carry that was burying his wife that time and the man noticed some movement in the coffin and took the lid off and his wife was there wondering where she was. She said he had nothing but his overcoat to put round her and take her home and she lived for long after that."

A shudder runs through the listener who hears these histories. Though American ships actually *brought* the moldy blight to Ireland, they also represented flight from a cursed land. To think of even the most basic elements of the time and place of these women is to realize the struggle of emotion and ambition that is *lived* history.

As with my impressionistic vision of Elizabeth, Adele's reality was probably far different than I imagine. You see, she knew how to write. She even had lovely handwriting, the kind one associates with "fine schooling." It's likely she was floating somewhere between the poverty of County Clare and the Big House plantations that marked Ireland's economic history. She may have been a more timid version of one Kathleen Coyle, who left Ireland before her, moving in the opposite direction, toward England and Paris. Coyle was part of a Big House family in Derry, one whose decline she described elegantly: "Its indications were tidal—and the tide was going out. Any chance of escape had to be both single and against the current. The process, of course, need not be deprived of splendour. We have but to regard salmon and eels to realize that they behave interestingly when they are going back."

Coyle was born in a "mixed" marriage, with a Catholic mother and a father whose religion was a "strict secret." She was born, like me, "in the strictest heritable sense of the term, from a generation of grandaunts." Kathleen was born in Derry, but went on to a life as a writer and traveler in Europe and the United States. Her eyes stare big and brown at you from the cover of her memoir *The Magical Realm,* which lay quietly dormant through most of this century until it was resurrected by a Dublin publishing house in 1997.

Adele, the strand that began my secret history of Ireland, was resident in Belfast in 1905, but longing for America. She may have been a factory worker, but she could also have been a piece worker in the textile trade, working diligently out of her residence, embroidering or crocheting lines that curved, circled, and knotted her life and passion. Sometimes I walked around the wet streets in Belfast's city center and wondered about what it felt like to carry your work into one of the dark brick factory buildings that made up the textile trade. Did the noise of the new, efficient looms invented during the industrial revolution assault her senses and rattle her bones? I wondered if it shook the fine threads of the table runners.

We're always dressing up history. We need it to fit our understanding of the present. We need it to secure our vision of what's right and wrong. *Long Shadows Cast Before,* by C. E. B. Brett, describes Oliver Cromwell's arrival in Ireland in decidedly mild terms, but then Brett's focus is family record. Curious time explorer that I am, I scorn Ireland's ancient patriarchy on behalf of Elizabeth, Adele, and Kathleen, casting it in the light of their struggle. Adele and Kathleen are like the women Edith Wharton and Henry James wrote about in their society novels. Theirs were creative lives cut short by upper-class convention. Grandmother Elizabeth, who stared solemnly from pictures of immigrant Boston, fled rural poverty for urban poverty. She had five daughters with Patrick and a son, Dennis, whose survival of World War I ensured that my father would come into the world, which in turn brought me to this century.

Of course, one day I did make a pilgrimage to the land of my ancestors in Ireland's mythic west. Amid the rock and sky, the wind and sun and sudden rain changing quickly into rainbow, amid the howl of famine echoes and the miles of crisscross wall and shadow of abandoned houses, I felt my modern disdain crumble underneath me and my knees buckle in a profound sympathy for their isolation and courage. What Elizabeth, Anna, and her sisters shared for the remainder of their lives in the United States was clattering kitchen conversation (Irish dialogues that Clare puzzled out from the next room). The words and memories fell apart with laughter at the end. No English allowed there. It was their sanctuary.

❦

I made my way one afternoon back down to the cramped confines of Linenhall Library. Two young women stood staring at a cart full of contemporary novels. Across the room by the newspaper section a young man in a T-shirt and jeans was curled up in a window seat like a greyhound. A red-faced man sitting across from me closed a leather binding holding a decade's worth of newspapers with a loud thud, then slid it across the table. He tapped it with his index finger and directed me to read it: "Look at that! You'll learn things you never knew!" Unable to resist, I lifted the binding and began scanning the *Belfast Telegraph* for June and July 1935. It was another riotous summer, but the editors managed to find room for a feature story on an amateur naturalist in Cranmore Park, South Belfast, as he struggled to capture a photo of the elusive little Grebe who very cleverly covers her nest where her eggs lay before hatching. Making my way through the summer stories, I noticed headlines and comments that were proof positive of a karmic repetition of annual conflicts. One headline read: "Belfast Death Toll Now Nine, Inquests on Seven Riot Victims." The coroner on the case claimed words were to blame, stating, "Provocative and offensive speeches reacted upon party passions, especially of the poor and ignorant. Bigotry is the curse of peace and good will. There would be less bigotry if there were less public speechmaking of the kind made by so-called Leaders of public opinion." Sound reasoning, I thought. I wondered how long he stayed in his position.

I caught sight of my watch and put the binder back on its shelf. I looked down at Colby's maps and memoirs. The *Ordnance Survey* would have to wait, I thought. I pulled my things together, left the library, and crossed the street to meet Dennis and Rene for a drink and some conversation.

"Edie!" Rene called out from her car.

"Hi, Rene."

"C'mon, luv," she gestured me to get in, "we'll go for a drink."

I climbed in.

"Hi there," I said to Dennis, who was behind the wheel.

"Hello, luv," he answered. Then he began to pull into the traffic. A BMW glided forward, blocking his way and coming to a stop.

"Now where the hell do you want me to go!" he yelled at the driver. I smiled.

"Dennis, don't you start!" Rene snapped.

I'm a Boston driver, so this exchange actually made me feel quite at home. I sat back.

Inside the pub, Rene handed me what she called a "small gift." It was another postcard.

"I bought one like this up the Donegall Pass!" I said, referring to an antique mart.

"Yes," Rene answered with a smile, "I thought this might be appropriate for you."

I turned the card over to read the text: "I am pleased to hear that you have received a line from the foreign port. What's going to happen?" It could have been for Elizabeth O'Brien, I said. After all, family mythology suggests she was *called* over by a departed love. I continued talking with Rene about the tall tale of her arrival. The barkeeper wandered over to the table. She was a bleached blonde with dark lipstick and a bit of a swagger.

"Hello, darlin'," Dennis said, sweetly.

"Whataboutche there, Dennis?"

"Dead on, Marie, we've got a friend here from America," he said, gesturing to me.

I was deep into my discussion of possible histories with Rene, who came from a family with a long history in Belfast. Her own grandmother had worked the mills I was imagining.

"If your postcard writer Adele *did* work those mills, she may not have lived to make it to America," she explained. "The life expectancy of the workers—at least in the carding room where my grandmother worked—was twenty-five. The puce hung in the air and was inhaled regularly, eventually clogging and choking their lungs."

"No wonder Adele wanted to leave," I answered. "Conditions were probably the same as the mills in Lowell, the factory city north of Boston," I said.

"Of course, in the Republic, the reason for wanting to go would be different," she said, referring to Elizabeth.

"Yes," I answered, "the poverty."

"Your great-grandmother's family probably didn't have the resources to feed her. There was no work . . . "

This was understandable, but still heartbreaking and an invitation to anger. Didn't poverty also push people to sell and abandon their kids? Could she have been sold? I mean, she was an unmarried daughter.

In the world of lace-curtain Irish America, such a suggestion is vulgar. It is beneath what we like to think of as our family heritage. Nonetheless, Ireland cannot lay claim to a history that honored women (I can't think of a place that can). The idea of selling may have offended my Aunt Clare, but it seemed a reasonable thesis to the barkeeper, who was, by now, politely waiting for Rene and me to finish our conversation.

"Oh, aye," she nodded, "the football pool. I'm going to take you to New York with my football winnin's, Mary." I looked up at her.

"My grandmother used to play the football pool in hopes of getting to America. You see, a great-aunt of mine was there—she was the one who had been sold."

But it wasn't to get to America that she was sold. Like some character in a grim and ghastly fairy tale, she was sold by her father at a country fair in Donegal for a bottle of "fine" whiskey.

"Well, she'd be damned," continued Marie, "she said there was no way she'd be treated that way and she ran off to America—alone."

And thus another American immigrant becomes a giant in my imagination, only this one leapfrogged over a bottle of whiskey and flew through the air, wearing black boots and a thick skirt. She must have arrived around the time of Elizabeth and Adele. Did she ride a slow steamer, like the ones pictured on postcards from the turn of the century? Did she wear black or cast grief aside for hope? It strikes me that she was unimaginably courageous and must have lived a life of great richness. This informal conversation is another bit of the secret history I collect as I move around talking with the Irish. I wonder if her family ever "spoke of" the great-aunt? Was she shunned, or did the women collude to keep their support for her new life a secret? Here America becomes the imagined place; it's the great escape, the "foreign port" sometimes heard from.

Eventually I stopped working so hard on my exploration of history through books. I stopped going to Linenhall Library, not because it had nothing to offer, but because its enormous content heckled me as I sat in the small wooden chair at the high table. I felt like a child at dinner eating thick meal out of obligation well after I'd had my fill. I looked at the lives of women and men, and the past mocked me with its unchangeability. I wanted to throw it away and hear another story about quick-witted comebacks and great escapes.

❧ ❧

In 1998, I discover the northern Irish through only a handful of media: dusty maps, poems, true stories, lies, my encounters with them on the streets, and through the looking glass of history. The looking glass is a curved mirror, somewhat like a strange funhouse contraption; there is a figure there, but we can't say what it is. We catch sight of something "normal" in a single motion in the mirror. It passes, and we struggle to bring it back, struggle to remember what we did to see reality so clearly, but then we are distracted again by the inflation of a limb, the extension of a neck, the way our teeth enlarge when bared, how frightening our eyes become, how foreign. You see, Ireland always shifts on you. For that reason, it is best to look at it only with your peripheral vision, to accept that things aren't quite what they seem, to admit that you didn't see the whole incident, hear the whole joke, or remember quite who was standing where. Leave it alone, the environment says, don't study it or figure it out. Freedom from ambiguity is an annoying late twentieth-century fetish. If you're caught looking at Ireland dead-on, it'll disappear or shapeshift into something you've seen a million times before, something completely expected and stereotypical.

But the mirror is something *we* created. We can marvel at its distortion, laugh at it, and shape it into something else, something equally distorted, but if we play long enough with the mirror, it will trick us into believing it is reality. We're such fools. Move and move again, reach back to the fleeting image and hold it in your memory. Underneath the stereotype, feel the gentle touch, the open heart, wait for it to shift again and you'll see the fragile-looking face.

Chapter 5

Autumn Evenings / Who's Irish?

The autumn turned out glorious. Temperatures rose most days to Indian summer warmth, and the sky filled with Ireland's gorgeous blue. People sat outdoors at cafés, and soccer matches were played on dry fields. One afternoon at Cargoes a silver-haired woman in a pale blue trench coat looked at me with a smile and said: "Can you imagine? Sitting outside on an October day having your tea!"

"Isn't it great?" I answered.

She split open a hot scone; the raisins were swollen to bursting and ready to pop out of the fleshy middle. Alison, one of our chefs, had baked the scones that morning, laying them in small, neat rows before she put the baking sheet in the oven. With a wandering eye and a hungry belly, I watched them brown through the oven door as we prepared to open the shop. After the scones had cooled, Alison placed them in a wicker basket, the raisin, or "fruit," scones peeking out from beneath the cherry and wheaten ones. She brought them out every morning, like clockwork, before she had her cup of coffee and took a break.

"Where are ya from, dear?" the woman asked me as she poured tea from her small pot into a milky cup and stirred.

"Boston," I answered politely.

"Do you enjoy it here, dear?"

"Oh, aye, sure it's grand." I answered, then blushed at my imitation Irish accent.

She smiled politely. While her tea cooled, she spread butter across half the scone, then added jam on top, the entire concoction turning reddish yellow as raisins and crumbs fell away onto the plate. I turned and walked away quickly, for fear I'd grab it from her and eat it myself.

I often felt you had to pick up and imitate the everyday chat phrases of local speech in Ireland. They rained down like coins, ringing against the pavement before they rolled and spun and stopped with a clink. The Irish dropped a turn of phrase like it was loose change they could throw at the verbally impoverished. Picking up is what they are there for, I reasoned with myself.

This tendency to change one's pronunciation may have seemed silly, or even offensive, to the Irish, but so many travelers did it. I often explained to friends that it made communication easier, but really it was a desire to feel a part of the place.

Before my arrival, I wrote in my diary of wanting to return to Ireland, but not knowing why:

> *I can only sometimes see and know myself in Ireland. By "know" I mean that all my senses are engaged on the ground and my spirit is present in the country. Perhaps it happens when I hear Irish music, perhaps it is the hum and roll of conversation, perhaps it is the sticky feel of a pub, the strange, musty comfort of ragged, worn carpet and the air filled with "somedays": a plan for someday working abroad, a story someday transformed into a stage play, a love someday realized. Perhaps I know myself to be at home in Ireland when I misuse the language, when I merge vowels and roll my tongue back just a little too far on my "r's." And though in Ireland banter is frequently mockery in disguise, I feel my heart lighten with the foolishness of my costume of words, and the Irish smile slyly and allow the game to pass.*

As October went on, the evenings closed in early, biting just slightly before the branches on trees threatened us with their rattle. The temperatures sometimes swung with the wind, and, unaccustomed to their rapid change, I still threw on my forest-colored Aran sweater each day, preferring its continuous warmth to the occasional chill. The radios and newspapers were full of rumors about the Nobel Peace Prize being awarded here, and media people were already camping out in Belfast hotels. You'd walk around Great Victoria Street or Royal Avenue and inevitably bump into a cameraman scurrying along. They never really looked like they knew where they were or should be going. What's worse, they didn't seem to know that the nominees, John Hume and David Trimble, were out of the country.

In the spring and summer, back and forth between America and Ireland, I had watched with embarrassment as the likes of George Will and Cokie Roberts—the American media's heavy hitters—asked questions about the Good Friday Agreement like: "Who'll benefit the most from this, the Catholics or the Protestants?" Policing and decommissioning were central elements to the changes taking place, but not a single analyst queried Talks Chairman George Mitchell about them in his many Sunday talk-show appearances. In Ireland, so-called experts were always watching and interpreting events in the

North. The Irish were unswayed by this, responding with any number of jokes. My favorite was: "If you think you know what's going on, you obviously don't know how things work here."

Many people outside Ireland remained unaware that a local government would be established after nearly thirty years of Direct Rule from London. The term was a comfort, perhaps, to those who felt the Union was appropriate. For people who see all of Ireland as separate from Great Britain, Direct Rule is to be held hostage to London. Another distinction in the media discourse was the convenience of religious monikers. Many Irish had, long ago, stopped talking in the categorical terms "Catholic" and "Protestant" when it came to politics (actually, many of my friends had stopped even thinking about politics). It was all about "Republicanism" or "Unionism." One evening in September, sitting in a warm apartment in North Belfast, a friend related the painful experience of a neighbor who was interviewed by an American news reporter about the death of her son. It took some patience for the woman to endure questions such as: "Do you feel anger toward Protestants?" and "Do you actually know any Protestants? Do you have Protestant friends?" She scowled and answered, "My son's death didn't have anything to do with religion."

My friend asked me what people in the United States thought Irish lives were like in the North today.

"Well," I explained, from my own initiation, "when it's talked about at all it *is* presented in those terms—the Catholics are oppressed, the Protestants are oppressors. And no one interacts with each other."

Viewed from the outside, Northern Ireland is deeply divided; even the geography (which may have been all the reporter could go on) reflected this division. One taxi stand in Belfast was for the Shankill Road (Protestant West Belfast) and another was for the Falls Road (Catholic West Belfast); walls were everywhere and you could easily meet people who would display the elements of this segregation and attempt an explanation. But people's private lives—those were something different. They represented a contrast to the formal institutions of division. People felt comradeship through any number of things: parenting, sports, work (when they could get it), unemployment. Division left its mark on many of these activities as well, but after talking with numerous people, I could not say they inhabited the "different worlds" claimed by so many outside the province. Not often on display, these lives could be described as no less diverse than what I found in Great Britain and the United States. In fact, I found many similarities. I knew fewer white

Americans who crossed color and culture lines than I did Northern Irish who, rejecting the bullying nature of parochial institutions, crossed social borders of class and politics. Nevertheless, Nuala, who had lost her son, wasn't about to take the time to explain her life to a heavy-handed reporter, and so it went . . .

Eventually, I came to believe this tendency is an aspect of the age. At the end of the century it is easier to think of this conflict in tribal terms. This is significantly simpler than looking at the tangled mess of patriarchy, government, greed, and injustice that marked the twentieth century. Prior to my travels, the terms "Catholic" and "Protestant" had never worked for me when I made the occasional observation about Northern Ireland (in fact, until recently, I never made them, studiously avoiding the discussion altogether). This rejection of categories puts me in the camp that sees the Troubles as a political conflict, not a religious one. I mean, wasn't it *always* about access to government? Why was no one asking about that?

In that fall of 1998, John Hume, who had been working to dismantle an unjust government and transform it since the 1960s, was said to be nominated for the Nobel, as was David Trimble, Unionism's spokesman and the nagging bane of Sinn Fein and the IRA. Trimble argued skillfully (and often) about the form of government in Ireland. In the Unionist community, however, there was talk that his first term as First Minister of the newly formed Assembly would be his last. He had come a long way as a politician and could easily be described as "coming in from the cold." As part of Orangism's power structure, he had helped bring down the government of Brian Faulkner in the 1970s and, more recently, had displayed gross triumphalism by dancing down a parade route after winning a contentious legal debate over the right of the Orange Order to march. At moments like that (and there were many on all sides), I concluded that the Irish aren't ugly losers but, even worse, ugly winners. Like many of the people he represented, Trimble was a believer in Baconian rationalism—that is to say, the belief that a thing was not true until it was proven so. This makes for particularly difficult negotiations. Later, when he made his Nobel speech, he would reference the thinking of Edmund Burke. Like many of Ireland's leaders, Trimble had one eye cast backward, looking both at the past and at who might be behind him.

John Hume cut his political teeth in the Catholic civil rights movement in the late 1960s. He had been participating in Northern Ireland's various governments since the seventies. His political efforts ran the gamut from economic development proposals to intergovernmental agreements to vigorous work on the peace talks that brought armed camps to sign the Good Friday Agreement. He insisted, since the dark days of the early seventies and the Bloody Sunday incident, that Ireland would be united through nonviolent means. For this he was threatened from every corner.

Listening to the rumors and speculation on the radio one evening I fixed my evening "tea," or supper. It would be the second time the Nobel was awarded to the area—with the first going in 1976 to Mairead Corrigan and Betty Williams, the founders of Peace People, a grassroots movement promoting nonviolence in the face of terrorism. Corrigan had started defying terrorists when her sister's children were killed before her eyes in West Belfast. Her sister was the final victim of the incident some years later when, after battling severe depression, she took her own life. Still organized, the group had an office down on the Lisburn Road in Belfast and remained active in the movement for a nonviolent society.

Often, on evenings like this, with their snap and wind, I craved the vegetable plate dinner my mother taught me to appreciate as a kid. With the radio going, I steamed fresh cauliflower, softened baby potatoes, and mixed them with fresh turnips, creating a nutty, rich taste that I seasoned with black pepper and butter. I ate the yellowish mash with fresh spinach or asparagus. The cauliflower soothed me, with its vanilla-like flavor blossoming on my tongue. The snap of the steamed greens broke up the flavors before they bled into and overwhelmed one another. I loved the reassurance of Irish food— it was padding against the wind and cold. As I did with the buttermilk scones we served in the café, I felt the urge to tear into my tea and not nibble at it. I listened to the news as I ate, and in the eaves the pigeons took shelter once again, crawling about and cooing softly.

Later, rather than "imagine," I went out and sat in a sidewalk café on Botanic Avenue with a new friend, Kathryn. Young women hobbled by in bulky platform shoes. Jackets off shoulders, mobile phones on hips, they called out to one another with the high-pitched anticipation of late adolescence. Though I loved the evening air, I wore a scarf and sweater to protect me from the wind, and I shook my head like an old lady as the young girls made their way down the street to a nearby disco. This so-called Golden Mile is still a rather schizophrenic cluster of high-end bars, unpretentious cafés, tacky discos, and fast-food outlets. In the evenings, neon lights battle for your attention with the soft color of European bistros. I leaned back in my chair and sipped my Budweiser.

"Kathryn, am I getting old or are those girls not dressed warmly enough?"

"I think so, too," she said, then started laughing, "but maybe they know something we don't."

As we sat and watched the evening unfold, I asked Kathryn if she was optimistic about things in Ireland.

"It's hard to say, really," she answered. I sat waiting for elaboration, but none followed.

An armored RUC truck rolled by, and I stiffened. The running boards were protected by wire nets to prevent thrown bombs from rolling under the vehicle, the front grill was as thick as a banister, and the body was dented, like a battered fighter.

"Y'know," I said, pointing my beer bottle with some spunk, "if I were on that Police Reform Commission, getting rid of those trucks would be the first thing on my list of things to do," I sipped the beer, " . . . I mean, they gotta go." As part of the Good Friday Agreement, the British Government had appointed former Hong Kong Governor Chris Patten to direct a committee investigation into reform of the Royal Ulster Constabulary (RUC).

Kathryn smiled and sipped her cider, then said, "You know, when I was growing up, I thought all police drove those trucks."

"You mean, police everywhere?"

"Yeah," she said, with a soft laugh, "I just thought all police were like that."

"It's less unlikely than you think," I answered. "Paramilitary training is part of more police forces than ever before."

The truck rumbled on, but I knew it would return later as bars closed and crowds of people rolled drunkenly out of discos. I looked at the parade of people.

"Hey, I know that guy!" I said loudly.

A man in a sport coat bounced down the sidewalk toward the door of Madison's. Earlier in the week he and I had chatted politely in the café. He had a kiddish demeanor and was quite handsome. A soft brown mustache and a broad smile kept his face so expressive and animated I was always on the verge of a laugh when I saw him. That day, while waiting for me to finish preparing his take-away sandwich, we fell into a conversation about travel. I mentioned I'd lived and traveled in Viet Nam. He acted politely impressed, said he'd always wanted to visit Southeast Asia, knew someone's doctor-son who now lived in Nepal, and wasn't I brave, etc., and then, with some comic vaudevillian overkill, he turned and headed for the door without paying and said, "Thanks very much for the sandwich."

"Oh!" I said, joining in the joke.

He turned toward me with a smile.

"What's your name?" I asked, feigning ignorance.

"Robbie Crawford," he said, waiting for the other shoe to drop. Then he rolled out with, "R. P. Crawford and Co. Solicitors."

"A lovely name, that. Well, R. P. Crawford and Co., that'll be three quid. I'm Edie Shillue. It's nice to meet you."

He laughed at my complicity, paid me, and said good-bye.

Then, like schoolmates reviving an old punch line, we chirped out the old Americanism, "Have a nice day!"

That evening at Madison's he caught my eye as I sang out a "Hi!"

"Hey!" he said, and put his hand out dramatically for a shake. "Edie Shillue! Man! I haven't seen you since Viet Nam!"

I laughed out loud.

"Robbie, join us if you'd like."

"I'd love to," he answered, "but I'm meeting some colleagues inside."

"Sure," I said, "I'll see you 'round."

He walked into Madison's a moment later and disappeared into a crowd, though occasionally I heard his loud laugh rising from the murmur.

A place is *peopled* after you visit it. Our minds, no longer content with imagining, are rewarded by this gift of memory. Countries become *un*-imagined, because once they are lived they can later be awakened for your memory with sound, smell, or feel. Viet Nam often came back to me, almost always with pleasantries: the taste of food, the singsong sound of its language, warm summer rain. Northern Ireland was already taking shape in a memory bank inside me, peopled by the likes of Kathryn and Robbie and his infectious laughter that helped get me through the day.

~≈ ≈~

Perhaps it is because I'm a teacher, but I think the autumn has always been a time of reminiscence and renewal. So for the remainder of the evening Kathryn and I talked about old lovers, drank beer, and thought about the future. Kathryn is a quiet woman who is also a painter with a great eye for bright color. Her work, which I saw often in her small apartment, betrays the passion she masks with modesty. Beautiful gray-green fish swam across turquoise seas on tabletops, sunflowers reached up from patches of bottomless yellow on chairs, and in her bedroom a warm deep red on the walls kept the winter chill away.

Kathryn also had the thickest, curliest head of black hair I'd ever seen. It fell in rivulets past her shoulders, and each time I looked at it I felt I was trying to find the source of a river. When she wore it up in a barrette, the curls spilled out wildly, like an ivy plant burying the confines of its pot. I was reminded of my great-aunt Elizabeth ("Betty") Shillue, whom I met through pictures from 1920s Boston. She stood on Carson Beach and looked at the camera with a wild smile, her hair falling like a long scarf as she tilted her head in the sun.

When I was with Kathryn I also thought of Queen Medb and St. Patrick, the Book of Armagh, and the Tale of Cuchulainn. Kathryn is from County Armagh in the southern part of the province of ancient Ulster, which is what connects her to those ancient Irish stories and events. She rode with me as I drove one Sunday to Belfast from Dublin, explaining that her family's new vacation home was located in the Republic and that it was great, today, to "feel a part of the place." She was a practicing Buddhist in a Catholic family with hopes not just of peace, but of a feeling of *belonging* in the Republic. I think this goes far beyond Republican politics—it's a daring hope.

As I listened to her speak, I remembered the experience of telling a Dublin woman that I lived in Belfast. She was a thirty-something professional, her clothing revealed middle-class status, and her soft face seemed kind, or at least generous enough for me to feel comfortable. We began with the usual chitchat; I told her I was American, living in Ireland, a writer working on a book about Northern Ireland. In response, she pressed her lips together, furrowed her brow a bit, and said dully, "Oh."

I pressed on, "Have you been up there?"

A sneer crawled forth briefly, "Yes, it's not my favorite place in the world."

Such a snobbish gesture meant I wouldn't be buying her a pint anytime soon.

"Oh yeah?" I answered awkwardly, " . . . well . . . "

Her disdain was part of something bigger than social status in Ireland. Many Irish I met from all traditions in the North were sadly apologetic about their own existence. For all their verbal saber rattling, they struck me as terribly insecure, like stepchildren. I could hear it in casual comments and everyday conversation. On one afternoon, a customer in the café meets a friend for coffee and talks about her first month at Trinity College in Dublin only to be met with the puzzling questions: "And how did the people from the South treat you? Were they nice?"

"How did they treat me?" she responded. "What do you mean?"

It was a point of debate both inside and outside the chattering classes— exactly what place did the North have in Irish society?

"Listen," says a man I meet in a bar, "I know we up here are just the poor relations of the Republic . . . "

I cut him off with a question, "I thought it was the other way around, isn't it the other way round?" (The North had a solid infrastructure and an economy that brought consumers over the border in droves after the paramilitary cease-fire of 1994.)

"Well, no . . . ," he said and halted. The conversation petered into quiet, and I wondered, as I often did in Ireland, if we were talking about the same place.

Some of the apologetic gestures had to do with what local community you were born into. Noelle, a friend from the Aards peninsula of County Down, blushed as we spoke about where she was from and said, "You'll hear about it . . . the snobbishness." I told Noelle that my hometown and the area it was in had the same reputation. But, in fact, it's not quite the same. Down is the heart of "Unionist Ulster" ("another imagined place" I said sarcastically to a friend). It's also gorgeous—and full of what people refer to as their "culture."

Noelle is what some Northern Irish refer to as "British"—something I'm still trying to get my mind around. It mattered little that her father was Protestant but Nationalist, and that they spent a large portion of the year in County Mayo.

"You see, we are not of here and not of *there*," another woman, this one from East Belfast's Stormont area, explained. She, too, was considered "British," though born in Ireland and with a personality I would describe, at home, as "very Irish." She was chatty, open, and very friendly each time we met. She had a teasing wit and was a hardworking woman in her professional capacity at Queen's University. She loved Ireland as much as any of the others I met—what was I to make of her categorization as "British"?

All of it was rather confusing to me at first, until I realized it was "ethnicity" they were referring to. Or rather, "ethnicity" was how *I* referred to it. I remembered a small incident the previous summer on the coast of County Derry: At a hostel outside Coleraine I sat thumbing through my guidebook, drinking morning tea, and looking at the beach outside the window. A young couple joined me at the table, asked where I was from, and began nibbling at their breakfast. The warm weather had brought them from Belfast, where they'd recently graduated university, to the seashore on a long weekend.

"Have you seen Belfast?" the young man asked. He wore a pink oxford shirt and belted khaki pants. As he ate his breakfast, I noted the starch in the shirt.

"Yeah, I arrived there." I answered.

"Do you like it?" he continued.

"Yeah, it was nice." I answered, less than enthused.

"Been to Derry?" he went on.

"Yeah, I really like Derry," I said with more enthusiasm, "I don't know what it is, maybe because it's smaller, more like Boston? I don't know, there's more art there? More . . . "

"More Irish?" he interrupted. His girlfriend blushed and looked down at her cereal, embarrassed by what was obviously a trick. I remained unaware of the sectarian jibe for only a few seconds, but continued on as if it went unnoticed.

"I don't know," I answered with obnoxious pertness, "I think I like the people better, you know? Like, I think they're more friendly or something, or maybe it feels like a real creative place?"

He was one of Belfast's young professionals. No doubt he is, today, making his way up some corporate ladder in the field of information technology, working in one of the companies investing—with substantial encouragement from the European Union—in both Belfast and Derry. Through his comment he was referring, in fact, to my own face, to my own ethnicity, my short, dark hair, my Aran sweater, my "Catholic" look. It mattered little that if you picked him up by his pink collar and plopped him down in Anywhere, USA, or even, for that matter, in Great Britain, within five minutes someone would be calling him "Mick" or "Paddy" by virtue of his face and his accent. What was he on about, I wondered, thinking he was British?

The next morning at the hostel I signed the guest book as I was leaving and noticed a telling comment. After the headings "Name" and "Address" was a column for "Nationality." In one of the spaces, a local man had wearily commented, "Irish, I think, but maybe I'm British." I wondered if he was so worn down by the debate that now he sought permission to be either.

The popular novelist Robert McLiam Wilson satirized such a debate in one scene of his novel *Ripley Bogle:*

"I learnt of a great many things on my first day at school. . . . I discovered that I lived in Belfast and that Belfast lived in Ireland and that this combination meant that I was Irish. The grim young bint we were loaded with was very fervent on this point. She stressed with some vigour that no matter what anyone else were to call us, our names would always be Irish . . . "

The debate and lecture continue throughout the lesson until Bogle makes a compromise to his own liking: "I dubbed myself 'Ripley Irish British Bogle.'"

When I thought about these things, conversation in Northern Ireland became the same social minefield I wandered so often when teaching international students attending university in the United States. This dangerous conversational arena is a place where all Vietnamese are Vietnamese unless they are Khmer, where all Japanese are Japanese unless they are Chinese or Korean, where Africans seem more European than any of the French or Germans I knew, and where all Europeans were just that: "European."

Irish British Noelle, from a Nationalist family in Unionist County Down, was a tall, energetic woman with a beautiful healthy glow and what was obviously a high life condition. She laughed often at both herself and the world around her. She was well traveled, had worked with British aid agencies building housing in Afghanistan, and had toured India and Africa. But after some time living in London, she became like my work colleague Alison, who felt alienated by the environment in England during her university years and who, in short, felt more at home in Ireland.

"I missed the openness," they both explained.

The debate over belonging was a strange and subtle form of innuendo that I thought for some time I was imagining. People were self-deprecating, but all around you was an open social discussion of local history, an incessant reference to Ireland and the histories referred to as "Green" and "Orange." You could go to a number of communities in Northern Ireland and see people handling the foundation of their cultural inheritance with respect and reverence. County Antrim had the highest number of Gailscoil (Gaelic-only schools) on the island, and Gaelic was spoken openly in public institutions. Ceilis (traditional music performances) were relatively common—sessions a dime a dozen. I was often receiving mailings from Linenhall Library for free public talks on any range of subjects, from local history and landscape to the linguistic structure of the Ulster-Scots language.

In addition, each season seemed to bring with it an arts or literary festival.

One autumn week I attended a lecture at the Down Heritage Center in Bangor on the success (or was it failure?) of the 1798 Uprising. It was, the historian stated, a well-intended but poorly planned disaster. Such a presentation was not unwelcome by those in attendance that night, but the speaker did tell us how badly his ideas were received in County Wexford, where the event was considered heroic.

Ulster Presbyterian intellectuals and activists had initiated this attempted revolution, inspired by ideas brought out from the European Enlightenment. In fact, Belfast itself was the birthplace of Irish separatism. Yet, today, the vision of 1798 is overwhelmed by the sentimentality that surrounds July 12, 1690—the anniversary of the Battle of the Boyne, the victory of William of Orange over the Catholic forces of Ireland. As the images of contemporary riots get broadcast around the world, Ireland's Protestantism is seen as a vulgar display of triumphalism. As Nadine Gordimer has noted somewhere, "Sentimentality is the obverse side of thuggery." The Orangism of the Boyne has been distorted into a brutal, bigoted sectarianism.

The East Belfast playwright Stewart Parker dramatized the human struggle of 1798 in the play *Northern Star,* restaged during my time there as part of the bicentenary celebrations of the rebellion. History of the event had tugged at Parker's imagination for many years, possibly as part of his response to the Ireland of his own lifetime. In 1976 he wrote with clarity and honesty of the cultural identity crisis he felt Northerners suffered under:

> We were supposed to be British, but when you visited "the mainland" (an insult in itself) they took you for a Canadian or a Scot. We were also supposed to be Irish, but when you went over the border to Dundalk or Dublin, they treated you humorously, as an exotic alien.
>
> We didn't have any country, we just had a Province. A very, very provincial Province—politically corrupt, culturally bankrupt, full of aggressive inferiority, sectarian, self-obsessed, and unutterably dreary.

Little wonder he left. I could still see evidence of this provincialism and corruption today, yet Belfast was home for Parker, so it was no surprise that he returned. The struggle to be part of either culture—Great Britain or Ireland—is something I can relate to in a general sense; America is the birthplace of the hyphenated identity, and when in Ireland I feel that keenly, both as embarrassment and pride. Everyone seemed familiar, but every*thing* seemed foreign. I was of there, but not of there. This is acceptable for the traveler who passes through an ancestor's homeland, but it is a painful insecurity for those *born to* a place.

My friend Kathryn's timid expressions of loyalty to what I called her "Irishness" were stark contrast to American Irish brashness and ethnic flexing. In fact, I often told Irish friends that to be born Boston Irish is to live with a burdensome mythology that glorified the tacky and misinformed you about history. In its kitsch, it robbed you of the wonder of reality, confining the best bits to the lace-curtain world of academia and leaving most of us stuck with Ireland of the Imaginations. (This pretty place floats above the water somewhere across the Atlantic and—this is so very American—it is *ours*.)

As Kathryn and I drove from Dublin to Belfast that Sunday, I kept thinking of St. Patrick and that gaudy March holiday celebrated in the States. We pulled away from Drogheda, through the winding roads of the Boyne Valley, and I took note of the number of flashy BMWs and long-haul trucks. "Overheated" was the current term for the economy of the Irish Republic. It was becoming manifest in high-end cars and vacation homes that would be termed "McMansions" in the United States. Hairpin turns in the Boyne Valley are always well posted, but still often brought us up short. I loved the edginess of such driving conditions.

St. Patrick's Day was a holiday often written about in the Boston media, and in recent years the celebrations had been riddled with controversy over, of all things, a parade. Nonetheless, the holiday was never one that I warmed to.

"In fact," I said, as we moved onto the N1 outside Dundalk, "it was one that, with some effort, went largely unnoticed in my family."

Looking around at the myriad greens and astonishing tangle of the country roadways, I talked about the only St. Patrick's Day that stays in my memory.

"Ellen was standing on the stairs and talking to me through the columns on the hallway banister," I began, talking about my older sister.

"How many sisters do you have?" Kathryn asked.

"Oh, four," I said, "I'm the last of eight."

"Oh, aye," she smiled, "the spoiled one."

I smiled back, unable to deny it.

"I was probably twelve or thirteen at the time . . . "

Ellen stood outside my bedroom door, and from my bed I could see she was wearing a shirt, a sweater, and a fancy scarf. She loved to dress up for school, striving to look like the women in fashion magazines. She spent hours in the bathroom putting on makeup and styling her hair. "Elllennnn," voices yelled in vain every morning, "how long are you going to be in there?" On St. Patrick's Day of that year, her lips shimmered with gloss.

Ellen didn't particularly like green and didn't really have any appropriate clothing for St. Patrick's Day at Scituate High School, where kids took their Irishness very seriously. But she had gained a reputation among her siblings for being a bit showy with her clothes and makeup (sure she aged by five years when she dressed herself up).

On most school mornings I lay staring through the open bedroom door and listening to the morning orchestrations from Elizabeth O'Brien's four-poster bed (inherited by my father and handed down again and again). My father was downstairs, like a character offstage. He puttered around the kitchen in the morning, trying to get himself fed, washed, and dressed with the eight of us storming around him. There were four girls pushing their way around, crying about hosiery, skirts, hair dryers, and periods. Paper-bag lunches made crinkly sounds from the kitchen while platform shoes thudded up and down the green-and-gold carpeting of the stairs and hall.

"Are you gettin' up?" Ellen asked me as she was walking down the staircase.

"What are you wearin'?" I asked, looking at a scarf tied around her neck.

"It's St. Patrick's Day," she said.

"So? Shouldn't you be wearing green?" I asked.

Whatever the motivation this day—adolescent attention or fashion statement—Ellen was wearing *orange*. After I questioned her supreme judgment, she began to explain to me, with the slightly uncertain disdain of an older sister, that "orange is the other color of the country . . . isn't it, Daddy?" My father mumbled something from the kitchen.

"Orange is gross," I said, from what I was beginning to feel was my throne.

"Don't wear orange," Daddy said, only half paying attention.

"It's different," Ellen said, her resolve shaking.

"It's ugly," I answered.

My father moved to the foot of the stairs to look at Ellen and render a decision on this very weighty matter. Ann, who was older and wiser than either of us, went storming across the staircase landing to register her disapproval by screwing up her face and letting out a groaning "ELLennnnn!"

"Don't wear either color," Daddy advised. "Wearing green on St. Patrick's Day shows you're the least Irish."

"And it's ugly, too," I finished.

My father hated the vulgar displays of Irish America, I just plain didn't like orange, but Ellen always wanted to be *different*. She wore a bright orange scarf that day, tied neatly around her neck and fitting smartly under her collar. I can see her in my memory: She's sitting at one of those small desks that are arranged in straight rows in plain, large classrooms. Her face glows with pride over the novelty of her choice, and she flirts mercilessly with boys in green sportswear who have spotty faces and bad haircuts.

I stayed on my throne that morning, listening to the bus pull away from the house transporting Ellen to bragging, boasting adolescent displays. I dressed, I think, in brown, and trundled off to junior high with a snobbish look on my face and my father's advice on my lips.

"Twenty-three years later, I like orange," I said to Kathryn, "I even wear it, and it looks very nice on me. It still looks awful on Ellen, but she's lovely, lovely in all different shades of green." Except, of course, kelly.

I imagined that St. Patrick's Day in Ireland was relatively low-key, in contrast to America.

"I don't suppose they've got a parade here for St. Pat's?" I asked Kathryn.

"Not here," she said, referring to the North with a bit of resign, "it's not a legal holiday."

"Oh."

We moved up the highway, but then, instead of crossing the border, shifted over to Carlingford, where we could view the granite Mournes across the lough in a sleepy end-of-day fog before we slipped into Newry, then took the A1 up to Belfast.

It no longer puzzles me that my father in a sense *rejected* "the homeland" of Ireland. Through my work in the United States, I have listened to the sighs and frustrations of immigrant parent and child both. The combined feeling of freedom and grief and the desire to pursue myths of America are always at loggerheads. Like so many of the first-generation students I taught in university, my father was unfamiliar with the landscape of Ireland and wearied by romantic portraits of the past. As I looked at the pictures of his grandmother and his aunts, I was not transported too far back in time. Our life was a move "from steerage to suburbia," to quote the American author John Gregory Dunne. In the curled and fragile old photos I inherited from Clare, Elizabeth's daughters Katherine and Betty looked burdened inside their twentieth-century Irish American home, but free and easy in those photos taken away from the family. Is this a young person's response to the world? For an immigrant, the home is a re-creation of the birthplace, where gestures, actions, and motions are carried

out in a different language from the wilder, open ways of the outside. So it may
have been with Elizabeth, Katherine, and Betty. Eventually the generational
gap would widen, and Ireland would really be a world away.

Declan Kiberd, a Trinity College academic and the author of the book *In-
venting Ireland,* created an insightful look at the literary images of Irish culture through time. He suggests that for most people, things "Irish" stood in
eternal contrast to things "British," and Irish culture's "otherness," its primitive, peasant source was a perpetual threat to the British sense of order in relationships and daily life. Its wildness, then, had to be contained as a British
response to the two cultures meeting. The Irish and the Anglo-Irish, in turn,
celebrated, even venerated, the practices, symbols, and elements of their
daily life. Thus, today in Northern Ireland, flag, shamrock, and harp are gestures of rebellion against a government that outlawed them. Among the population, they are "tradition."

Now, after all these years, I realize my adolescent St. Patrick's Day experience stays in my memory because it was the day I discovered that I didn't
know what the Irish flag, the tricolor, looked like. Nor did I care. Still, none
of us had been educated at school, church, or home to know who St. Patrick
really was, only that he "drove the snakes out of Ireland" (and I have a vague
memory of learning at some time that the shamrock was adopted as a symbol
of Patrick because he used it as a metaphor for the Holy Trinity). Ireland was
nothing more than silly symbols to my adolescent mind. The tricolor was as
unimportant as the landscape, of which I knew nothing . "Ireland" was really
a group of women I knew through my father. They worked for priests in
Boston, spoke with brogues, and spoiled my older brother, Brian. That my
parents would give up these symbols meant that my siblings and I were free
from what I still see as the *burdens* of tradition. In 1998, to discover that so
many, from both British and Irish traditions in Northern Ireland, were just so
burdened evoked in me enormous sympathy.

Kathryn's desire to feel "a part of the place" in the Irish Republic fascinated me precisely because I had never had that desire, and even after visiting Ireland—the ethnic homeland for "colleens" like me—I still didn't feel
it. What piece was missing from her, then? Or was it from me? Everyone was
familiar in Ireland and in the North; in fact, it was a place I liked. But I didn't
long to be a part of it, as so many other Americans did. I was aware of part of
me looking down on so many of Ireland's elements. Still, the power of Ireland's ancient history pulls at you, and eventually it humbled me in my modern-
day arrogance.

Looking through literature on Patrick, I discovered that his arrival in Ireland was through slavery. He was sent over from Roman Britain and forced to work in difficult and lonely conditions. On the mountainsides of Slemish, in County Antrim, he was said to have had a vision and to have converted to the Christian faith.

"Will you look at that?" I said to myself with a soft laugh, "he was a Brit."

Patrick eventually left Ireland, but returned later to preach and practice Christianity. After converting a large part of the population, he eventually set up Ireland's first bishopric in Armagh. His firsthand understanding of the horror of slavery was a key element in his compassionate action and included an awareness of the nature of suffering of women: in his "Confession" he writes: "But it is the women kept in slavery who suffer the most—and who keep their spirits up despite the menacing and terrorizing they must endure. The Lord gives grace to his many handmaids; and though they are forbidden to do so, they follow him with backbone."

He is said to have performed extraordinary feats that one can only imagine as miraculous in the Ireland of the ancient Celts—that is, a decrease in intertribal warfare and violence as well as bringing a halt to the slave trade between the island, Great Britain, and mainland Europe. I often drove on my own around Armagh, Antrim, and Down (where he is rumored to be buried) with Patrick in mind.

When driving through the countryside, I'd often stop for a rest or a snack at the side of the road and wonder about how we see the past. One day it was outside Downpatrick, one day it was on a detour through Ballygowan, once I got lost in Kathryn's hometown, Armagh. And as I looked around at the farmland of much of the six counties, it struck me as no wonder that the island produced so many scholars and poets, for the emptiness causes you to turn inward, and the drama of Ireland's weather causes you to wonder about the forces that make up the universe. Kathleen Coyle's memoir *The Magical Realm* touched on just such images and experiences of landscape. Riding a horse home one spring afternoon in her childhood, she feels herself fulfilled by simply looking at the physical world around her. It is a world defined less by green than by a stunning, liberating blue:

No blue is cleaner than the northern blue. Other blues may be deeper and richer but the blue of the north has the sea and the wind woven into its texture. Even the flax fields maintain it. They offer it with the full chemistry. The slightest motion of the stalks reveals it. It is a substance rather than a colour. It has the quality of form, of cranes carved upon a Strasbourg steeple. In Ireland it is needled upon the land with an amazing subtlety. It performs the miracle of restoration. It returns what has been taken, so that no monument is needed.

I stood by my car one afternoon outside Omagh, staring at the blue sky as a small rain shower fell on a field across the road. (The day before, at a bus stop in the city, an older man had turned to me, pulled up his collar, then commented, "We've the four seasons in a single day here, so we do." And so here it was again.) The sky above me was a startling blue, making me think of a painter's canvas.

I thought of Coyle's story, its ups and downs, her dry wit, and her lonely exile from what she found so deeply beautiful. Breaking up a portion of the sky, a brown-gray rain cloud moved toward me across the field, and as it approached, I decided to stay outside. The rain fell slowly, with drops that tapped lightly, then the charcoal smell of the pavement rose above the musty smell of grass and sheep. The water ran down the back of my neck, soaking my collar, hitting the brim of my cap with a soft *plink*. It passed quickly over me, and with a smile I wiped the residue off my face. I looked down at the newly beaded stitch pattern on my sweater. The water acted as a prism against the wool. I shivered with a brief chill. On a hill nearby, some sheep bleated dully. I took a deep breath. For me, Ireland is "God's Country," not in spite of the mixture of beauty and violence, love and hatred, that we can see today, but *because* of it.

I listened and looked some more, but I was misplaced in the countryside. Something in me is unsettled and impatient there.

"Good God, wasn't Patrick bored?" I muttered to myself in the quiet as I stepped back into the car.

St. Patrick was not born in Ireland, but I think he must have been the first drop in the huge diaspora that Ireland would provide the world. He left and came back with a love and passion for the people. He had become, in the words of the American historian Thomas Cahill, "an *Irish*man" whose writings provided a look at the people of the island well before it was colonized. He frankly admires beautiful women, referring to one he baptized as "*pul-cherrima* (extraordinarily beautiful)" and "noble, by birth Irish." Later, when Coroticus, head of one of the petty kingdoms on Britain's west coast, invaded northern Ireland and made off with thousands of Patrick's new converts, Patrick begs for help from the rest of Britain. Knowing full well the horror of slavery, he asks for their freedom and contends that they, too, are children of God: "Is it a shameful thing in their eyes that *we* have been born in Ireland?"

That Britain did not see the Irish Christians as human beings is no surprise. There are very few world powers that see those outside their boundaries with any degree of humanity. The French had colonized Viet Nam with a cruelty that still echoes in people's memories. The Japanese had colonized Korea with such animality that even today the Japanese language is outlawed in that nation. And, at the end of the twentieth century, the United States is still arrogantly debating the status of free people in its own hemisphere, as Puerto Rico, like Northern Ireland, votes to stay or go as part of our country.

I made my way back to Belfast to meet Rene for a coffee. We began a discussion about the parades in Derry—and in Boston.

"The parades are a celebration of tradition," Rene said to me in frustration, "it's not something long gone."

I said young people I met didn't feel connected to them. She said young people she knew did.

"Think of St. Pat's Day in New York or Boston: people get together, they have a good time, they get drunk, they celebrate, they want to be happy."

I'm one of the few people I know who doesn't love a parade. The Boston and New York City St. Patrick's Day parades are very political. It is a foolish elected official in either city who won't participate.

"Those parades are a display of political clout," I said, "and they're as tribal as it gets in the States."

Her face fell, "I thought they were a celebration of being Irish?"

"Well, they're not," I said, bluntly. "They just look that way."

The U.S. parades were a response to the "No Irish Need Apply" environment people had landed in—they were a display of power after years of being shut out of the economic and political life of the United States. I suppose that makes the contemporary versions all the more triumphalist, given that pollsters are now tracking something called "the Irish vote."

"Their victory in America is all the more reason to celebrate," Rene scolded.

"No, NO," I said with a scowl, "these things exclude," I continued, referring to both Ireland and the United States, "they don't celebrate anything. I mean, to participate you have to somehow prove how Irish you are . . . or aren't. And they always exclude groups! Some celebration. It's awful in Boston. Politicians and community leaders strut around making people 'honorary Irishmen' one day a year, then denying them political access for the other 364."

Rene sipped her coffee. I thought I should change the subject, "I think those parades are embarrassing."

Sometimes I was deeply annoyed by Irish America, sometimes deeply moved. In Boston I knew working-class women who had been humiliated by WASP elites and endured it with a continuous, subtle humor so they could put their kids through college. And as I grew, I learned that I belonged to the same community that gave the United States Al Smith, the populist governor of New York, and Paul O'Dwyer, one of the premier civil rights attorneys in the country. And I often boasted of the creativity and resistance of Grandmother Anna's sister Nora Kilcoyne, who occupied Boston City Hall in protest of funding cuts in city child-care programs. She rapped on the door of the city council, with a dozen toddlers in tow, and asked where, exactly, they were meant to be cared for. My father knocked me out of bed with a yelp when a photo of her protest appeared in the next morning's city paper (but I knew from its tenor that it was admiration masquerading as scorn). From these things I knew what it is to be Irish. But I also know of Boston police officers who put shamrock insignias on their guns as a form of muscle flexing. When challenged by others, they claimed that was "celebration," too. This is a hard sell. It is rather difficult to reconcile the symbol of St. Patrick's analogy of the holy trinity with a gun. Symbols are hardly "harmless" in the United States or in Ireland; they bind people together and hold them hostage at the same time. The resulting tension plays out in violence.

Each spell of time I had in Ireland I heard of "another American," someone who wandered through the community and then settled and stayed. There was a poet up in Antrim, a woman who lived on the Ormeau Road and wrote a piece for the American edition of *Newsweek,* there was a singer that I often heard about and was told I'd like, and a woman who worked in a bookstore downtown. Each time I heard about these people I was told that we should meet, but I couldn't figure out why. I often replied politely to this suggestion and, out of habit, asked what the Americans were doing in Ireland.

"They think they're Irish," Rene's son Malcolm said to me one evening.

I laughed out loud. "Oh, leave'em alone," I answered, imagining a circle of us from the States traveling backward in time until we began speaking in mock Irish accents and trying to play fiddles. I did it myself each time I handled some piece of what the Irish called their "heritage"—fingered a piece of linen and imagined it traveling through the British Empire stained with the sweat of factory women. I did it when I looked through Colby's Ordnance

Survey and imagined him hypnotized by the landscape or when I wandered in the footsteps of passionate warrior queens or of the shawled women captured in a stone frieze in the County Down heritage center. Was it "the Irish in me"?

I don't know. Not long into my trip I could no longer tell what "Irish" was. My family appeared out of Ireland—an island across the Atlantic—and they were characters in a series of powerful, painful scenes. Anna and Nora were bullet dodgers, Patrick walked across a continent, Elizabeth survived rough waters only to resettle in Boston just as a flu plague was ravishing the city. They were composed of something that made us "Irish," but, really, it didn't have anything to do with a color. Still, it was impossible to put my finger on it, so I put aside its symbols in favor of a future I could shape for myself in America and in the world, with its millions of possibilities.

The stories of family and past are like clips in old film run on a 16 mm projector. It hums and ticks and sputters; everyone seems to move like small mechanical figures. The film eventually slows and stops, the core running out and the people frozen mid-gesture or halfway through a laugh. Then you're left to your own devices to finish things for them, to feel the warm release of tension that laughter brings, to slacken the jaw in wonder.

As I puzzled out the debate over who belonged in Ireland and how to record who actually lived there, I realized I was "taken" with the place. I wrote: "I've been thinking about how Ireland now captures my imagination and how—contrary to what I assumed most of my life—it has a depth and complexity, a kind of thing unfolding to other thing."

The effete, awkward turn of phrase belied my increasing attachment to Ireland. The truth is, the place leaves you speechless. A thousand stories unfold in front of you in any number of forms. The stories told, the poems written, the laments sung, the paintings and tapestries created, the political speeches and pamphlets delivered, the pub story told with its missing details and exaggerated tenor. The Irish hypnotized me with their words, left me dazed and astounded by the simplest conversation. It was narcotic in its effect, and I sometimes just stared at them, feeling slightly stoned by contact. The meaning became secondary to the roll and rumble of sounds— anger drummed, seduction sang, intimacy was mumbled and whispered—it gurgled underneath things like water over rock. A terrible resign was woven through so many thoughts, like a bass weighing down a music set, dragging you into a darkness that you didn't want to visit. Then this was coupled with astounding sentimentality.

All these contradictions puzzled me. Then, one autumn night, I dreamed of the new friends I had made in Belfast, Armagh, and County Down, and what made them Irish was more than I could ever have imagined. It was a complicated mix of the ancient and the modern, deeply political and personal, annoying and beautiful at once. I dreamed of my friends from Belfast: Pauline's car sprouted wings, and she and the girls circled around the six counties shaking their fists at soldiers and other symbols of war and injustice. Lizzy's hair was pulled neatly back as she leaned forward in the seat and looked out the window, then shouted directions to her ma. Aisling quietly watched from the other side, her hands placed on her lap as the action unfolded, waiting, as many a champion does, for the right moment to act. My colleague Alison wandered like a cat onto a doorstep, carrying a soft carpet bag. She sighed and said she was happy to be home. Noelle sent postcards out to all the places in the world she had visited. She was smiling and laughing so much that all of dour, snobbish County Down became infected by it and even fat, old patriarchs wobbled like bowls of jelly. Kathryn of Armagh became a paintbrush. Her body lay stiff, her thick hair splayed out against white linen canvas. She is painting Ireland as a sleeping infant, one that dreams of its glorious past and sees the infinite potential of its future.

Chapter 6

Twisted Landscape / Macha's Curse / Eleven Plus

"Oh, look, the colors are different," Alison said.

I put the map down and looked again at the road in front of us, then took a quick breath.

"Oh my, you're right!"

We were on our way back through a town called Clogher, trying to find the A28. I studied the winding lines and marks on the driver's map once more, then looked out at the countryside. Though we were driving the A4 from Fermanagh to Armagh, and though it was the exact same road we had taken from Belfast out to Enniskillen, the color had changed when we turned back. In the light of early Sunday morning, when the roads were empty and silent, the landscape across Counties Down and Armagh was a riot of orange, gold, green, and blue. But the afternoon, when sleepy crowds moved en masse out of churches, saw me marveling at the subtle tones of aubergine, gold, gray, and mossy green. I folded the map back into its fanlike holder and put it aside. The best part of driving in Ireland is, in fact, getting lost. Looking at the trees as they began to shed leaves, the pine ridges on the hillsides, and the roadsides that were a combination of hedge and soil wall thick with ivy and berry bush made me wish again that I was a painter, not a writer.

I had to admit I was "enchanted" by the Ireland of these country towns. I was lulled into a sleepy state of relaxation by the hills that muffled the chaos of the world. I liked the hedgerows, plants, and trees that had forced road builders to curve things this way and that, and I loved the moist air.

We came around a curve, and Alison lifted her foot off the gas so we could drive slowly through a military checkpoint. An RUC officer stood waving people on, while British soldiers lurked behind their army vehicles cradling Uzis. Farther down the road two more armored trucks were lined up on a side road, looking squat and ugly, like toads waiting for rain. Alison was raised in northern Ireland, and I am well traveled in a few rather dodgy corners of the world, but still we both fell silent for some minutes after passing the trucks.

That the landscape color would change didn't surprise me, but that it would change so very dramatically in so short a span of time made me feel as if I had been asleep at the wheel.

"Ireland's always shifting on you," I said, quietly.

"We're to turn at Augher, right?" Alison asked.

"That's what the map says," I answered, wanting to go to Armagh, but not *really* caring if we ever arrived. I threw the worn paper into the back seat. In Ireland, maps are not simply useless, they are undesirable. Alison smiled and said we would get there eventually. Like me, she loved driving around Ireland, but, also like me, she was a toodler behind the wheel. We drive along out of curiosity, not any real desire to arrive—sometimes we chitchat like it's a tea party, sometimes we sit silently and watch the landscape around us as if it was a film.

From behind her tortoiseshell eyeglasses, Alison always looked a bit tentative. She had a small frame, mousy brown hair, and a small mouth. She was very intelligent, had received a university degree in modern Irish history and politics, but preferred the kitchen to the classroom and was working as a chef. She kept her ideas and thoughts to herself most of the time, but like so many women I know, she let them loose when the conversation was private. Then they came out in rich, full force, and she jabbed and pushed along with me, cutting me off, asserting her ideas and opinions, and speaking with confidence. Occasionally, she pursed her lips and widened her eyes as she came to a conclusion, pleased with her discovery, as one is with a gemstone found in rough soil. I spent most of my time with her repeating casually again and again, "Y'know, you really ought to become a teacher. You really should."

Her own education was something she looked on with ambivalence. She once mentioned, in passing, that during secondary school she and her classmates were taken on a tour of Castlereagh Holding Facility as part of a study project on policing. Castlereagh is famed among dissidents as the site of torture and unjust imprisonment by the British government. It had been written up in human rights reports by Amnesty International a number of times.

"You're joking!" I said, in shock.

"No," she answered, "it was all very stage-managed. Everything plain and simple."

This strikes me as not so much surreal, but obscene. You know, a strange community relations project on the heels of the infamous "Stalker Affair" (an investigation in the early 1980s by a British Deputy Chief Constable, John Stalker, into a possible shoot-to-kill policy among the RUC—the investigation was stopped at a certain point, Stalker's work conveniently discredited, his career destroyed). I imagined with a shudder what kinds of words came out of the mouths of police officers and tried to envision a similar scene in Los Angeles or New York.

"Oh yes," Alison continued, masking unease, "things like that happened." Then her voice rose a bit in irritation, "mind you, I had never even been taught who Michael Collins was either."

The latter seemed to bother her more. As they say, history is written by the winners.

"Oh, I know what that's all about," I answered, "indoctrination starts early."

As I talked to friends about their elementary and secondary history education, I started to see it as *less* unique and more like that of other places, the United States among them. Selective history is par for the course around the world. White Americans learn about "treaties with the Indians," not about land seizure and genocide. On the other side, encountering what I call your "political karma" is a disconcerting experience. This is when you bump up against the perspective of "the other side." A Dublin friend once said jokingly to a London tour guide, "You don't have to tell me who Cromwell was, I'm Irish." The woman responded with a blank look, as if the connection was lost on her, then answered, "Oh, yes, he did go to Ireland, didn't he?" A young Japanese woman once told me of her terrible embarrassment after innocently asking a friend about a war memorial in the center of Singapore. She blanched over her ignorance when she discovered that the country had been invaded by imperial Japan. When I was living in China, indoctrinated university students insisted to me that Tibet "was always part of China. We *freed* those poor people!" Still, in Ireland there was something terribly unseemly about filling the blank space in a young woman's schooling with a public relations theater of the absurd.

"Well," Alison continued, "of course I always knew things were abnormal here. I knew enough to realize there was something wrong with our society during the worker's strike. I mean, 'Mommy, why is the milkman wearing a balaclava?'—these kinds of questions don't get asked here. Not in Presbyterian homes, anyway. I'd look over the window's edge—from behind a curtain—it was terrifying for a little girl. Then we'd go into the city and get searched going into every store. " She lowered her voice in slight bitterness and muttered, "Is it any wonder I stopped eating?"

I was unsure how to respond to her comments in much the same way one would feel a sense of wordlessness when a friend reveals a family dysfunction. The Loyalist Workers' Strike was a labor protest that shut down all public services for a full fourteen days in May 1974, thus bringing the province and the power-sharing government to a grinding halt. As it dragged on, Loyalist political and paramilitary groups subsequently provided services, such as milk delivery, to select communities.

Still, Alison explained, it was less politics than religion that kept her family silent. Their "Ballymena" Presbyterianism was a strict type of Christianity that called for complicit silence about human imperfection. No discussions of abuse, no references to "someone who wasn't quite the full shilling," no skeletons in the closet, and—this was sheer artistry—*no war*. In a tony suburb of Belfast, the Workers' Strike and a milkman with a balaclava might just be someone's first contact with that elephant in the room.

Alison continued, "It's a strange sort of analogy, the Troubles were an outward showing of deep cultural problems, which, for much of life, by one's actions, one sought to ignore, and . . . " she paused, " . . . my . . . anorexia, an outward showing of deep cultural problems of another sort. Those cultural attitudes of tightness, I suppose, were both a contributor to and a function of the Troubles."

The reference to what later hospitalized her explained the spidery frame and a two-biscuit breakfast that, from then on, made me rather nervous. Alison, like others, killed her curiosity because it could alienate the ones she loved or, out in the world, get her killed. But she kept going. She killed her appetite until doing so almost killed her. It was around this time that her lips could no longer be held tight, and she burst out with the query: "Why are we supposed to hate Catholics?"

"Yes," she explained patiently, as I queried her further, "I was hospitalized for six months. I'm all right now," she continued, "don't get alarmed." She touched me as if to reassure me. I felt confused, then realized people would have been policing her *eating* after she got sick.

"Oh, do people get hysterical about your eating?" I asked.

"Oh, yes." She nodded.

"Well, gaining weight's hard. I've tried it. I dropped down pretty far myself once," I explained, "purely by accident, not anorexia, but it was damn hard getting it back."

"Oh, aye," she said, still patient.

The burden of institutional stagnation meant those raised in northern

Irish society would cope in various ways—celebrate identity, rebel against identity, distort the myths and facts that are presented as history. A person who didn't accept the categorizations and despised the militarism thrust into her life might just do something else.

For the literary critic Edna Longley, the environment both north and south of the border meant anorexia personified Irish women, who, in her words, were "starved and repressed by patriarchies like Unionism, Catholicism, Protestantism, Nationalism." I am haunted by the image of Alison as a child, killing her curiosity from behind household drapes, sitting in a warm house out near Stormont; visiting police interrogation centers; and reading signs over and over that read: Sorry for the Delay or Don't Blame Us, Blame the Terrorists. Who's the bogeyman in that landscape? Alison's resistance eventually freed her. The anorexia, though damaging to her body, would be confronted and she would become, of all things, a chef living happily in the Republic of Ireland.

After many a turn in the road, we arrived eventually at the fort at Emain Macha. It is the site of the capital of ancient Ireland, near the seat of its high kings, and it is also the locale of legend and myth. For historians and archaeologists, it is an endless series of puzzles to be solved. For the romantic or the storyteller, it is a setting that speaks of events told and retold, colored and recolored, changing like the shifting landscape.

I complained that history was beginning to take center stage in my writing: "I mean, St. Patrick, maps of Ireland, old newspapers, and, now, Guy Fawkes."

I had recently looked through Antonia Fraser's *Gunpowder Plot*, the story of the famous Guy Fawkes, accused of plotting to blow up Parliament. It is a compelling account, written with a novelist's flair, of the earliest forms of terrorism and religious strife in Great Britain. Take state-sponsored persecution of Catholics, add subversive action by those interested in putting a Catholic on the British throne, put in some priests running underground in town and village, and you have the makings of a thriller. Reenactment of the uncovering of the plot itself is the centerpiece of an autumn festival that includes Halloween and Bonfire Night (on the fifth of November). The anniversary came and went as I read the book in my damp apartment. Stories of interrogation, hidden clergy, and palace intrigue were supplemented by dark nights filled with a rainy wind that slapped against my old windows and left me unsettled.

Autumn rested in piles of rust-colored leaves and brought a chill into my apartment. The trees that formed a beautiful canopy on my street threatened me with monsters and ghosts as I returned home from work thinking of the rise of Protestant Queen Elizabeth I, the Papal Edict declaring her a bastard child and welcoming her murder, her death after a glorious tenure as queen, and later the struggle of the Catholic King James II and the brutal acts of violence made in the name of religion and political power.

By the end of the twentieth century, few that I met, with the exception of Alison, had any interest in James or religion or King William III or even the pope, previous or current. All of which led me to firm up my suspicion that as interesting as history was, as fascinating as struggles for power in the seventeenth century are from our lucky distance—they've got nothing to do with the Troubles or "the current phase of the Troubles," as some put it. But they do serve to remind us of the tangle that is politics and religion and how it always seems to sacrifice justice, especially when it claims it is trying to preserve it.

"Well, nothing is wasted," Alison advised me about my copious notes, "you can use some of your writing for some other book." This was wise counsel, but hardly reassuring, since Ireland, real and imagined, was unraveling in front of me, and I was beginning to feel overwhelmed.

"Such a small place," I said again and again, "but so big, so damn big."

❦

Patrick isn't the only one whose footsteps echo around Armagh. Nor are the Troubles Ireland's first struggle for power. I asked Alison if she had ever learned about *The Tain*, ancient Ulster's great epic poem. It tells the tale of a battle royal over—of all things—a bull.

"No," she answered, then caught herself, "wait, is that the poem about the Hound of Ulster?"

"Oh, is it called that, too?" I asked.

"Well, I don't know," she said, "is it about someone named Cuchulainn?"

"Yeah," I said, "same poem."

Whichever name one chooses, *The Hound of Ulster*, *The Tain*, or *The Cattle Raid of Cooley*, this poem shows ancient Ireland and the oral traditions at their finest. It is the story of Cuchulainn, a young man so big and powerful that he is able to defend ancient Ulster against an army composed of the remaining three provinces of Ireland.

Naturally, a woman started it all. Queen Medb ("Maeve" in English), over in Connacht, was overcome with greed when she heard that there was a bull in Ulster whose might surpassed that of her own. She would offer the owner anything to have it, including, as she brashly and fabulously put it, "my own friendly thighs on top."

The Tain shows us ancient Ireland and the Irish memorizing their landscape through chant and stories of warfare. How could Medb win the bull she wanted so? By following Fergus, her advisor who knew Ulster, Cuchulainn, and the Murtheimne Plain. And reading it aloud, imagining it chanted and sung, you can feel every footstep and every curve in the roads leading to this corner of the island.

> That Monday after Samain they set out. This is the way
> they went, southeast from Cruachan Ai:
> through Muicc Cruinb,
> through Terloch Teóra Crích, the marshy lake bed
> where three territories meet,
> by Tuaim Móna, the peat ridge,
> through Cúil Silinne, where Carrcin Lake is now—it
> was named after Silenn, daughter of Madchar,
> by Fid and Bolga, woods and hills,
> through Coltain, and across the Sinann river,
> through Glúne Gabair,
> over Trego Plain, of the spears,
> through Tethba, North and South,
> through Tiarthechta,
> through Ord, "the hammer,"
> through Sláis southward,
> by the river Indiuind, "the anvil,"
> through Carn,
> through Ochtrach, "the dung heap,"
> through Midi, the land of Meath
> through Finnglassa Assail, of the clear streams,
> by the river Deilt,
> through Delind,
> through Sailig,
> through Slaibre of the herds,
> through Slechta, where they hewed their way . . .

It was a long and confusing march for Medb and her soldiers as Fergus tried to avoid Ulster's hero while they pursued a bull they would borrow for only a year. He advises the queen:

> I take these turnings as they come
> not to bring the host to harm
> but to miss the mighty man
> who protects the Murtheimne Plain.
> Do you think I don't know every winding way I take?
> I think ahead, trying to miss
> Cuchulainn son of Sualdam.

The novelist William Trevor notes the comedic possibilities of the route of avoidance that Fergus created for the safety of the army of Connacht, "Had Shakespeare ever discovered the story of the two bulls there would at this point have been a comic interlude, three or four military yokels scratching their heads over hills and trees that looked remarkably like the hills and trees of a week ago."

All across the counties that made up ancient Ulster there are soft earth pathways in areas where the epic is said to have taken place. Places with names like *Trumpet Hill, Sleivenaglogh, Windy Gap,* and *Black Cauldron* all refer to the fantastic events in the story, events which, in turn, refer to the topography of the landscape, creating a map of sorts for travelers through time. Maps are a literature all their own in Ireland, and the country's literature is full of a landscape of references.

So few of my friends in Ireland knew of *The Tain.* It had been relegated to that quiz-taking part of the schoolchild brain where a few key moments are recalled as a measure of knowledge. It takes great effort to capture and connect the rhythms of the past with today's world, to speak in such a way that the likes of Alison or even a visitor like me can be touched. I felt moved by Medb's passion and ambition—though these are considered the cause of her downfall.

The contemporary poet Nuala Ní Dhomhnaill wed all the elements I so like in *The Tain* in a great feminist poem, *Medb Speaks:*

> War I declare from now
> on all the men of Ireland
> on all the corner-boys
> lying curled in children's cradles

their willies worthless
wanting no woman
all macho boasting
last night they bedded
a Grecian princess—
a terrible war I will declare.

Merciless war I declare—
endless, without quarter
on the twenty-pint heroes
who sit on seats beside me
who nicely up my skirts put hands
no apology or reason
just looking for a chance
to dominate my limbs
a merciless war I will declare!

I will make incursions
through the fertile land of Ireland
my battalions all in arms
my Amazons beside me
(not just to steal a bull
not over beasts this battle—
but for an honour—price
a thousand times more precious—
my dignity).
I will make fierce incursions.

In literary and academic circles, much has been made of *The Tain* and this ambitious queen. However, Medb is hardly the only woman worth remembering in Ireland, real or imagined. You can read about the tale in tourist brochures, follow along paths and trails listed in the poem, find landmarks described in the poem with typical exaggerated detail and drama. But in all this talk and encouragement to explore a mythic past, people manage to gloss over the story's finest element and its true hero: Macha, Medb's predecessor and the woman who passes on the "curse."

The literary quality of *The Tain* is often studied, as is its oral telling, its powerful portrait of war making, and the passionate greed and violence portrayed in it. Even the damn bull is studied and explicated, creating, as he does in the myth, so many of Ireland's landscape marvels. But little is made of Macha's curse. She is easily overlooked, coming at the beginning as she does, then being overshadowed by the warrior queen, who delivers the lessons of unapologetic arrogance and selfishness. Macha plays a bit part in the epic, but she is a woman who, had she lived, could have taken on brutal Queen Medb.

Now, as far as I know, Macha's timeless curse makes its first appearance in literature from her mouth as she lay suffering. Many women nod in agreement with the idea that the world would be a better place could such a curse be made to stick—for we've all made it at one time or another. In this scenario, it's a man who started it all.

Macha's husband was full of big talk and, naturally, one day it got *her* into trouble. Drunk and loud at a king's fair, he boasted that his wife could outrun the king's chariot. When challenged, he insisted it was true, so Macha was summoned to prove his boast. One small problem gets in the way: she was "full with child." To the reasonable person, this would appear to be a bit of a burden.

"Burden?" says the king's messenger, "your husband will die unless you come."

"A mother bore each of you!" she cries to the people gathered at the fair. "Help me! Wait till my child is born!"

The crowd, however, was unmoved by this request, and she was forced to race. Naturally, she won, but at the end of the race, she fell into labor with twins. The poem records her agony and response: "As she gave birth she screamed out that all who heard that scream would suffer from the same pangs for five days and four nights in their times of greatest difficulty. This affliction, ever afterward, seized the men of Ulster who were there that day, and nine generations after them."

How often I have endured the indescribable pains of menstruation and shuddered to think of childbirth and then, when encountering vulgar machismo, whispered Macha's curse with the hope it would stick. In *The Tain* it did stick, and Cuchulainn's shaken, whining, and dopey soldiers lay strewn about Ulster as Medb and her army approached. The entire male population of the province, with the exception of Boy Wonder, were defeated by the wish of an abused woman who rose up in defiance at the moment of her greatest humiliation and pain to ensure ultimate victory. May her tribe increase.

It was to this place—with its war, storytelling. and superstition—that the slaveboy Patrick was sent. As I walk around on muddy and overgrown footpaths I can feel the earth pull at something deep inside. Perhaps it is the angry, passionate and creative pulse of a warrior queen. As we made our way home that Sunday evening, I thanked Alison for doing so much driving.

"My pleasure," she said sweetly.

Back in my apartment, I stared out at the landscape as the day was ending. The palette outside my window was a line of green, speckled with brown and orange. Trees were spotted with the chilly light of winter creeping in from the horizon. Clouds and mist began to descend over the hills, and the tiles on nearby roofs darkened with mossy patches. I gathered my afghan around me and waited for the rain.

~∙≈ ≈∙~

In the following week, winter began to make a creeping progress across the hills and streets. On sunny mornings, my windows glittered with frost, and the landscape outside looked cold and scratchy. Trees pressed their branches against the sky like hands reaching out in frustration. I rolled quickly out from under my duvet, went from room to room turning on the small gas heaters in each, then hopped back into bed and listened to the morning news. The 11+ exams were being given to schoolchildren, and people were complaining about them. The exams would determine where young students would be placed after they left primary school, but their value was being questioned by both parents and educators.

"Oh, little one . . . " I said softly into the morning air, remembering a small boy in the café the day before. Patrick had short brown hair and tortoiseshell glasses. Standing in front of the deli counter, he looked up at me with patience and politeness as I wandered about getting ham, coleslaw, and salad for the couples sitting at tables and waiting in line for take-away food.

"I'd like a ham roll, please, to take away," he said quietly.

I leaned over the glass case because I couldn't hear him. He wore a lovely bright red sweater and gray pants. "To take away?" I asked loudly.

"Yes, please," he answered, backing away slightly.

"Okay, babe, I'll be with ya in just a minute."

He stood still in front of the case, waiting patiently.

"Ya see that wee one, Edie? He's going to be an ace footballer," Annie told me as I passed her behind the counter. Annie ran a soccer team during the spring and summer seasons and was constantly talking about "football."

"Yeah?" I said, "He looks more like an engineer to me."

Annie passed by me quickly with a plate for another take-away order.

"Be right with you, Joan," she called out as she wandered back into the kitchen.

I looked up to see one of our regulars. It was the woman with a cane I had muttered about to Gillian some weeks before. Joan stood quietly waiting over by the kitchen doorway, wearing a trench coat and leaning on her cane. In the interim, I had waited on her once. It was rather awkward, since she was hard of hearing and couldn't understand my accent. She snapped back her answers in the rather unfriendly way people do when they can't understand or be understood, and I just stupidly raised my voice. As I made young Patrick's sandwich, Annie wrapped up a hot meal and carried it out to Joan's car for her. From the corner of my eye, I watched Joan walk, dragging one foot and limping, across the shop floor. Annie came back in after she drove away and marked off her tab. It took a strange and awkward conversation with my colleagues for me to remember that in northern Ireland limps have horrific sources, and Joan was one of many who were in the wrong place at the wrong time. (One of the notable characteristics of the Irish in the North is that they understand *without* asking. Outsiders have no such humility or awareness. I felt like an idiot pretty quickly, and from then on didn't ask.) Joan had survived the Abercorn Blast, a retaliatory bombing by the IRA in 1972 that targeted a restaurant in the center of Belfast on a Saturday afternoon. Another regular, a quiet, dark-haired man who came in weekly, was also pointed out to me as a survivor. "Oh, the Colombian coffee man," I said to Gillian, who took me aside one day to explain it all. "Yes," she said with gentle understanding, "that's him." Mr. McNaul was a nice customer who came in on Fridays for a quick cup of Colombian coffee and a sweet snack. On occasion, he chatted politely with me, but for the most part he just treated me with a distant courtesy. I could see him nod to Joan when they were in at the same time, but it was a strange club they belonged to, and I'm sure they were enormously reluctant to acknowledge it.

Patrick continued to wait for his sandwich while his mother sat enjoying cappuccino and conversation at one of the tables. As the lunch crowd began to queue up, he resembled a shaky little sapling in a grove of trees.

"Sweetie, I'll bring it to you at the table, okay?" I said, finally.

"Yes," he said politely, then walked over to his mother.

That day he didn't strike me as confident enough to be an athlete, but after hearing about the exam, I finally understood. I got the impression that, like many of the tests in the United States, the 11+ exams were said to measure skill but were ultimately an exercise in gatekeeping. I disliked the U.S. tests immensely, since they generated such a fear of exclusion. In Belfast the results were similar. Boys and girls sat in the café tapping their feet together in nervousness, wringing their hands in fear, worrying far too soon about their "future"—that amorphous thing so profoundly affected by the present, the thing held so threateningly by mothers and schoolmarms over the heads of young, irresponsible kids. "What are you going to do in the future?!" voices seemed to call out with the cold wind. Little boys were turned to piles of slush in the face of these educational tests, and little girls worried and gnashed their teeth in fear. The exams determined what community within a community they would belong to. What blazer and skirt would they wear? What tie would show their place in the pecking order?

I rolled over as the radio news went on . . . *another American software firm would open up an office in Belfast, providing X number of jobs for university graduates. American manufacturer Fruit of the Loom was closing its Donegal factory, taking away X number of jobs for workers. . . .* Another news story mentioned the closing of the Whiterock army base in West Belfast. My ears perked. This was great news, I thought. The encampment was a horrific sight that loomed over the community on a hill just above the City Cemetery. My first approach to that neighborhood, on a summer afternoon in 1997, was a shock. I stood on the Falls Road, looking at my map and guidebook, trying to figure out where I was, then looked up to discover I was at the corner of Falls and Whiterock Roads. The scene struck me as some morbid piece of contemporary art, the kind meant to shock you by its realism. The cemetery looks like a grotesque carpet laid at the feet of the military base, with the headstones and crosses stepping up the hillside leading to the terrible blot that is the barricade. Further down to the left is Milltown Cemetery, with its row upon row of Celtic crosses and burial plots of Republican guerrillas.

Military and police stations in poorer areas of Ireland were enormous structures that were hastily and callously placed in the heart of people's lives. They were fenced in by dark corrugated iron and wire mesh and at the corners were watchtowers that looked like nightmarish cyclopes. Police stations in other parts of Belfast and elsewhere in the six counties had the same look, and each time I saw them, and the armored vehicles that moved in and out, I shuddered. To hear that Whiterock was coming down was, to my ears, wonderful news.

It struck me that day that the imposing nature of the military and police was softened in South Belfast, where I lived. Less than a block from my house was an army base that I mistook for a tennis club when I first arrived. I had the same foolish response to the RUC station on the Lisburn Road. Walking up the Malone Road I looked with wonder at the brown fencing and mistook the gun turret for a gazebo perched on the corner. My face was curious and inquiring, but soon turned pale and shocked as I walked toward the structure and recognized a pasty white, mustachioed face in a beret staring out from the small wire window. I crossed the road quickly and tried to suppress my laugh at the absurdity of it. These naive mistakes often served as comic relief to my anger over the presence of so many military and police institutions thrust into the lives of good people.

I got up and prepared for work as another news story unfolded a week-long sports saga. Donegal Celtic soccer club, located in West Belfast, had recently elected to play a cup match against an RUC team. This was politically controversial and deeply emotional for some.

"Annie," I inquired later in the day, "what do you think of that match?"

"Mmm," she muttered, suddenly uninterested in soccer. She closed the drawer of the cash register, absorbed in recording some numbers.

"I mean . . . ," I started, but she had walked away.

She held some money up in the air and said, "I'll be back in just a tic, Edie. I'm just taking a wee nip up the road."

The soccer match was seen by many as a small mark of change, but it came at a time when there was vigorous, painful debate over the reform of the police force, with people in the Republican community demanding that the RUC, with its (para)military status, be disbanded. It had virtually no credibility in Nationalist and Republican areas, since it was allowed, by law, to violate basic tenets of human and civil rights. It was, in short, *the oppressor*. I was terribly wishy-washy on the matter of the match. I sort of agreed with opponents, since I had heard and read about community meetings with Chris Patten's Reform Commission and was particularly touched by the testimony of seventy-eight-year-old Emma Grove, who was blinded by a plastic bullet to her face. There was other testimony, too. Young people were gunned down inside their homes. People were picked up, interrogated, and tortured during periods of unrest or when changes in the law demanded changes in RUC powers of arrest and detention. The latest charge of corruption was a shocking story of murderous complicity in Portadown. One December evening in 1997, a young Catholic man named Robert Hamill was assaulted and kicked to death in the town center. Witnesses claimed that when they approached the RUC, who could see the assault from where they were situated, calls for help went unheeded. It wasn't the first time they were accused of looking away. To others in the province, the police were heroic under war conditions. When Patten eventually recommended, among other things, a change in uniform and name for the service—no more crown on the shield, no more "Royal" in the name—the political howling continued for months.

However, soccer players and fans could not make this connection, did not see the relationship between sport and politics, and wanted to have the match go off. I couldn't say I disagreed. I still think that one of the greatest moments in the history of sport was when the American runner Jesse Owens won four gold medals in the 1936 Olympic Games held in Hitler's Germany. It was eloquent, if silent, testimony against tyranny and racism. Less than a week after Donegal Celtic voted to play, the club withdrew its decision "in the interests of player safety." It seemed that "pressure" from Republican community groups had mounted in the wake of the original vote. These euphemisms annoyed the hell out of me. In Ireland, like nowhere else, intimidation works.

Annie swung through the door onto the street as Robbie Crawford walked in. I smiled at him as he called out "Edie Shillue!" and took a seat. He was becoming a regular in the café, and time spent talking to him was strange relief to my weary brain. Each time I saw him I felt as if I were meeting a Beckett character, as if I had been running quickly through battlefields of conversation and I could dive into a foxhole that he alone had occupied for years. He was a young man, but with a weary face. He struck me as having been through his share of battles, though I never asked for specifics and he never offered.

Completely unpretentious, he was lawyer to both the down and out and the up and coming. He took on asbestosis, probate, basic worker's compensation cases, and more profitable business law. He filed people's insurance claims, did the paperwork for their divorces, requested restraining orders to protect abused women, tried to help men in custody battles over their kids. His office was located on the Antrim Road in North Belfast, an area referred to repeatedly as an "interface." He was a soft touch, and I knew more than a few of his invoices had gone unpaid. He was grand craic, and I felt I could arrive at his side in any state of fatigue, hysteria, or confusion and he would let me know I wasn't insane, as if to say, "Yes, you're absolutely right, Edie, this is tragic."

"Isn't it?" I'd reply, referring to nothing and everything at once.

"And, y'know, we've been doing it for some time now."

I shared my observation about little Patrick, the boy taking the 11+ and hoping to become a soccer player.

"Ah, the wains, Edie," he said with a smile, "that's the key to lasting peace here. We'll never have real peace until the kids are educated together."

This was a comment people made in the streets and pubs frequently, but it was an issue wholly ignored by politicians. Like language debates, it seemed a matter of less urgency when held up against weapons decommissioning or the reform of a corrupt police force.

As we sat chatting, a driver from the "AAA" cab company wandered in. Robbie gave him a nod, and he walked over to say hello.

"Whataboutche there, Robbie?"

"Hello there, Michael."

I smiled, then introduced myself.

"Is that an American accent, pet?" he asked.

"Aye," Robbie answered, "Edie's a writer; she's here *checkin' the scene out*," he said, imitating an American accent.

I blushed. "Enough about me," I said, quickly, "how's business today?"

"Kind of slow," he said.

"Really?" Robbie asked.

"Even with this weather?" I asked.

"Yeah. You take this mornin'—bad weather, but no calls for school."

"Really?" Robbie asked.

Michael began to scorn the new generation of schoolchildren. "They're all bein' driven by their mums! Do you remember our school days?" he asked Robbie. Robbie laughed and nodded.

Michael continued and looked over at me, "We wouldn't be caught dead having our mums drive us to school! Oh, the teasin' you'd get! But not these ones, today," he finished with a tone of dismissal, "Yer mam's got to drive you!"

Outside, the wind was sending birds in wild, looping arcs. The café emptied as quick as it filled sometimes. The take-away orders overwhelmed the kitchen, but we were left twiddling our thumbs over the empty tables by one o'clock. Robbie talked about how times were changing in the city. Eager to reminisce, Michael brought up a favorite memory.

"Hey, do you remember the summer it was sunny?"

"Oh, aye," he answered, "cease-fire summer."

"No," Michael corrected, "summer *after* the cease-fire."

"Oh, Edie," Robbie said with a laugh, "you should have seen it! No one knew what to do! It was sunny and mild almost every day!"

Michael laughed out loud. "You'd see folks sittin' in cafés at three in the afternoon—half of 'em drunk—they didn't know what to do with it!"

Robbie laughed along with him, adding, "And everyone was pink!"

Michael slipped further into a laugh. "Oh, aye, no one could get a tan. All those faces and arms—pink as salmon!"

I got up to get Michael a coffee, delivered it, then returned to the counter. I started cleaning shelves and rearranging packages and thought about other places where reconciliation was undertaken. I shifted bottles of olive oil and ran a damp cloth across the metal shelf. Belfast was changing, certainly, but everything seemed so unstable—or was reported to be unstable. After all, who knew how peace was created, really? The Basque separatist group ETA had recently announced an end to its guerrilla war against the Spanish government, crediting Ireland and the political party Sinn Fein with influencing its decision. Gerry Adams was to make a trip over there to advise them as they began peace negotiations with the government. South African Archbishop Desmond Tutu had recently visited West Belfast, and after listening to people talk about obstacles and difficulties in the post-Agreement period, replied: "Why did you assume it would be easy?"

As I talked to friends from communities all over Ireland, I found myself struck by the similarities between them and friends in other parts of the world. The more I looked at it, the more they seemed similar. They all had a sense of resignation I would never feel, coming from a country with a stable government. They struggled with anger and hatred in a way that startled me. Having experienced violence firsthand, many couldn't easily put the past behind them, though they were often advised to do so. In Saigon, close friends and colleagues used the words "Hanoi" and "Northerner" with such venomous contempt I was taken aback. At the same time, one snowy evening in Boston I watched with shock as the gentle and generous face of a friend from Hanoi suddenly hardened as she talked about the American War and suggested that postwar suffering in Saigon was deserved. In Taipei, an old roommate of mine displayed a 2–28 sticker on the back of her car, reminding people of the government's use of force against the population on February 28, 1950. She also patiently explained to Americans that she was *Taiwanese*, not Chinese, and that Taiwan was not part of mainland China, though it had been occupied by Chiang Kai-shek's forces in 1949. Something similar went on in Korea and, again, I thought of my own country and its relationship to Puerto Rico; from northern Ireland, the idea that Puerto Rico would become a state was upsetting. I ran my cloth over the bottles of oil and placed them back on the shelf, then lifted jams and pickles and shifted them to the counter. Military bases were a complaint here; in Vieques, it was live bombing runs.

From the streets of these varied locales I could see that all the movements and events reported in the news were still, at bottom, made up of a mix of people. There were greedy people, idealists, justice seekers, revenge mongers, insiders, outsiders, arms dealers, corporate swine, pious holy people—it was an astonishing mix. Underneath this melange, where the wheels of history turned, were regular people trying to live ordinary lives. They wanted to play soccer with the passion and adrenaline that went with athletic competition, the primitive, physical push of muscle and speed, not of revenge or hatred. They wanted to perform well in school, challenge their minds with the plethora of numbers and possibilities in maths or the unraveling delight of storytelling that went as deep as the soil here in Ireland.

I thought the departure of the military base from West Belfast was as important and historic an event as the recent promise to build a new campus for the University of Ulster system that would straddle historically sectarian communities. That the military presence was declining and the educational one growing was a sign of hope and development I considered as significant as the increasing investment in Ireland made by information technology companies from around the world.

"We'll see," a friend said about the university campus, "it's all talk right now, y'know. They could back out."

Pessimism and cynicism about the promise-letdown patterns of politics are natural responses in Ireland. Even when the Nobel Peace Prize was awarded, people spoke of it as "premature." David Trimble looked as though he had just bitten into a lemon. No one seemed capable of talking about the future with hope, only with the steely determination to get away from the present. After a while this attitude bored and annoyed me, and I found myself repeating my mother's line to me when I rolled on about politics at home. "Edith," she said, "could you just say something pleasant?"

Listening to responses like "premature" when the gracious answer might have been one with more appreciation, or having it pointed out to me (an outsider) that the actions of the British government based on a promise of change were not enough (not fast enough, not sincere enough) was painfully disconcerting; talk came to a bitter and sudden stop. Fatalism was so strong, both personally and socially, that I think peace was believed to be a stolen season. I turned away from these sour comments in disappointment and disgust. They rolled out of people's mouths naturally, almost as if they were unaware of what they were saying. I finished with the shelving and began to wash the fridge. I pushed hard against the glass, shaking the bottles of juice.

My optimism was frequently dismissed as a novice's foolishness, but Ireland was in better shape than most people knew. Having spent time in the collapsed economies and infrastructures of Southeast Asia, I found myself tut-tutting the Irish as they overlooked what I saw as good fortune: a solid infrastructure and a place in a stable economic system, reformation of dysfunctional institutions, and tools to address injustice. But I was, at a deeper level, mistaken about this thing called hope, too. I could come and go as I pleased in their stop-and-start world. As I watched things unfold and read books about ages past from the remove of my South Belfast apartment, I realized it was easy for history (and resentment) to take center stage in life in Ireland. Stepping back, I looked through the display case and around the shop. A basket full of French baguettes stood out. They weren't selling, and I knew by the end of the day they'd be hard and stale.

Chapter 7

Fish and Chips / Fergus / The Fitzsimmons Sisters

Reading about the ancient while watching the contemporary helped me as a map of the island began to take shape in my head. The roads curved and twisted in on themselves in painful and confusing ways. Annie walked back into the shop and changed the drawer on the cash register.

"Edie," Robbie said, startling me from my theorizing, "you wouldn't be free this afternoon, would you?"

I smiled, the café was empty, and he knew I could type.

"Are you flirting with me, Mr. Crawford?" I asked.

"I have to go to court . . . and . . . ," he answered, with a blush.

"You need some transcriptions done?" I asked. He breathed a sigh of relief, and I laughed at him. "Perhaps for a few pounds," I continued.

"Ten quid," he offered.

I snorted and dismissed him. "Twenty, plus a meal at the end of the day." He smirked. "Listen," I said with a smile, "I'm a very busy woman, places to go, people to see!" I gestured to the empty café.

"I'll be back in an hour."

Just as I was feeling pleased with myself, he left the shop, mumbling something about the workday at R. P. Crawford and Co. ending at 9:00 P.M.

I walked back behind the counter and into the kitchen. Annie, who knew Robbie from his frequent trips into the shop, laughed at our exchange.

"Y'know, Edie," she said, "some people are just craic unto themselves."

She was right. Robbie was good craic. He went to law school at Queen's (classmate of Irish president Mary McAleese), had an entire file of low-life lawyer jokes, and could play the acoustic guitar and do stand-up comedy at the same time. His capacity for keeping a joke running floored me. A single line could run an entire week, popping up unexpectedly in conversation over and over again, like a shark always returning to the surface of water. As winter set in, he referred again and again to the cold water flat above his law office and the death from hypothermia of a newly acquired pet polar bear.

"Oh, that's how damn cold the place is," he said, "poor Reykjavik, he's dead as a doornail."

Robbie showed up an hour and a half later ("sort of right on time, for Belfast," I joked as we pulled away). I was actually quite pleased to do a bit of work for him. His firm was relatively new, and as he was really the "and Co." of "R. P Crawford and Co.," I felt I should show him some support. Robbie's decision to "hang out a shingle" (which is our American slang for going it alone in the legal business) instead of staying with larger firms brought a smile to my face. My father was a lawyer who had hung out a shingle. Early in his career, Father was part of the multitude of workers in Boston city government who had small-time political connections. That is to say, he knew a few people, but no Kennedy or O'Neill, and his career might well reflect it. Landing himself a job in this way meant that he would only be as secure in his work as the political climate was stable. Summarily let go when he reached middle age, he had no alternative but to do local work in our hometown. Despite its two country clubs and the yacht club at the foot of our street, our town provided more mundane legal work for my father, and a paltry bit of it at that. After some time, it became necessary for him to enlist his children as workers, and so, off I went to his office—located conveniently above a pizza joint—where I typed out wills, articles of incorporation, and other legal documents. Through a mottled glass door, I could hear my father talking with a faux expertise about anything that concerned his clients: Would a will be legal if it was changed? Would a small business be able to expand? Would a workman be able to collect compensation for back injuries? The questions were often simple enough, but Daddy was "the lawyer" and had to explain some obscure local exception to a foolish state law. The clients often muttered their gratitude through a bit of confusion, then left. My father handled all these people and their personal lives with a degree of grace and respect I came to understand fully as I grew older. "Don't ever forget where you came from," he would say to me, scornfully, when I embraced local elitism. Where I came from was neither a yacht-club suburb nor "the old country," but rather, a way of being in the world that meant I had to recognize the impermanence of good fortune and the lasting value of humility.

Robbie and I chatted about his business and other things as we drove to the office, and I felt that narcotic experience of language again. I shook my head in wonder. Sometimes I encountered the thing called "culture" in conversation. It was so elusive in this form that when I met it, I froze, as if it were a bird unwittingly landing near me in a garden. Music, voice, history, and

even *future* all spun forward out of individuals in such a flood that I was
dumbstruck. The woman I met in September in Donegal left me in just such
a state—inarticulate, unable to describe even the simplest conversation. So
it went on occasion in the city, too. Stories and jokes from Robbie—a head-
spinning series of simple exchanges—struck like flash floods, then withdrew.
We were driving through the downtown area on the way to the office when
Robbie explained that he had to drop off a writ at his brother's firm.

"I've got to stop by my brother's," he said, "then there's a pile of files calling your name at my office, Miss Shillue."

"Oh, it's what gets me out of bed in the morning, Mr. Crawford. I can't wait."

"Now, will you look at this!" he said, pointing to traffic detours.

"Laying cables for the Internet age, my friend."

"Right. Changing phone service, electricity, you name it."

"Welcome back to the world," I said.

We pulled down Great Victoria Street and turned in by the Castle Court
parking garage. Robbie hooked around a side street, then slowed the car.

"Edie, I'm going to pull over to the curb here. What I want you to do is
get out of the car, knock over that RUC officer over there, and take over the
wheel while I go in and rob that bank."

I giggled.

"No, I'm going to run upstairs and drop this off. If 'the cawp' asks you to
move, just drive around the block."

"Got it," I said. As I waited, the afternoon news announced an investigation of punishment beatings and recent murders in the city. When Robbie got
back in the car, I asked him what he thought of the situation.

"Edie, it's a sorry state, but the truth is, we're not shocked here anymore."

I knew that he had recently stopped taking criminal cases because of the
hazards of the occupation, and I wondered to myself if it was combat fatigue.
He changed the subject. "Boston, eh?"

"Yeah," I said.

"I was in the States once."

"Yeah?"

"The Catskill Mountains—it was a summer jobs program."

"Yeah, there're loads of those for college kids," I answered.

"My mother's family actually lived in America. In Canada. We probably
could have moved there—at least my mother would have been willing to, I
think. But my father said he'd never leave."

One of the more bitter ironies of the Irish diaspora is that it provided safe haven for those suffering in the Troubles. I began to think of the "What if" scenarios for Robbie's life, but as if catching me at it, he turned on the jokes, and I swung from downhearted to lighthearted.

"I'd be Canadian!"

"A Canuck," I laughed. "You could be a resident of Manitoba."

"It would have made Reykjavik happy."

"I once had a dog named Manitoba."

"You named your dog Manitoba?"

"Yeah."

"What kind?"

"Black lab mix . . . probably about the size of your Reykjavik there."

"Yeah?"

We pulled up in front of the office.

"Oh look, Edie, there's yer man McGinty waiting on me. I'll blame the lateness on you, okay?"

"Deal. What's he here for?"

"He has business with me," he answered with a sideways glance.

Mr. McGinty was as polite as you please when we went into the office. Robbie's paralegal, Marie, looked up from her pile of work and gave me a smile. She smoked furiously, so was perpetually surrounded by a haze of bluish smoke. Her face pressed through the fog with a greeting.

"Well, if it isn't the Marines!" she said, then gestured with her hand to a pile of folders and a tape recorder. "Take that beachhead, would you?"

McGinty entered quietly behind us. He was a tall, good-looking man— dark hair, dark eyes, arms like tree trunks.

"Hello, Mr. McGinty, whataboutche?" Marie greeted him.

"Dead on, Marie."

"Would you like a cup of coffee, Edie?" Robbie asked as I was about to sit down and start chatting with Marie.

"No, Mr. Crawford," I said, springing up and smiling sweetly, "but can I get you fellas one?"

"That would be lovely."

I fixed the coffee, brought it into the office, then returned to the desk to do some transcriptions.

"I haven't had my damn lunch yet," Marie said. "C'mon, let's go," she said, grabbing me by the arm.

"Robbie!" she yelled out, "we're away." Then she quickly pushed me out the door. I laughed at her bravado.

"I work almost ten hours a day for that bastard," she said as we climbed into the car.

Though many Irish I met demurred on politics as a topic of conversation, Marie was one of a handful who spoke with a loud, brash voice about its many deals and the contradictory details interwoven in it. We jumped right into conversation on politics, local "gossip," street-level analysis of the infamous, and the enduring "peace process."

"Yer man Adams . . . " Marie said, "he goes from the Armalite to Armani and suddenly he's Mr. Charisma . . . what's that you Americans say? . . . *Yeah, right.*"

"Do you think he can deliver weapons decommissioning?"

"No. No one can," she answered.

We stopped at a set of lights.

"We'll go to Malone's and get some fish and chips." She turned right and pulled up to the sidewalk.

I mentioned the rumors of the Nobel Peace Prize going once again to someone from Northern Ireland. It seemed clear that things would turn out as the media predicted, and it would be awarded to John Hume and David Trimble.

"David Trimble?!" Marie screeched as she drove, "I'd like to take David Trimble to that mermaid statue and shove it up his ass!"

"You're thinking of Copenhagen," I said with a snicker.

"Copenhagen?"

"The Nobel is awarded in Oslo."

"Well, Edie, I'd like to fly to Oslo, pick up David Trimble, take him to Copenhagen, and shove that mermaid statue up his ass."

It was not easy to embrace Trimble as a leader unless you could also warm to the Unionist Party's policy of grudging, minimal compromise. It was akin to accepting the moral absolutism of a bullying patriarch.

I was getting more and more curious about our handsome Mr. McGinty, so I tiptoed around the subject as we entered the shop and waited for the chips.

"That McGinty's a good-lookin' one, eh?"

She muttered softly.

"So what's his story?"

Marie laughed. "Who knows!" she said. The waitress brought our plates over. "Well, y'know, McGinty's all right," she continued, sprinkling salt onto her chips as we sat down, "at least he's got morals, know what I mean?"

"No," I answered. But really I did. McGinty fit the profile of businessmen and nightclub owners I met all over Boston.

"He doesn't do 'political' crime, and he's not a bigot. He'd help you out of a jam at a moment's notice."

"And not let you forget it?" I asked, popping a chip into my mouth.

Marie waved me away. "Who would? He won't squeeze you, though. I like him. He treats me like a lady." She lifted her bottle of Coke and cracked the seal on the cap. I confessed that McGinty seemed all right to me, too.

I never learned the score on McGinty, but he looked like so many men I met in Northern Ireland. He was like the cabbie who had chatted with Robbie the day before, one of many working-class guys who were not a "part of the Troubles," but rather survivors of same. Today, with a cease-fire on, they had various means of getting ahead that might not endanger their lives. McGinty's was just more of what kept him going in the first place. For others, there was construction work, cab driving, night work as a bouncer at local clubs, the occasional "antique" sale.

Most of the men struck me as the walking wounded, with the leathery hands of rural farmers, but pricklier characters. On sidewalks, women would encounter the occasional lascivious stare, or the odd and alien howl of blue humor rising up from the dust of work sites. Such workmen were all over the city as buildings went up in the new, changing economy—apartments, office blocks, restaurants, and hotels. The skin of their hands was often gray with plaster, thickened with the mixing of cement, scarred from accidents or fights. They were tree-root hands at the end of fence-post arms. At the close of a workday, glaziers spent their early evenings picking shards of glass from their palms. Occasionally, joiners earned extra income by driving cabs or banging heads together for gangsters.

Through talk, analysis, and the push-and-shove that passes for dialogue in Ireland, joiners and glaziers (the "regular blokes") became the bottom feeders of the Troubles industry—replacing doors and windows after a blast or a shoot-up and getting paid by insurance money. A joke running around Belfast in the 1980s was that the police often tailed them because they were tipped off about bombings. This, too, explained the high number of BMWs in the city throughout the decade. These working mobsters and their henchmen, apparently, were making a killing (figuratively speaking).

But if the calloused, shard-speckled hands of glaziers represent corruption, you're *really* joking. The facade of "democratic institutions" and the mini-industry of Troubles analysis might focus on these jagged-faced, beefy men, but that was simply the distracting gesture of a stage illusion. Eyes focused on ugly ruffians, we're unable to question what exactly grew out of the conflict. It is a well-known maxim that war is a money-making proposition for a handful of providers. The government might scream about fiscal black holes, but its contractors likely did not. When asked by a local paper if she believed in success for the peace process, a woman from Belfast's Shankill Road dismissed such naiveté by saying, "No, no. There's too much money being made."

Most of these and other working people approached the door of Robbie's Antrim Road office with the sorry slouch of the powerless. They walked in and softly greeted me with a "Sorry, luv." And though the British government has established damage awards for a whole host of strange disasters (deciding, by a complex series of insurance configurations, on their relationship to the Troubles), filing papers and getting a refund made you feel you were one of those tiny fish that feed off the barnacles growing on the back of a lumbering whale. These clients were the people who swept up shattered glass on unsafe streets while lawyers and executives delivered the bad news from downtown. Each case was a consummate portrait of the little guy fighting "the system." And he always lost.

I could see both elements of the population as I moved around town. Some walked in the delusion of empire still: jacket and tie, smart looks, a belief in the honesty and integrity of government written across their faces. Others walked slowly, heads down; trousers speckled with dirt, paint, and plaster; faces soured irrevocably with lines and grimaces. They had spent their lives on industry—working at places called Mackies, Londonderry Power, Newells (later Monsanto), and a famous place referred to rather benignly as "the shipyard." Self-deprecating in the extreme, these workers may have been the very ones to spread another local joke: "If it weren't for the skills and dedication of the good people of Belfast, the *Titanic* wouldn't be where it is today."

From the distance of a worksite, the younger guys heckled women like orangutans behind overgrowth, but that very morning two came into the café, and their demeanor shapeshifted within the tile interior of the shop, with its neat shelves and white walls. I looked across the counter at their dusty figures, and out it came: hands held as if a schoolmarm was present, they softened suddenly and in place of "hello" they muttered "sorry, luv" (as if their custom were imposition).

"What can I get for ya?" I asked.

"Two cups of tea to take away, luv."

(Of course, they tossed some coins in the tip jar. Later, an Ulster preppie wearing jacket and designer tie stood before me and, in response to the same question, mocked my accent.)

We finished the chips, and Marie lit another cigarette. The waitress came over and cleaned our table.

"Work," Marie said, pointing with her cigarette, "that'll bring decommissioning," then she sighed, "maybe."

We went back to the car and drove to the office.

⤙ ⤚

Later, I was just finishing a file when two men walked in saying they wanted to see Robbie. One was portly, mustachioed, and chatty. The other was a young man, carrying a guitar. The older man walked in, shook my hand, and introduced himself in a deep voice, heavy with a country accent.

"Name's Fergus. It's a pleasure to meet you."

"Edie."

"Yes, yes, Robbie's mentioned you'll be giving him a hand."

"Has he?" I said, "that's news to me."

"He also said you're a helluva good-lookin' woman, and I'd say he was right."

I smiled at the flattery, then explained that Robbie wasn't available, but they could wait, and gestured toward the chairs. Fergus took one, then lit a cigarette.

"Robbie tells me you're from Boston," he said, while his younger, blond friend sat quietly.

"Yes," I explained.

"A fine city. I liked Boston, but y'know, I preferred New York."

"Who wouldn't?" I answered with a smile. I moved my hands to put the recorder on again so I could continue my work. He was unfazed.

"Y'know what I really liked about being in America?" he asked.

"What?" both the younger man and I asked.

Realizing he hadn't introduced us, Fergus said, "Edie, this is Donal."

"Hi," I said.

Donal gestured with his hand, but looked away.

"What I liked about America," Fergus continued, "is everyone thinks it's great to be Irish."

I laughed softly. "Yeah," I said, "I suppose it's one of the better places to call yourself 'Irish.'"

"What about your people, Edie? Where are they from?"

"Grandmother from Galway, great-grandmother from Clare."

"The west," he said, impressed.

"The west," I said, with a nod, though I was still unsure of my Irish credentials.

Robbie had mentioned more than my hometown to Fergus, it appeared, because out of nowhere he plucked the question, "Viet Nam, eh?"

"Viet Nam?" I answered.

"Did Robbie mention that you lived in Viet Nam?"

"He may well have," I said, "I did."

"Ho Chi Minh!" he said, as if the name were self-explanatory.

"Yes?" I asked with a smirk, "what about Uncle Ho?"

He smiled.

"Did you know he was the only person to tip his cap for Terence Mc-Sweeney?"

"No," I answered.

"He was a dishwasher in London."

"Who—McSweeney?" I asked, egging him on.

He snorted a soft laugh and eyed me again.

"McSweeney was the first Irishman to go on hunger strike for the rights of Irish political prisoners. Ho was in London when he died, y'know, and when the body was paraded through the streets, Ho was the only one to take off his hat."

"So the story goes," I said.

He put out one cigarette and lit another. Donal, sitting to his left, continued to finger the strings of the guitar.

"Ho Chi Minh—he was good craic," Donal said, with a wink toward me.

"Che Guevara," Fergus said.

"Another revolutionary," I said quickly, thinking this was a word game.

"And an Irishman."

"Yeah," I said, with a snort and a dismissive laugh.

"He writes of it in his autobiography," Fergus said, "says his grandmother was Irish, and he attributes his politics to the blood of Irish rebels running through his veins."

Given that the Caribbean was a landing place for the Irish labor diaspora, this is not so far-fetched.

"Well, then, you'll have heard of the San Patricios," I said with a smile, proud of my own nugget of history.

Donal began to hum a straggling tune.

"Christy Moore," Fergus muttered, recognizing the piece.

"Aye," Donal said, then put the guitar down. "Look, Fergus, you promised to drive me downtown to Dixon's," he whined.

"After I speak with Robbie," Fergus said. At which point, Robbie came out of his office.

"Fergus, hello," he said, shaking his hand, "what can I do for you?"

"Just a few questions about the house in Tyrone, Robbie," he answered, walking into his office.

"What have you done now?" I heard Robbie ask as the door shut behind them.

Donal picked up the guitar again and asked me what kind of music I liked, did I know who Christy Moore was.

"Ireland's Bob Dylan, right?"

He scowled at me. "That phony! Moore was writing and singing *before* yer man Dylan. He *influenced* Dylan."

"U2?" I offered meekly.

"The greatest band that ever was!" he yelled, putting me on.

Robbie and Fergus came out of the office in short time, Robbie patting Fergus on the shoulder as they said good-bye, Fergus hesitating further.

"Dixon's, Fergus!" Donal said, "I've got to go downtown to Dixon's."

"All right," he grumbled.

"Are you driving into town, fellas?" Robbie asked. "I need a few things. Can I send Edie with you?"

He gestured to me.

"C'mon along, young lady," Fergus said, happy to extend his history lessons.

Robbie handed me a list of office supplies and fifty pounds.

"Now, I want change, Shillue."

"Oh, right," I said, with a wink to the lads.

We walked out onto the sidewalk. Fergus pointed proudly to his Toyota Celica and said, "What we've got here, Edie, is what we fellas call a shaggin' wagon."

Donal rolled his eyes while I suppressed a laugh.

"Well, y'know, you should hear what we women say about 'em."

They both stopped and looked. "What?" Fergus asked.

"You've never heard?" I queried, in mock surprise, "we say, next to a motorcycle, it's the single best sign of a midlife crisis."

With that bit of slaggin', I won Fergus's respect. He let me sit in front. As we drove into the city, he pointed to the architecture on Great Victoria Street, "Y'see this here, Edie? Bombed to shit in the seventies—the Europa—"

"Most-bombed hotel in the world," Donal piped in from the backseat.

"Did I tell you about the day I got stuck down here?" he asked, looking into the rearview mirror at Donal. "I'm driving along and turn onto this street and all of a sudden the street's empty, and a soldier he yells out, 'THERE'S A BOMB!!!!!' I don't know how I ended up in a cleared area, but I turn to him and say, 'Right, I hear ya buddy,' and gun it all the way down the street."

I wondered if he shouldn't have just turned himself around, but didn't want to touch the story.

"I've done a fair bit of travelin' myself, y'know, Edie," he continued, turning to me. "I went to Mexico City to see that monument to the San Patricios. I like to go to New York a lot—every St. Pat's I head over."

I began to see the pattern. Fergus followed the many footsteps of the Irish diaspora. We pulled into the parking garage of Castle Court shopping mall, and Fergus quickly found us a spot. He set the parking brake and said, "They wouldn't have even thought of building a place like this in the bad old days."

"Aye," Donal said.

We got out of the car and walked over to the mall.

"Let us buy you a coffee and donut before you head over to the stationer's, Edie."

"I really should get this done and go back."

"Oh, c'mon," Fergus said.

I agreed, and we entered the mall, went up the escalator, and joined a line for Dunkin Donuts. I turned to Fergus. "So, El Macho, how is it a good Irish man such as yourself never married?" I asked while we waited.

He laughed quietly. "I'm still a young bachelor, Edie, y'know. Forty-eight is young by Irish standards. Beside, I like my freedom, y'know, Edie? And what about you? A lovely slip of a girl such as yerself, never married?"

"Well," I said, "there was that one unfortunate incident, but we're divorced now," I joked.

He smiled and nodded.

"Well, that's it, then," Donal piped in, "Fergus's a Catholic, y'know, he'll be unable to propose marriage to you now—as he no doubt hoped."

I blushed and broke into a laugh. Flattery and slaggin' by turns, I thought, this is out of my league. I could see the conversation was about to head into high gear, so I decided to fall back. And it did, moving along so quickly that it resembled a Chinese Ping-Pong match, with words clicking and bouncing so fast I didn't know what was where. This form of dialogue is an orchestration of language in Ireland that comes out so naturally and spontaneously that it is truly a marvel for me when I encounter it.

Young Donal began talking of his home village in Fermanagh—how the pub was his playground, the hobnailed boot his punishment for the infraction of pinching or biting the customers whose attention he wanted. The stories come out like water over falls, and I think he cannot be for real, this one. I cannot believe that the place he speaks of, with its exquisite details—the wood of the bar, the voice of the woman who gave him his first job, the glasses he collected for change—they cannot be real. He learns music, singing, and Irish in the village. He talked about the craic, and I wondered at him, thinking to myself that just listening to him was grand craic; just listening to most Irish was grand for me. Here was a story, and in it was a character and he "was the worst laiyer (liar) you ever heard. 'I once shot a man with a .357 magnum,' says he, and I ask him, 'Where's the safety on a .357 magnum?' (He elbows Fergus.) 'He says, 'Safety?' Oh, he was a terrible laiyer. When he was a cub, he was good-hearted, but stoopid, y'know, and our ma . . . " And the story shifts to the woman known as "our ma" and her golden heart but sharp tongue, and the cub's gone to America now, but Donal, he's got no plans to go, and life here's all right, and he works for an engineering firm, worked once in the eastern bloc countries, helped out a bit in Croatia before things blew and then Slovenia (and here I point out to Fergus that now he can pay a visit to Slovenia, since we can all connect an Irishman to it). And Donal is talking now about his other brother, and is he a musician, too, I ask, and he says, "That man wouldn't know a bar of music from a bar of soap."

To slow him down a bit, I ask if he knows the controversy about "Danny Boy" aka "The Londonderry Air," did he hear the story about . . .

" . . . how it was written by a peasant?" he asks.

"No, that it's really "The Limavady Aire," I answer.

"No, but it was written by a Prod . . . "

" . . . who heard it being played," I add.

"On a whistle," he says.

"On a doorstep," I say.

"Probably by a peasant," he finishes.

And as the young one talks, Fergus gets a gleam in his eye, proud that a torch is being passed—he's got the gift, this one.

Where in some places a loosening of the tongue such as this might come out as a type of nonsense, it is pure orchestration here, music of a grand sort, the babble of water on rock, and it thrills Fergus that for this kid, born in 1974—it's *okay* to be "Irish." Only in America had he, Fergus, felt that. Meanwhile, Donal wanders through the city shopping center and talks on and on about needing to buy a tape player for his Da, and Fergus shifts uncomfortably while we wait for him to finish buying,

"Downtown, here, I feel like that Indian in the movie with Burt Lancaster, what was it? *Apache*. When he wanders into town and stares at all the white people."

He hitched up his pants, waiting impatiently. I keep thinking of his age and the context in which he grew up, his recitation of things Irish—history, culture, and identity became a lifeline for him. He was a suspect by virtue of his address, was stopped and searched regularly, his family careful not to own anything that would be cause for arrest—no books, no music that could be called a threat to the British Crown. He was a Republican who, I presumed, found the notion of "physical force tradition" perfectly reasonable. Though not a member of the infamous Felon's Club on the Falls, he was happy to give them his business.

"Donal!" he snaps at "the cub." "We gotta go."

Donal walks toward us with his bag and nods to Fergus that he won't keep him longer, then, turning to me, he finishes our conversation about music in a teacherly manner: "At the end of the day, 'ere's none of 'em you can't find a controversy over," says he, meanin' the songs.

❧ ❦

After leisurely attending to my own errand, I hopped into a cab and made my way back to the office. As we pulled up, I could see two older women walking in the door. They carried worn shopping bags and moved with a deliberate slowness.

"Hello, ladies," Marie said politely as I walked in behind them. The women were startled out of their conversation. "Our Edie here will let Mr. Crawford know you've arrived," she said, then walked quickly into the back room.

I hung up my coat and smiled awkwardly, then walked into Robbie's office. He scowled at me from behind a pile of files and asked if I enjoyed my extended break.

"Yes," I answered with a giggle, "uh, two little old ladies are here to see you."

"Oh," he said, "the Fitzsimmons sisters. Tell them I'll be with them in a minute."

I closed the door. "Ladies, he'll be right with you."

The younger woman, wearing an orange trench coat and blue suede sneakers, turned to me before she sat down next to her sister. "Is that accent Canadian, pet?"

"No," I said, with a smile, "I'm from Boston."

The older sister had gray hair and a gentle, wrinkled face. Her eyes were pale green and made her look vaguely distracted. She held on to her shopping bag and mumbled quietly as her contribution to the ensuing conversation. I slipped into a sense of ease immediately, liking them both.

"I've been to America, y'know," the younger sister said.

(*Oh, yes, yes, been to America,* the older one mumbled with a roll of her eyes.)

"Yeah?" I answered.

"I spent most of me time in Canada, but I took a visit down to Graceland."

"Did you?" I said.

"Oh, yes."

(*Oh, yes, of course, look at the shoes,* the older sister added.)

"Was it great?"

"It was wonderful. I saw everything."

I smiled, imagining Graceland, warm weather, and loads of velveteen.

"And can you imagine?" she continued, "I've met people that have spent their whole lives in that country and never seen it."

"Oh, yeah," I said, beginning to feel uncomfortable, for I was one of them.

(*Oh, no, heaven forbid, heaven forbid you don't go,* she said, with a shake of her right hand.)

My discomfort grew.

"You've got a lovely figure, pet," the older woman said, apropos of nothing.

"Oh, thanks!" I said, relieved, "that's nice of you to say."

"Whaddar' ya doing here, pet?" she continued.

The mystery of my choice was never resolved by folks in Belfast (though elsewhere it was not questioned), but I had learned to say sincerely that I liked the place. This brought a laugh from her, and she mumbled, *Sure you're joking.*

"Ladies," Robbie said, coming out of his office, "I'm so sorry to keep you waiting. Come right in."

They gathered up their shopping bags and went toward Robbie's office.

But the older woman lagged behind a moment and then walked toward me. Occasionally, today, I can still see her in my sleeping and waking life. Her lips are moving, and she is burdened with bags on each arm. She holds her hands up like a woman releasing enormous grief, but her eyes are calm and lovely. I get confused for a second as she mumbles and begins walking toward me. After a few more steps, I realize she's talking *to* me. As I lean toward her, she cups my face with rugged and bony hands before kissing me and saying, "Aren't you beautiful . . . "

~§ ~

I could no longer see Ireland as a floating image in the North Atlantic; it had too many faces now. Some were plain and nervous; others pale and crabby; some were children with white, white skin, fine curly hair, and pink cheeks that looked as if they had been painted on. I rolled through the words of history books and the chant of poems, the stutter of contemporary truth and the silence of hatred and felt myself settle in with the rest. I had just begun to emerge from the numerous and fragile touches I experienced in Asia. The Irish had such harsh and heavy words, I failed to see their gentle, sentimental thoughts. I waited. Sometimes patience rewarded me, and in Ireland's powerful, long, and warm embrace, I found myself at home.

Chapter 8

Poison into Medicine / Homesick /
Peace Comes Dropping Slow

Winter was setting in. In my apartment, I curled up by the fire and wrapped myself in blankets as I read history and listened to the crackle and bang of the cold outside my window. I felt more confused than ever when trying to understand these relationships and cultures, when hearing the bitter expression of disappointment at negotiation and compromise, or when reading the "informed" analysis of journalists and political scientists. I bounced around the stories in the newspaper and on television like someone trying to get her bearings underwater. I reached out to touch things, thinking them solid, but they pulled away with the water's current. "Both sides" was a vague and dissatisfying reference to communities I was coming to know. "Across the Divide" was a sorry cliché.

"The Irish have harsh words, but gentle thoughts," my friend Seamus from West Belfast observed one day. I met him in the café one busy Friday, and we talked on occasion over coffee. He insisted that I stop by his house, so one day I finally made my way into the maze of streets in Finaghy and Andersonstown.

At six feet plus, Seamus is large and imposing. His gray-blue eyes often looked at me with suspicion from over the counter. His voice is deep and loud, he says "fuck" a lot, and even after I spent more time with him, I often stood defensively when he approached with his heavy footstep. He told me once that he'd lived in London, describing his tenure there as "the neighborhood's local fucking Paddy." Still, he liked the British and didn't point the finger at them when discussing Irish history. "Hundreds of years of killing each other," he said with scorn, "and we blame them."

These were powerful words from a man whose family had been in Belfast for generations and painfully damaged by the Troubles. Standing in his front room, he pointed out Hannahstown in the distance and explained to me that was where his brother had been killed by an IRA bomb.

"My family owns a large part of that mountain. My brother was driving along that road," he pointed with his finger, "you see that white house straight ahead?"

"Yes," I answered, following his hand.

"In 1972, my brother was driving a truck along the road that runs behind there, and he pulled over to let a school bus full of kids pass. When he started his truck again, the bomb went off."

As he explained, I got confused, "His truck was bombed?" I asked.

"No, fuck, he was a totally fucking innocent bystander," Seamus explained, turning away and sitting down in a chair. "The army explained to my parents that his truck, when he fucking started it up again, must have vibrated and triggered a fucking bomb that was nearby. He was blown to bits."

My confusion about the details of the story prompts questions, but the words to form them are kept at bay. I want to ask for more details, but I can't. "Responsibility" and its daunting moral overtones appeared moot to me. The bomb lay in wait. Would it be a van driver or a bus full of children? Truth is stranger than fiction—every traveler knows that—and when I encounter these tragedies, I handle them delicately. "Caught up" is a phrase used to describe some tragic deaths here as that vortex the Troubles sucks in another victim.

I looked out the window at the mountain, wondering what might have happened had he not pulled over (I mean, suppose it had gone off *in front of* the bus?) and thinking about how it must feel to see that mountain every day when you walked out your door.

He continued with his contrast of British and Irish personalities: "The British have gentle words, but harsh thoughts." Then he got up to illustrate his point, "Look, follow me. I'm going to show you something that I hope will focus your mind."

We walked out the back door of the house. He explained that he never used the front (answering my unasked question). Coming around the building, I was startled by the sight of the mountain. We then walked a block down his street.

"This," he said, gesturing to the air as we walked, "will be poison turned into medicine."

I didn't quite understand his point, then realized he meant the closed nature of the rebuilt neighborhoods. He stopped and turned dramatically to give an illustration. "I can hear a child's voice from my open window and know exactly where she belongs. Mothers can call their children home from out the kitchen window."

In a 1987 piece in the *Manchester Guardian,* the journalist David Hearst described the two-sided nature of West Belfast's neighborhoods. At the time, one billion pounds had been spent there on raising housing standards. That meant 80 percent of West Belfast was rebuilt. There was a catch, however, and Hearst didn't let it pass, noting: "Although it also means that estates can be sealed off by police Land-Rovers and moving security gates within minutes, limiting the number of escape routes gunmen can take, the design is generally popular in areas like the Ardoyne, a Republican stronghold." I'm much less cavalier about inhibiting freedom of movement, but then I've never lived in anything referred to as a "stronghold." The latter effect of the engineering design was a point all residents were aware of and had accommodated. However, it was something that would, on occasion, send *me* into emotional depression and, when I got lost driving around the area, screaming exasperation. Here was Kimberly Street, off Kimberly Drive, leading to Kimberly Close, circled by Kimberly Circle. It's not conducive to visitors, let's put it that way. But Seamus was right; it meant all the difference in the world to a family-oriented community. *Poison into medicine, a mom calling her child home.* We walked further, and these elements of idyll hung between us as hope. We took a left and another right, until finally we hit a dead end. The street was blocked by military fencing.

"This," he said dramatically, and here I joined in, lifting my arms to gesture too, *"is a Peace Wall!"*

It was heavy green corrugated metal, the same material surrounding Whiterock. In this neighborhood, it kept one group of citizens from interacting with another. The government claimed it was at the citizens' request, it was for their own safety, it was *a necessary measure.* Perhaps it was. Who was I to say? I stood looking at it with my hands on my hips.

"And they better take it down soon," Seamus continued, "because it's starting to annoy me."

I didn't ask how long it had been there, for I knew it was most of his life.

Gentle words, harsh thoughts. I agreed and thought of this line again and again as local politicians appeared on the news, dug into their uncompromising positions, and blamed each other about the failures of the new Assembly. Tony Blair flew in from London, Bertie Ahern flew up from Dublin, and everyone said they wanted to help the peace process. "Tell them to shut up and deal," I muttered to the news readers.

I had been up in the hills of Hannahstown, behind the city, after I first arrived. On that summer afternoon, the sun split clouds, and dogs prowled and sniffed in tangled hedges. I drove further up as the day ended and saw a small farm with piebald horses lumbering around an enclosure. From there the city struck me as the bundle of contradictions for which it is famous. It was a sprawl of brick housing estates and old factories. The peace line snaked through neighborhoods, like the spikes that rise from the spine of certain dinosaurs. Yet, up in the hills—only a short walk from Springmartin and Andersonstown—a lovely quiet prevailed. Chickens wandered about, their voices rolling softly. A dog lay resting in the sun. I could feel, again, the tug of the countryside, though traffic hummed an urban soundtrack in the distance. It was—how else can I describe it?—*peaceful*.

Spending time with Seamus helped me to see that the most divisive words in contemporary discourse were the most mundane. Who, for example, were *they*? What were *victims*? *Genuine victims*? Sometimes everyone sounded broken to some degree. "Fuck" ricocheted through all conversation like a bullet bouncing off armored plating. I shuddered a bit at its frequency. Such vocabulary was emblematic of a community's helplessness in the face of militarism from within and without. The walls, the road designs, and the murdered sibling were all things that caught people by the collar. Militarism or "the cause" was shoved into their lives like meal forced down the greased throats of geese.

But, being in Ireland today is to hear history echo and see change come inexorably. I could go to the hills over the city today and see a landscape completely different than on that summer visit. It would be marked by a host of tragedies. Nonetheless, as Seamus noted, poison could become medicine. I had been visiting it for one year, and in that time, peace talks were established, an agreement was reached, and the outline of a new government was put in place. Change is like the hoofbeats of approaching horse herds, and it arrives in spite of us. But the echo of the immediate past haunts everyone; it is the sobs of family grief as soldiers leave and the fences around bases get pulled out. It is the "fuck" that spits from every sentence and the curl in every lip of the unemployed. It is the gravelly testimony of the blind, and it is the slip-slide limp of the injured.

─≺ ≻─

In late winter, Ireland's moist air met up with northern cold. The two created a fog that frosted the landscape, so that the green, brown, and black of hedges and turf walls looked like the grizzly, tobacco-stained beards of old men. Moss turned to a slick film on tree trunks, and the red berries on bushes faded into pockmarks. Wood pigeons rested on leafless branches, and I imagined they were contemplating ways to dig out food. Each morning, light waited to break the night until eight o'clock, but a single bird woke me with its trill at 6:30. It must have rested on the tree-filled slope outside my bedroom window. As I walked to the café in the rising light, magpies darted around among the neighboring houses. A helicopter often gnawed its way through the sky around different parts of the city. Here they flew singly, but they flew in pairs in the countryside, hanging over neighborhoods and towns like dragonflies over stagnant ponds.

Walking to work was a simple pleasure. I could hear and see children making their way to Victoria College, the school across the Malone Road. I watched the traffic turn into a long queue that snaked along into town, the red taillights shimmering on foggy days. On one memorable morning, walking through my house to the door with my usual cloudy head, I caught sight of a fat, waxing moon hanging in the sky over Black Mountain. At eight in the morning, it was still wrapped in a cottony cloud and looked as large as an October harvest moon rising in the evening. I stopped dead in my tracks on the way out of the house, then again as I made my way down Marlborough Park toward the Lisburn Road. I stood outside a neighbor's house, still and staring, then caught the smell of cinnamon toast making its way out a nearby door. Three schoolgirls took no notice, wandering around me on the narrow sidewalk as I stared at the sky and sniffed the air.

"So I said . . . "

"My mam said . . . "

"I hated her; she was so mean . . . "

As I hurried past another corner, two window washers were unloading a ladder from their truck to begin cleaning. One started whistling "Norwegian Wood," and it floated through the air as clear as birdsong. Everything went silent as he rolled through the first two refrains, then circled around and began again. *"I once had a love or should I say she once had me . . . "* Eventually, his colleague began whistling harmony. I wanted to join in, but I restrained myself. They did not know I was listening, and I'm sure the addition of my shaky whistle would have spoiled things. One of the ladders rattled during the song, and then it faded away. A door banged shut. Homesickness rushed over me; I shook it off and hurried on to the restaurant. But I couldn't release myself from the tune and spent the entire morning working with a grin on my face.

"Edie's Irish, you know," Gillian said to a customer later, during lunch. This was meant to be a tease, and I smiled at her.

"Oh, aye," I answered, looking up at the woman from my work. I placed a spoonful of Greek salad next to some colorful rice and vegetables, then added mixed greens and dressing. Gillian handed me a plate with rounds of French bread and two squares cut from a wheaten loaf. I wiped the olive oil and mustard dressing from the edge of the plate, then handed it to her to deliver, adding a smirk as I did, "You're very funny."

"Do you have relations here?" the woman asked politely as I wrapped some croissants for her.

"My folk come from Galway, but I don't know of any that are still there."

She smiled as I handed her the bag, then she headed out into the windy day. Outside the window, clouds moved swiftly, sometimes letting the sun in, but mostly keeping it out. Occasionally, rain would fall in sudden, solid sheets, coming from somewhere between earth and sky.

"Aw, I was just taking the piss," Gillian said, returning to our station after the customer left. She leaned forward on the counter. Gillian has a classic Rubenesque figure and long red hair. She walks and talks without the least bit of physical self-consciousness and laughs at herself (and others) with an inviting ease.

"I used to work in this pub in Manchester, and British people, ones who'd never set foot on the island, were always walking up to me and telling me, 'I'm Irish, you know,' like I was supposed to feel some sort of great kinship with them. I haven't got a nationalist bone in my body."

If Fergus was right and it was great to be Irish in America, England was a different scenario altogether.

"I'm just not interested in that stuff," Gillian explained when I asked her about Irish ethnics in Manchester. So she did not pursue her cultural interests with a revivalist's fervor, but rather with an imaginative curiosity that, by its nature, couldn't be partisan.

She shrugged off the experience with a soft laugh. The politics of cultural identity is fertile ground for contemporary critics, and it has an eerie way of mirroring more rough-and-tumble politics, like, say, war. The edge so often associated with "northern" personalities, both in the Republic and in Great Britain, verges on a classic stereotype of the Irish (and Scots) from across the centuries. They are raucous, rude yobs, violent and riotous. There was a set of signifiers that were perpetually rerun by the global media, and they had come to define everyone. Balaclavas, truncheons, graffiti, and petrol bombs came to mind when one said "northern Ireland." What sort of people would we project onto such a place? The latest literary incarnation was Frank

McCourt's *Angela's Ashes,* a best-seller in the United States. Central to the story is an abusive father from the North who is brutalizing and alcoholic. In contemporary Irish and American television and film, the "bad guys" were always northerners, though in the United States there was still an air of romance about them as "struggling for the cause." British popular culture fared no better in my eye. Contemporary film and television had generated what I called "the rise of the Belfast gal pal." This was a new role popping up in story lines everywhere. She was a minor character in film and television stories who went by her first name only and stood loyally by her better, more British, friend. A source of comic relief and a vehicle for moving the story forward during a crisis, she was sexually deprived, a bit overweight, outspoken but observant, and nonintrusive. She came to the rescue of teary girls like Gwyneth Paltrow and told off their emotionally impotent boyfriends when it needed doing. Her accent was the key implication in her unknown history—Belfast or northern Ireland suggested tragedy of some sort. She is without family, lacking a lover, but full of emotional generosity and endurance. Once, in a television mystery series about a police pathologist, she had the chance to take center stage—a beautiful professional woman who, again, had an air of sadness about her. Her Belfast roots slipped out in vowels or diphthongs hidden in words like "about" or "down," giving the game away, like the "ax" of African Americans or the "prease" of Asian immigrants. These creations are a reflection of both limited imagination and lack of access to platforms of cultural expression.

Northern comedy found fuller voice in Belfast and Derry, with groups like The Hole in the Wall Gang, who performed parodies of Irish history and contemporary political debate with side-splitting good humor. More enduring than visual media, literary canons being formed in the North were almost exclusively male and Troubles oriented. In 1999, Seamus Heaney's sixtieth birthday was cause for celebration and tribute on both sides of the border, but there were far more who received little attention. One understated writer named Mary Beckett was almost erased from reading lists, but she wrote stories and novels such as *A Belfast Woman* and *Give Them Stones* that showed the slow impact of local hatreds and parochial institutions on personal relationships. The women in her stories had the kind of humorless endurance that devastated me as I read.

"Sure it's bad in the States, too," I said to Gillian, continuing our conversation. I knew the Irish found the ethnic longing of pub conversation irritating and alienating, "but y'know," I said, "there're worse annoyances."

Attempts to embrace a shared cultural kinship were awkwardly received by the Irish I met, but worse still was a hunger to offer armchair analysis of current politics. This is a great pastime of Americans, one which I often embrace. But I have learned through experience that the receiving end is less than enjoyable. When I was twenty-five, I undertook a year's study in Yorkshire, northern England. There I had my first (but not last) encounter with white British liberals who felt it necessary to tell me about the heinous crimes of my government and the appalling state of race relations in the United States. This was easy for me to embrace and agree with in my twenties, with my naive liberalism in full force, but I was hardly very experienced at that time and failed to point out to my lecturers the presence on the world stage of one Margaret Thatcher, nor did I mention hunger strikes at the Maze, the Stalker Affair, or race riots in Brixton.

By 1998 these same comments would come at me from Cool Britannia, enhanced by the boast that fabulous, multicultural Notting Hill was their home. My naive liberalism had blossomed into a radical-left political perspective by then, so I tolerated these comments for only a moment before I said, "West Belfast, Bradford, Brixton, and Stephen Lawrence." Meanwhile, Margaret Thatcher was having tea with Augusto Pinochet and telling him he had "brought democracy to Chile."

More difficult to handle today is that being Irish is in vogue in Great Britain (as well as in the United States). Thus, the people I met were repeating over and over that northern Ireland was on their list of must-go places; after all, the Irish were so "inspiring," what with the Good Friday Agreement and all.

"I really, really want to see it," one London woman said wistfully.

I wondered where she and all the others were in the eighties, when it was so much less trendy to be inspired. Then again, where was I?

How can they stand this? I wondered, about my Irish friends.

"Oh, people have been saying they'll come visit for years," a Belfast friend doing graduate work in London explained. It seemed the British were almost apologetic about it.

"Now I just reply with, 'Well, you come over when you're ready,'" she said. Naturally, the condescending tone does not go unnoticed, nor should it. No sanctimonious screeds had been delivered for my enlightenment from Britain's long-enduring "other" in northern Ireland. Neither "Orange" nor "Green" gave speeches on policy, race, and justice in America. The worst corners of Belfast and Derry still could not compare with certain housing estates and neighborhoods in Bradford. Though the British Army made a habit of sending its Sandhurst graduates to Belfast each summer for training, there were increasing numbers of riots on what they called "the mainland." The United States, and, I'm sure, European nations, also provided war tourists and various hangers-on who might come to northern Ireland because they believed in romantic myths of war as an expression of all of life's passionate extremes—something they had seen in the many movies about the Troubles. In fact, it is really quite the opposite. In northern Ireland and elsewhere, war is an utterly dreary and dispassionate series of decisions that slowly drain the life of communities. Recognizing the charade, soldiers sometimes puffed themselves up, gritted their teeth, or offered other forms of showmanship for tourists out to see a "war" up close, knowing, after all, that it was merely that ghastly twentieth-century creation called "acceptable levels of violence."

Politicians and decision makers often failed to recognize the disparity of numbers in proportion to tensions—all the while knowing it was a perfect real-life training ground for contemporary urban warfare. Guns fired or not, young men would be trained in toting heavy packs through urban areas, widely recognized as the "war of the future" by industry analysts.

No wonder British friends are unclear on who the northern Irish are! Of course, to be any kind of Irish in Great Britain or the United States is to have two very different experiences altogether. In the former, it is a handicap; in the latter, a boast. What makes it so is a puzzle. The "Irish passion" referred to by a British friend some months earlier was beginning to make sense to me. Its differentness was great relief to Britain's staid and stodgy south or its repressed and dreary Midlands. Better still, its Europeanization was making Ireland open in ways unheard of in its parochial past. Contemporary cultural observers had posited Ireland and the Irish as England's opposite—disordered where England was ordered, lively where England was dull—but it was not a new insight. English influence on Irish culture is historical fact, but the English perspective is indoctrination. Even Samuel Johnson's authoritative *Oxford English Dictionary* defined the word "Irish" as the following: "Resembling the Irish, esp. with reference to their reputation for illogicality."

Still, in the United States none of the imported symbols of lovely Ireland reflected what I felt it was to be Irish. One evening, after wrestling with stereotypes and representations and my own experience, I challenged myself to write down what I thought of as "Irishness." Of course, what first came to mind was a wake.

I once imagined myself at an Irish wake at my mother's childhood home on Hyde Park Avenue in Hyde Park. This was part of Boston, home of the diaspora and way station for the Cliffords before they lost the house and moved to the south shore, to Summer Street in Weymouth and the house with the gabled front.

The Cliffords, so I'm told by Mother, were "half-fares"—those who only had fare to Canada. The ride was cheaper, but—and the Irish didn't know this—less safe. Mother said that was all she knew about the family history, and "no, we never talked about any Irish ancestors," but someone said, somewhere along the line, that a Clifford owned the deed to the property that Westminster Abbey sits on. In history books, "Clifford" suggests Kerry or Clare or—Mother would love this—Ascendancy Irish.

Nonetheless, in the front room in Hyde Park was a corpse, an unnamed corpse that would haunt my mother well into this lifetime, my lifetime, so that on a weary summer afternoon, while the Red Sox play on the box, the ghost taps Mother and then she taps me and says, "Don't sleep here, Edith, if you're going to sleep, go upstairs! You look like a goddamned corpse."

In my imagination, the wake is an odd affair. Grandmother "Diamond Lil" takes the stage as you enter, a gracious and witty hostess, a relative of the deceased and an excellent bridge player. She was also renowned for taking in strays—an abandoned husband, an unmarried woman, a rogue kicked out for the last time—and letting them rent her attic room. In pictures I see she poses like a duchess for a painting, head turned to semiprofile, a regal look on her face. There about the room at the wake are her children: Dickie and Spike, Mary Ellen (who in later years becomes, simply, "lovey"), Ralph, Nat, Arthur, Jimmy, and Edith (Mom). Her husband, aka the Silent Butler, lurks about the kitchen, brooding perhaps, while Lil tries to make it a funny occasion by tossing one-liners back and forth with Auntie Jo, and all the while Jimmy is taking in the jokes and Mother is restraining her nervous laughter, and Jo finally decides to play a tune on the piano, and people move in and out of the room talking about the corpse and complimenting Lil on the food, looking at the picture of the sacred heart and the ceramic figure of the Virgin. The subject of the half-fares comes up and then passes away, since the story is sad and sorely in need of some elaboration. Someone somewhere suggests that no one's any the wiser as to who they were and, well, didn't one of the earlier ones go across the water the other way and a little later hold the deed to a little piece of property in London? This thread is picked up and carried across time, perhaps by the ghost, until it lands in my hands, passed on from my mother as the land Westminster Abbey sits on today. A lovely idea to my young, wandering mind, and I pass it on in Ireland, where it is smiled over, but the wake is still stuck in my mind as a simple, strange, slightly amusing affair. I dwell on the image, and the room becomes crowded with Cliffords. Cigarette smoke creates a fog, and the hum of voices rolls gently, broken by a loud laugh, prompting a raised voice as a story reaches its climax. Mother's hair is brown, and I myself am many births away, just after the snobbish owner of 41 Damon Road, in a town called Scituate, tells the newly arrived neighbor—pregnant for the sixth time— "You don't know when to quit do you?" From inside her, I kick, and she smiles and says she'll probably have even more kids, that's why she wants to buy the lady's house and what is she asking?

The wake moves then from Hyde Park to Scituate—very lace-curtain Irish now—and the ocean is close enough to hear and Mother checks it from the widow's deck "just to make sure it's still there," and because we're lace-curtain Irish now, the wake is a somber affair, and I've never been taught how to be at a wake, but a few gestures here and there make sense to me. Still the scene is foggy, and now ice clinks in glasses of gin and the laughter is a little more polite. Kerry people, I'm told, Kerry folk, and a book taken from the mantle of a fireplace in Belfast goes even further and suggests Fermanagh, but Mother dismisses the old country with a wave of her hand, relieving us of the burdens of tradition, except for the odd one-liner and a goddamned good argument, and by now the room is very crowded and the voices belong to me and mine and others pass politely through and someone somewhere somehow knows just when to wave and smile and say, "Safe home."

For a while I thought that's what it was to be Irish. The use of "Safe home," like "Da," was inexplicable for us in the States, but it lent a rhythm to our lives. It rolled off the lips on cold nights in lieu of "good-bye." To some in the States these things mean a great deal. Surprisingly, to some northern Irish citizens living in Great Britain they mean a great deal as well. In the oral history collection *Further Afield: Journeys from a Protestant Past,* one Belfast citizen discovered just how much: "After four years in Lancashire I found that I was gravitating toward Irish bars . . . one day I turned round and saw a childhood friend. The last time I had known him he had been a militant Loyalist and a member of the Ulster Volunteer Force. Now he was sitting in the corner listening to diddlidee music and talking to an old fella from Kerry. He had gravitated to Irish bars for the same reason I had. He was a paddy as far as the English were concerned." What in England made him a paddy, other than bigotry? What border in Belfast said he couldn't be "Irish"?

What made me use a wake as a vehicle for describing my Irish family? There are those who would say they define a people and their "culture." I'm sure they do, but another million unnamed, untouchable things make culture in contemporary Ireland. "Culture" is also the mundane elements of daily life in the North. It is the door being open to guests in spite of the violence; it's what people do in spite of difficulties and how they—in their own words—"watch out for each other." It is a neighbor walking down the street to feed the children of a friend because she knows Mom has been drinking too much lately. It is another neighbor picking up kids from school for you on a moment's notice, another parent dropping by after the school exam period to see how your kids did; it is giving over household goods and furniture to new neighbors or young married couples; it is empathy with hard times, but not much sympathy, since we'd all been through it at one time or another and sympathy was no help. All this awareness of others' vulnerability existed in spite of the obvious presence of blatant bigotry and hatred. Northern Ireland sometimes seemed the heart of the conundrum Is it the institution that gets transformed or the people? Which gets changed first to bring the peace? From where I often stood, the gestures I so admired were daily acts of subversion against a machine run rampant.

A perusal of the newspaper archives at Belfast's Linenhall Library for March 1972 revealed the shock and horror of the Abercorn Blast in exactly the same way the media brought home the pain of Omagh when I arrived. The Abercorn was the one I could put faces to, could "connect" with, because I had encountered the survivors. I could walk through both those sites and talk with British friends about the repetition of history, but we would never come to know Ireland that way. Though some people fought over the Orange and the Green, most I met in Ireland never even thought of their "Irishness," indeed found it annoying that others would.

❧ ❧

Unlike her British and American acquaintances, my friend Gillian was born in Dublin and had spent her childhood playing there. She told me about it as we ended our long workday.

"We used to dress up in boas and high-heeled shoes and stroll around the Liffey, lipsticked up to the nines and wandering about O'Connell Street in wobbly shoes," she said, wrapping up salads and cheeses. Alison walked out of the kitchen and opened the cash drawer to start counting the money. She ran the tape, then walked over to the door and locked it.

"Catherine," Gillian said, gesturing to her friend, "turn up the music."

I began pulling chairs together to pile them one atop the other. Dublin is now in its European heyday, but within Gillian's own lifetime, it had been a grotty little town with few opportunities for people.

"Mom moved us up here when I was about twelve, I suppose," she continued. She spent her afternoons and evenings making her way round the corner from her house and across Lagan Meadows in girly, fashionable shoes of the eighties, to climb a fence in the early evening and show up on a friend's doorstep for TV, snacks, and the occasional indulgence as a melancholy bedroom DJ.

Catherine, whom she palled around with still, was born and raised in Belfast and lived now in her father's flat, while he was away working in the States. Like Gillian, she had a round voluptuousness coupled with an unpretentious laugh. In fact, she was a magnet for laughable situations, and working with her was always a small adventure. I walked into the kitchen and talked with Alison as she did the bookkeeping. Catherine is, I explained, what my mother always referred to as "a character." As if on cue, her rosy-cheeked, wide-eyed face hung in the round window of the door, and she stood there staring at nothing. She mouthed words, but I couldn't hear them over the music.

"She worked in an antique shop on the Donegall Pass, too," Alison said in response to my comment. "She wanted to open her own near the university, but never quite got it together." She stirred a tomato sauce simmering on the stove. "Now she's managing her bills by working in two Belfast shops."

Besides working what seemed endless hours at two jobs, Catherine and Gillian partied in nightclubs all over the city, and both performed together in the Belfast Philharmonic Choir.

"It's not a group you see twenty-somethings joining!" Alison said with a laugh.

I looked out the window and saw their reflections as they swept the floor. The night fell quickly, and their images grew clear against the dark. In combination, the two had voices like angels, a sound that could stop the murmur and chant at parties, I thought.

I walked out of the kitchen with a mop and bucket to clean the floor.

"Did you hear?" Catherine asked as I swung through the door.

"What?"

"I said, Gillian's the cure for writer's block. A customer said so today."

"Frustrated poet?" I asked.

"Not anymore," Catherine said with a bawdy laugh. Gillian rolled her eyes. The music ended, and Alison made a request.

"C'mon girls, give us a song."

They refused modestly.

"Edie, give us a poem!" Gillian said, cornering me, "You're a writer."

"Oh, I can't remember any," I replied truthfully.

"Aww, sure you can, give us a poem, please!" Catherine persisted.

Remembering only Yeats, I said, *"I will arise and go now, and go to Innisfree."* Gillian and Catherine joined in, in harmony, then Alison.

"And a small cabin build there, of clay and wattles made;"

"Nine bean-rows will I have there, a hive for the honey bee,"

"And live alone in the bee-loud glade."

"Oh, Alison, was Yeats on the curriculum?" I asked, a winking reference to her schooling. She smiled, pointing at me with her index finger, then replied, "Anglo-Irish is still Irish."

We continued moving mops and brooms and feet, dropping coins, and folding bills.

"And I shall have some peace there, for peace comes dropping slow,"

"Dropping from the veils of the morning to where the cricket sings;"

I lingered for a moment over the last line, then couldn't remember the rest, so let the others continue without me.

"There midnight's all a glimmer, and noon a purple glow,
And evening full of the linnet's wings.

I will arise and go now, for always night and day
I hear lake water lapping with low sounds by the shore;
While I stand on the roadway, or on the pavements gray,
I hear it in the deep heart's core."

It's a standard, that one. Memorizing a sentimental poem warms us on cold nights, mingles longing and grief to create a beautiful song. The girls moved on to a song, forgot the words, then switched to "Down by the Salley Gardens." I sat up on the counter, smiled, and sipped a well-earned cup of tea. A poem, a song. That was good craic, that.

The next day Catherine came scurrying into work late, with a smile and a hello and a "Sorry I'm late." It was quiet, and we floated about the place, wiping down counters, sipping coffee, dusting off shelves.

"Should I choose some music?" she asked.

"Yeah," I answered, casually, "play what you like."

"I want to play Bach's cello concertos. Where is the cassette? Have you seen it?"

"No," I answered.

"I'm going to start cello lessons again," she continued.

"Oh yeah? That's great," I answered.

"I really want to learn to play Elgar," she said, referring to the British composer. "Here it is," she said.

"Bach?" I asked.

"No, Elgar."

She put the tape in the player. Elgar's Concerto for Cello moved elegantly around the shop, and I understood why it would drive a young woman to take up the instrument. In it even my untrained ear could detect a narrative line, a story unfolding from a deep, slow opening to dramatic emotional heights.

"No wonder she wants to play." I said while listening. It was full of love and passion.

In their first few years after graduating from Victoria College, Catherine and Gillian determined to find a way to study the cello. But it came to pass that they couldn't get instruments, and eventually Gillian relocated, for a time, to Dublin. This sent Catherine into a small spin (like death, separation reminds us of all that we have left undone). But as a result, Catherine managed to arrange cello lessons for herself and, determined to keep their original arrangement, called Gillian on the phone and insisted she listen to her practice. This is so very romantic to me, and after I heard it told, I held on to the story for months—imagining Catherine, with her foggy look, soft makeup, and strawberry blonde passion, trying to connect with Gillian, who was, so it seemed, a world away. I could see it in my mind's eye.

After dialing the number and chatting for a bit, Catherine explains that she's learned a new piece and Gillian should hear it. She cocks the phone just so—the mouthpiece set gingerly atop a book so that Gillian could hear clearly. Then, poised on a chair some feet away, she rests the cello on her leg and proceeds to play a tear-jerking piece. Catherine gestures with her arms the way she thinks a cellist should, head is bowed, strands of hair fall across cheek, shoulder falls forward with a dramatic, if inappropriate, thrust of the bow and a gentle draw back. The resulting sweet-sour sound is the squawk of eager desire encountering inexperience.

Though it was told in passing, this story stays with me and brings to mind a running joke from the supposed Anglo-Irish in me, the Clifford family, holders of great wakes and long-running gags:

My grandmother Lillian was enchanted with her son Dickie's singing and often stood listening from the kitchen as he rehearsed.

"His singing brings a tear to your eye, doesn't it?" she commented to her son Frankie.

To which he replied: "Yeah, 'cause he's trying so hard."

This oft-repeated story may be the source of my own shyness about singing. It ran through my mother's head like a tape, and each time I sang as a child she had to leave the room quickly. There I was, an eager adolescent, looking at the shape of my mouth in the mirror, trying to do scales or some warm-up piece, and she'd scurry away. It was no use; there was nowhere she could hide. The gentle giggle snowballed under suppression, then a laugh crept around the ten-room house until someone else was infected. I caught it, like a shiver, and it broke up the soprano piece I was trying to sing in baritone. ("I want a deep voice," I explained, "like the blues singers.") To this day I can't sing without breaking down, at some point, into a laugh at myself. That, I suppose, is my inheritance.

Frankie, the wiseacre, went on to a life that looked typically "Irish" in Boston. He married a lovely girl (daughter of a Clare woman), became a bricklayer, and fathered a brood that rivaled my family. He was one hell of a golfer, so I'm told, second only to Dickie, who is still listed as the record holder at Weymouth Country Club, south of Boston. In fact, Dickie died while playing. It was sudden, but of natural causes. He was struck by lightning. After a newspaper reporter reached his wife with the news before the hospital did, they waked him in Weymouth and left his name engraved on a small metal plate at the country club for all to see.

I walked home after work that night, breathing in the cool, damp air and laughing, still, over the music and banter of my friends and thinking about the elegance of cello concertos. The daytime beauty of the gardens turned chilling in the dark, but I looked and listened closely to the whisperings of the plants. In these quiet moments, I admitted to myself that I would never capture the "Irishness" peculiar to this part of the island, and I felt a mixture of emotions.

As the street darkened closer to my house, I thought about Joan's limping walk and the shy politeness of the Colombian coffee man. I heard my friend Seamus open his door onto the mountains over Belfast, and I saw all of it in a haphazard rhythm, as its own sort of dissonant music. Their collective beauty was in the survival of each of them, a survival that demanded that they among all others must live lives that were tributes in their richness. My feet brushed along the gritty driveway, and I stopped to look up at the sky. The evening was cloudless so I could see the Plough, following on from it to find Orion's belt.

Empty all day, my apartment was freezing cold when I walked in. I dragged myself to the second floor and drew a bath. The hot water created a warm fog that steamed up the stained-glass window and mirror. Pouring bath foam into the tub, I could feel my spine stretch and relax. Often, while waiting for the water to cool, I stood practicing a yoga stretch called "the reed." With my arms extended over my head I moved like a reed gently pushed left or right by flowing water. The exercise was accompanied by the sound of wind through the bushes outside, and as I exhaled I could feel a sense of release and harmony.

I often sat in the long porcelain tub and, instead of relaxing my mind, re-played comments and stories from the news and my own daily encounters. Occasionally I recited poetry or read aloud from a novel. Sometimes I imi-tated people I knew—one moment I was husky-voiced Pauline, the Dub-liner with the Belfast accent.

"Whatir youse doon?"

"Hey, girl, what's yer crack?"

The sound burst the bubbles. But I broke up the sequence by falling into a laugh as I remembered the tail end of a conversation I heard in which eleven-year-old Aisling yells out, "No, Mummy, it was *me* who taught you how to get the football scores with your pager." Once I tried to imitate my friend Rene, her stout figure shaking a fist at a helicopter, her delicate hands then splayed in front of her, cigarette smoke rising, as she at once imagined and explained a stage world. Then I recited her poem, written in quick re-sponse to the comment from the infamous Colby about "memoir" supple-menting map:

> The memoir stays when the map is truant
> But only the land *lives* on,
> in the shapes of its weather,
> its worn and woven fields, roads
> in its wrought rock and walls
> worn by our passing.

Then I began to hum a tune: "I once had a love or should I say she once had me . . . " I had overcome my shyness about singing over the years, but still dis-liked soprano pieces and their drama. If you are an ethnically identified Amer-ican, you're always trying on a culture's symbols and traditions to see if they fit. But to be an "American" is to have some other unnamed drive, too. It was to have a soprano voice—"angelic" like Karen Casey, who sang old folk

ballads in both Irish and English. When she sang an air, you could feel yourself floating through an oak grove. But what you *wanted* to sing with was
something entirely different. For me, this unnamable element was personified
by the blues singer Susan Tedeschi—another suburban white girl from outside Boston. Hers was a voice that could burn a house down. She did "Angel
from Montgomery" like a melancholy Janis Joplin, and I envied her. She sang
"Crazy" and made Patsy Cline rise from the dead. Only in Ireland was soprano singing appealing to me. "She Moved through the Fair" and "Down by
the Salley Gardens" slowly revealed the strength of heart in its tremulous
wobble. Gillian and Catherine both sang the high notes beautifully, their
songs a set of grace notes to the rhythm of the day. My life condition was high,
and the music stayed with me through the sudden weather changes, the peace
process "in peril" hyperbole, and the evasive answers of political leaders.

My friends' voices rose above the crumple of folding maps and newspapers I sifted through each week. I hummed along with them as I listened to
the sound of the wind and the running water of my bath. Finally, I reached
tentatively through the fog, my feet probing the bubbles for the shock of water. As I lowered myself into the warmth, I could hear the echo of their music above my own weary sighs.

Chapter 9
Panto / Article 25 / The Fountain

Work in the winter was a schizophrenic combination of hyperactivity and deadly quiet. During the busy periods, we were snapped out of our winter fog by the preparation of hot dishes like baked pasta or leek and pancetta risotto. Spicy lentil soup went down well with customers, as did the carrot and coriander, with its warm orange tone and sweet smell.

"What's this?" a man asked me one afternoon, pointing to a menu item, "Spicy Italian sausage with tomato sauce."

I described the dish for him in the fancy language of the restaurant world, where spuds are "fresh baby potatoes" and gravy is a "tomato, olive oil, and seasoning" dressing.

"Oh," he answered, "it's bangers and mash."

A woman with a pram made her way into the shop, lurching along with an infant and two toddlers. The look in her eye said she was begging for adult conversation and relief from what was already a long day.

"Cappuccino?" Annie called out from behind the counter.

"Yes, thanks, Annie," she replied.

An older woman entered quietly, and "Hello's" rang out again.

"Coffee for Mrs. McCluskey?" I asked.

"Yes, and a fruit scone," Annie said, automatically. "We'll be with you in just a minute, Mrs. McCluskey," she called across the room.

"Ach, Annie, you're all right," Mrs. McCluskey said, lifting a newspaper and pulling out a chair to sit down. Annie immediately relaxed.

It took me some time to catch on to the social courtesy "Ach, you're all right," though it was sprinkled generously throughout conversations in Ireland. In the café, I'd try not to keep people waiting (particularly at lunch), try not to hold people up as I worked in my different rhythm. But with the Irish, being wrongfooted in social circumstances, or even a little behind, seemed to prompt only a reassuring "Ach, you're all right" and a wave of the hand. For me it came to represent the complete unpretentiousness of people in the North. The more I heard it, the larger the scenarios it encompassed. It was not just a simple embarrassment or failure that prompted the phrase, sometimes a collision with egos or a simple loss elicited it as a way of reassuring others. It repeatedly reminded me that here everyone knew that underneath it all, situations were a complicated web of circumstance, power, poor luck, misunderstanding, and desire, and we—well, we were only human—we would just keep going, regardless. The expression said, *"You'll get a new job, a new lover, go to a different school, try a different course of study. You're a child of God—Ach, you're all right."*

I brought Mrs. McCluskey her coffee, then walked back behind the counter. The door swung open and a chilly breeze swept in with a deliveryman, who tried to manage a crate of vegetables around the toddlers fiddling and fussing in the pram. Newspapers snapped, voices rose in caffeinated chatter, and chairs scraped against the tile floor. I moved around slightly startled by the customers. Winter often sends people into hibernation, and my mental state could best be described as, well, a bit of a snooze. But the physical nature of real work awakens those of us so often stuck inside our heads. Lift the boxes of Colombian coffee, stir the cumin-filled soup, reach over to keep the sugared cranberries from overboiling, and you can feel your blood begin to move.

As the winter days trudged on, Annie ran around the café, moving as if she was dribbling a soccer ball and calling out dramatically, "I'm beehind yoo!" It was a running joke, bringing to mind the theater cry, "He's behind you!" from holiday pantomime. It always brought a grin. Winter may have set in with its gale force winds, power outages, and hospital closures, but panto season must go on. Pantomime, or "panto," is Britain and Ireland's people's theater par excellence—it breaks up the winter with larger-than-life cartooning. It is referred to as "children's" or "family" theater, but it is still full of bawdy punning and drag. There's a dame that must be a man and a male lead that must be a woman. There're tacky sets and a narrator who harasses the audience, who, naturally, yell back as an unapologetic foil. In every piece, be it *Snow White* or *Jack and the Beanstalk,* there is a moment when the hero gets approached from behind by the villain. The audience, in its vital role, must warn the poor fool so the great chase can start.

Walking from the café to downtown Belfast on Saturday afternoons, I often passed the opera house just as the panto matinees let out. Families wandered down Great Victoria Street toward restaurants or sweet shops, toddlers being teased by their older siblings:

"You were scared, weren't you? Yeah, ya were!"

"No, I was not."

"Just a wee bit?" the Granny adds, initiating a consoling hug.

"Aw, ya baby!"

The child turned his face away and I caught his eye. I smiled at him as he discovered I was within earshot of the taunt. Taking out his frustration on me, he screwed up his face and stuck out his tongue. Granny gasped.

I made my way into Belfast center each week to do any number of things. Often I wandered around the city center to run errands and linger in book stores. I walked to the waterfront area, passing the courthouse, moving back up around the City Hall and then onto Royal Avenue. I went in and out of shops while vendors yelled out sales of the street magazine *The Big Issue* and people listened to the mournful sound of bagpipes played by a white-haired man wearing a green tartan kilt. I wandered around Boots the Chemist thinking about makeup and hair-care products; I fiddled with little perfume bottles and smiled graciously as salesgirls drifted toward me with an offer of assistance.

I floated freely around streets and shops, enjoying the freedom of movement as a simple pleasure. I breezed into the Tesco supermarket and bought some fresh vegetables or a sandwich. If the weather was clear, I would sit outside City Hall and watch people or read a newspaper. The headlines were full of stories of recent winter storms knocking down power lines and the subsequent controversy over their slow repair. I found it a welcome relief from the argument over decommissioning.

To me the question was a red herring. I couldn't see any man addicted to violence giving up his drug. Politicians were no different. In Britain and the United States, the governments themselves are the biggest weapons dealers in the world. Ireland's heated economy contributed to the plague through an increase in the manufacture of weapons and weapons parts for American corporations. In fact, without so much as a nod to irony, John Hulme and David Trimble smiled as they opened a Raytheon facility outside Derry less than a year after winning the Nobel Peace Prize.

The majority of sectarian crimes being committed each week in the six counties were largely done with homemade weapons anyway. Pipe bombs went through windows, bats were used for punishment beatings, houses were set alight with fuel. Decommissioning was a demand that reflected something other than a desire for peace. Even David Ervine, a Unionist Assembly member and former terrorist, referred to the debate as hypocritical, focusing as it did on the IRA and Sinn Fein. There was a private army on one side, a very public one on the other. Who would drop their weapons first?

Among my small circle of friends and colleagues I was the only one that even thought about the subject; everyone else, having lived with it their entire lives, simply rolled their eyes.

By arguing over the implementation of the Agreement, politicians were creating a political vacuum; matters that affected ordinary people on the mundane level of the everyday were being eclipsed by the debate over weapons. The National Health Services in Great Britain and in the Republic of Ireland were said to be in dire financial straits, and hospitals servicing rural communities were closing. In the meantime, patients were told surgery would have to wait.

I moved on from City Hall, making my way up the Dublin Road to Donegall Pass and into the weekend antique market. It's a rather nondescript building holding three floors of dealers who trade in everything from Edwardian trinkets to picture postcards to fireplace mantles and ceiling fixtures. I walked up the narrow staircase to the second floor, through a room full of cabinetry and wrought iron, and on to the back, where there was an array of collectibles, textiles, and furniture. Cast-iron Victorian coatracks stand like oaks beside a glass case full of antique medicine and perfume bottles (one marked, seductively, "blue poison"), old tablecloths and linen napkins, crocheted tea cozies and table runners. I wandered around the dusty clutter with the other bargain hunters. The floorboards creaked on occasion and tables wobbled. It was hardly a scene from *Country Living* magazine, with estate furniture displayed unpolished and chipped, chandeliers abandoned and looking like wilted lilies. I loved it. People poked and prodded the goods. On a small table, mother-of-pearl sign letters were in a messy pile. A scamp in a blue windbreaker arranges four of them to read "TITS," and an old lady gasps. All the suburban customers, in for an expedition in their Land-Rovers, pretend it's not there. A blonde woman with a black headband walks by, slightly dazed, and stares at the table until she realizes what she's looking at, then moves on. A man in a tweed sportcoat and cap looks twice and mutters, then backs away. The room filled with a polite quiet. The silence was enough to send me into a suppressed giggle. I moved away from the table, but social courtesy pushed in on me and I couldn't stop giggling (or, as I told the story later, "tittering") until I was red-faced and laughing out loud at a framed copy of the "Sligo, Leitrim, and Northern Counties Explosives Act of 1875." Finally, I moved away like the others and began thumbing through postcards.

Amid all the postcards filed together in the antique shops on Donegall

Pass, up in the market off Pump Street in Derry, and at the occasional Antique Book Fair was what I called the Veronica Series, a set of cards written
to "Koko" from Veronica, "with best love and kisses." They were never
posted, but I assume (from the handwriting) that they were hand-delivered
to a granny nicknamed Koko. I bought one that afternoon written from
Lough Gill. Veronica notes, "It was a lovely day, and the lake looked beautiful." It's a beautiful card, a color photo made in the fashion of the early part
of the twentieth century, with the colors painted onto the negative. Veronica
is eager to write her adventures—you can see it in the expansive lettering and
thick ink and the love and the kisses. I bought the card, then made my way
back to the street for a ramble.

To make your way around the city or the countryside towns in Northern
Ireland is to willingly engage in a walk through a civil engineering maze.
Roads were frequently laid out in patterns that defied logic and didn't en-
courage ease of movement. Donegal Square, in the heart of Belfast, led in all
directions to dead ends or turns that wound on to a wall or a one-way street.
Standing in front of City Hall facing the waterfront, you could see the new
modern design of the concert hall. It hovered like a spacecraft between buildings, but you couldn't reach it without driving *around* the block in front of it.
The city courthouse was wrapped in metal fencing and barbed wire, and
its Victorian gates stopped cars and rerouted them to the Queen's Bridge or
forced them to go around the St. George's market and back toward the Lower
Ormeau Road area (formerly known as "Murder Mile"), where a housing estate had only a few entrances and those all led to closed areas where you had
to stop or slow for the many speed bumps and stop signs.

The stops and starts you engaged in were the point of the exercise. Joy-
riders were stopped, and gunmen couldn't escape. But it was a strange and
terrible reasoning that built these estates. It was as if they were painting
people into corners. I tried to rationalize it as being no different than the
older cities and towns in the United States, where nineteenth-century planning
was insufficient for twentieth-century traffic patterns. In fact, Boston was
famed for its nineteenth-century cowpath-wide streets. But in Northern Ireland, none of the town layouts came across as "old town design meets the
modern age." The Westlink Motorway, leading to the M1 and M2 highways,
ran between the center of the city and the north and west sides, further iso-
lating people—similar to New York's Cross Bronx Expressway or the isolation of Cabrini Green in Chicago.

The urban and suburban landscape in Belfast is one final, lasting tribute to war: a trap within a trap. As I crossed these ugly, clumsy streets on foot, it oc-curred to me that attention to such fine details is the cornerstone of what is elsewhere called an "oppressive regime." At any rate, people had to endure encountering walls and borders at every turn. So I became aware at a certain point in my stay that I could no longer explain away the multiple three-point turns I made while driving, or the infinite number of times I was forced to stop walking and turn around because I had encountered a dead end or found myself on a road to nowhere.

The realization of a lawless goading, defended by what the government would refer to as "practical and necessary measures," occurred to me early on as a purely intellectual observation. It passed then into a justice-seeking alarm—the moral outrage of political consciousness—and finally, after some time had passed and the place was peopled with friends and "folk," it became a heartbreaking nightmare. I slumped in defeat and bitterness as I realized what was creeping into my consciousness: I would follow a single path to only certain corners of the city; I had a mental border, a set of blinders that kept the landscape limited to certain routes. It began to impinge on my curiosity, kept me from looking down roads, since they led only to a block of brick housing or a small factory. It got me thinking ahead only so far and so much. For me, as a long-term guest, it was an annoyance, but I believe for the citi-zens—Catholic or Protestant, Republican or Unionist—it is the enemy silently outposted in your head.

The other element of alienation for the outsider was the intimidation fac-tor of Ireland's panoply of symbols and colors used as war cries. It finds its expression in flag flying, graffiti, and painted sidewalks. These symbols have been analyzed to no end by people inside and outside the conflict, but I recall them only as the things that cut my stride, slowed my pace, and alerted me to dangers real or imagined. The painted sidewalks of cities and towns were a reflection of local sectarian borders. The red, white, and blue of the Union Jack ran through Loyalist areas, and the green, white, and or-ange of the Irish tricolor ran through Republican areas. They intimidated me as much as the gang colors or the coded signal of sneakers hanging from telephone wires in U.S. cities. They all unnerved me when I encountered them on my walks. Painted sidewalks were, essentially, a line drawn in the sand for other people, and they were coupled with murals and flags that re-flected, rather than loyalty or courage, a desire for violence. They often de-picted men wearing balaclavas pointing guns at the viewer, or Republican soldiers shown killing members of the British Army. In one mural on the

Donegall Pass, "King Billy" (William of Orange) was painted riding a white horse, wearing a smile as he trampled on the body of a dead Irish man. Even some of the less violent ones offended me, bearing such slogans as "Ireland for the Irish." In the States, such sloganeering is often the cry that initiates racist segregation.

Since the murals were speaking to the entire community, they had none of the mystery messages of American graffiti writers, nor did the "artists" choose to dress up the letters so they were indecipherable to the reader. "Lest We Forget" was a typical memorial phrase for fallen paramilitaries, but if it was painted beside a gun-carrying "guardian," then the reader was reminded not of any heroic gesture, but of exactly who ruled the roost in the neighborhood. I often walked by these murals and wondered how women could raise sons in such an environment without fear of losing them at an early age. I suppose they didn't.

⇜ ⇝

Later that evening I met with Dennis and Rene and their troupe, The Shankill Theatre Company, as they rehearsed for a performance in a Dublin panto on the weekend. They were invited to perform the intermission entertainment in Dublin's Shankill Theatre (that Dublin has a suburb called Shankill came as a surprise to me). In Belfast they practiced regularly in the Woodvale Cricket Club off the Shankill Road. For this evening the group was relegated to a locker room for rehearsal of an original piece, and the small space quickly filled with a fog of cigarette smoke.

Rene, who was directing, is stout and matronly, a dame of the theater without any of the pretentiousness that goes with such a title. She smoked like a chimney, but held her cigarettes like an American film star of the forties, gesturing in a way that brought to mind some dramatic black-and-white film about espionage in World War II. It was that same hand that had pointed a finger at a Loyalist gunman who accused her of ingratitude for denouncing paramilitary violence.

"Don't you tell me about 'the Cause,'" she answered, "I didn't put the gun in your hand."

Rene wrote poetry, plays, and stories prolifically and recited one of her favorite poems easily when we met.

> The sun came to visit me today.
> It shone through my window and warmed my desk.

It was written by her son Gideon when he was six. The lines bring a smile to my face, also, like a simple haiku. Malcolm, Gideon's brother, was a stringy adolescent, present that night reciting lines, making wisecracks, and sizing me up with the occasional glance. When he felt comfortable, he introduced himself, then looked me in the eye and said that he collected exotic pets and how did I feel about snakes and tarantulas. Knowing I had been to Southeast Asia, he said he hoped his next acquisition would be a gecko. He was showy and dramatic, with many of the same physical gestures as his mother. Walking around the benches with his tall, skinny frame, he announced his genius to me, evidenced by his epilepsy, with which it is frequently associated. He explained this correlation as clear proof of his bright and successful future. I smiled, thinking of Oscar Wilde's pronouncement, then added one of my own:

"You're in good company. Genius is often associated with left-handedness as well," and I waved my writing hand at him.

I had grown increasingly fond of Dennis since our first meeting. On that afternoon, he had growled at me from behind a clenched fist: "Suppose the Native Americans wanted their land back, eh?" He was referring to Republican calls for a United Ireland. I smirked and answered, "Well, you've certainly picked the wrong side in that conflict!"

"Dennis, I told you we weren't going to talk about the Orange and the Green today!" Rene snapped.

Of course, Orange or Green was not the point. The point was: Americans are only partially informed, and, as they say, a *little* knowledge is a dangerous thing. I agreed with the underlying challenge, but put it in terms of civil rights. White Irish America can't have it both ways. They can't see Northern Ireland as a civil rights fight or a battle against injustice, but look away when it comes to matters of class and race in the United States. It is another hard-edged debate. In fact, Irish tourists to America often found themselves "shocked" when encountering racist white opinions and gestures in the United States. They occasionally confronted me with this observation, as if I could provide an answer to the mystery of it. What can *I* say? Particularly from an Ireland in the middle of a surge of anti-immigration sentiment and a United Kingdom exposing itself as riddled with "institutionalized racism."

Dennis's attempt to rattle my cage still brings a smile to my face. All the more so because I caught him looking sentimental over Belfast's still ratty waterfront and market district and later, in one of the province's poorest housing projects, playing the prince to a roomful of women.

At Woodvale, around nine that evening, they began rehearsal of a piece Rene wrote that they'd performed at theater festivals the previous summer. Helicopters hovered over some not too distant spot, and as the actors' voices rose to compete against the noise, I could feel a frustration rise inside me.

Article 25 was the title of the play, a reference to the Universal Declaration of Human Rights, with particular focus paid to Article 25, section 2: "Motherhood and childhood are entitled to special care and assistance. All children, whether born in or out of wedlock, shall enjoy the same social protection."

It was interesting to consider such fundamentals in the Western world, with its obscenely high incomes and medical advancements. In the United Kingdom, 1999 began with the overt rationing of health care. Hospitals were closing everywhere, including the Jubilee Maternity in West Belfast and South Tyrone Hospital's maternity wing. In addition, people were being put in unreasonable queues for orthopedic surgery (largely repair of hip and thigh fractures among the elderly). While they waited, people were doped up on painkillers and asked to be patient. Eventually, a stopgap measure was instituted, whereby patients were taken across the water to Glasgow, Scotland for surgery, since it was cheaper than extended hospitalization locally. I had a hunch, as the stories were told in the media, that neither mothers nor *grandmothers* in Northern Ireland were entitled to "special care and assistance."

Rene wrote *Article 25* in the 1980s out of concern for the lives of her own children and a sense of despair over the harsh realities of life for street children in São Paulo, Brazil. It is a series of monologues that are both harsh testimony and beautiful tribute. I pulled my knees up as I sat on a corner bench and watched. I smiled weakly, trying to escape the sour irony of the helicopter's presence nearby.

~≈ ≈~

In addition to running the theater group in Belfast, Dennis and Rene worked regularly with the Fountain Women's Group in Derry. They drove the two hours from Belfast every Wednesday evening, grabbing a take-out dinner on the way and swallowing it down quickly before the workshop started. The Fountain is a housing estate in Derry that lies immediately outside one of the gates of the city. It is the last of the Protestant communities in Derry to remain on the west side of the Foyle River. The others have moved across the river over the years, effectively segregating the city. The location and architecture combine to make the area a ghetto. In fact, like some corners of Belfast, it has the lowest housing standards in Europe.

Housing estates, or "projects," as they are termed in the United States, have historically been built with the most callous disregard for the inhabitants. The conditions of tower blocks or the long, snaking balconies of low-rises are probably the last thing middle-class civil servants would want to live in. So why do so many politicians often contend that such ungracious accommodation is *bestowed* upon sponging inhabitants?

The brittle experience of enduring public housing manifests in the voice and gesture of the inhabitants. The scarred existence of what we call "kids from the projects" was magnified for me in the Fountain, where I felt trapped, in a physical sense. There is only a single road entrance, the city wall rises up behind you, the army security tower is always within sight, and the estate itself is a set of dead-end blocks. You can, quite literally, go nowhere. This is the heart of the "painted sidewalks." Here the colors are red, white, and blue; in another part of town, the colors are green, white, and orange.

Before we entered the basement of the community center, I looked uneasily up at the turret that hangs over the neighborhood. A dark-haired woman began pulling chairs together, setting up a table for tea and snacks. Another woman locked the door as she entered, then someone joked, wasn't Dennis the lucky one, locked in a room full of women. After the group milled about for a few minutes, Rene graciously introduced me, and everyone said a polite hello. Then it got quiet for a moment, and a woman with dark, cropped hair and a hard-edged look to her face said, as if she had thought about it for some time:

"Welcome, we're honored."

I stared at her in shock. *Was a visit so rare? Did no one ever come talk with these people?* Their isolation hit me like a brick.

Sitting in that circle in the basement of a housing block, I realized that even more than being loved, people want to be understood. Ministers and priests exhort us all to "love one another," but those words sound so simplistic in the face of harsh reality. Over the years and in different parts of the world, I've heard stories begin with a gesture that says, "I'll try to explain." Invariably, the storyteller will begin by apologizing. She starts by apologizing for her inabilities, then ends up apologizing for her existence, her presence, her life. I can't tell some of the stories that came to me from the painted sidewalks; they would be too much to bear. But the bits and pieces will sound familiar. These voices of the violence of urban poverty, of people labeled by sociologists as "disenfranchised" or "marginalized"—here they are the poor relations of both Great Britain and the Republic. They have tough edges and fractured, unfaithful, bleeding hearts. They speak in the cryptic lines of those accustomed to not being heard and look at you with eyes like hawks, open wide, as if they were lidless, robbing the women of the luxury of looking away.

I married a British soldier, and he beat me and my kid. . . . I married him, and he took me to England. . . . I thought it would be great . . . he took us to England and beat my kid until he was dead. He killed my son. . . . I married a British soldier. . . . I was a British soldier. . . . My son died, and the doctor thought we had beaten him, when it was him wouldn't take my call when the baby was sick days before . . .

"You travel?" my host asked me at one point.

"Yes," I answered hesitantly, for I knew what was coming.

"Sure we only travel by looking at the pictures, right girls?"

I thought of my rental car sitting outside, my casual drives around Sligo and Donegal, my weekend rambles. Freedom of movement is a complex layer of things beyond my worldwide trip taking. It's about money and confidence and starting your car and not getting stopped. It's about curiosity and welcome and freedom from fear. It's about "getting out." In the Republic of Ireland, it is currently fashionable to reject your "Irishness" in favor of a European lifestyle. Among young elites around the globe, physical mobility allows them to transcend borders and, if they're willing, escape the intellectual myopia that might come with village life. However, people without the economic freedom to move about are constrained, and their bitterness is understandable. Who are we to tell them to *love thy neighbor*? It wasn't our house that got burned; it wasn't my kid who got beaten.

Chain-smoking, coughing, and sipping gallons of tea, the women smile at nasty jokes and share a dirty laugh, as if it's jam sweetening dull bread.

Beatings, dirty buggers, paras, fucking social workers, teachers, burned buildings, hits, hands, red hands, across the divide only for the cameras. What are ye? Taig bastards, Prods? What about us? All these big politicians walking round the city, what about us?

Them soldiers, everyone thinks them soldiers is so great. . . . I wouldn't hurt anyone, so I wouldn't. My boy died suddenly, and the social workers and doctors thought WE did it?! Our boy's a soldier . . . my boy's got epilepsy . . . she's got asthma . . . oh, my lad has asthma, too. . . . I can't walk down the street without being harassed, called a stinkin' Prod. . . . This is such a damned bigoted city . . . you can't go anywhere without gettin' it. . . . We were just out for a bit of fun. . . . What about us?

Everyone's broken by war and violence, but some are more broken than others. And middle-class citizens can't hear these stories without imagining they're tales from another country. Today, in basements of community organizations, at wobbly tables, and sitting on broken chairs, people talk and scratch out hundreds of stories, trying again and again to get it right, to make sure they are understood, to make it clear that something *really did happen*. So we know that it is true that a woman was beaten on her way home from work for no reason whatsoever except the chance to bang her head against pavement and call her a "stinkin Prod." So we know that a small boy was blinded by a bullet, or that an old woman stood up in her own home only to have her face smashed by a plastic bullet through the front window.

But, as the disappearing man in the pub said, "Here's the craic, luv": the stories match each other. Furthermore, they match stories I hear in Boston, from Saigon, from Hong Kong, from Port-au-Prince, from Medellín, and from São Paulo. There are guns where there shouldn't be and paramilitary mafias keeping their own kind of order in the absence of effective government; there are moments of safety violated by threats and the repeated phrase, "You're not wanted."

Here's a "wee something" from Creggan, another stronghold in Derry. But here the sidewalks are painted green, white, and orange.

"I'm only twenty-one and I've seen sixteen people killed before my eyes." (I do the math: that's one killing a year since the age of five.) . . . *"Oh, I could tell you stories . . . there were these three old folks on our street, this one bachelor who used to have dinner weekly with these two other neighbors; they rotated meals. Well, one day he doesn't show up, and they're worried about him, so they go to his door, and he doesn't answer and they're very worried, so your man decides to climb through one of the windows and, well, the whole place just* blows . . . *it was booby-trapped for the police. That's three old ones killed right there. Oh, geez, that was a bad day. . . . And I've talked to the soldiers, too, y'know. They don't want to be here. Some guys just break down and cry when their names are drawn for service here."* I thought about this landscape. Grocery story bread racks double as cages to keep rubber bullets at bay, and milk bottles are filled with petrol to make bombs. You're thirteen years old, and you've seen heads blown apart right in front of you . . .

As he talked, I could feel myself back away and knew my eyes were about to glaze over, as if I were listening to a foreign language. I hid in the topography of Derry, thinking: "Creggan is up above the Bogside, if you move toward Brandywell, there's a soccer pitch, go up Creggan St., there's the wall of St. Eugene's, move right away from it and you're headed toward Magee

College. The Fountain is just outside Bishop's Gate, St. Columba's Cathedral is near there and that fucking watchtower above the army base, and moving around, I'm back at the Bogside . . . blah-blah-blah." And all the while the testimony continues, but I'm too scared to hear it.

"I'm sorry, I can't describe it."

"I'm sorry, I don't know how to explain it . . . "

"First, I want to apologize because I can't speak well."

"I don't know as much as others."

"I'm sorry, I don't understand."

"I got nothin' to do with anything, why the fuck do they want to kill me?"

I realized that night that back behind the cameras and the towers in Derry is Londonderry, with men and women white-knuckled and ready to fire, but apologizing to me first for their very existence and blinded by something no one can explain. In ghettos everywhere, working people kill each other and outside the walls others throw up their hands and say something about "small-minded people" or, perhaps more frequently, "let 'em kill each other, the fucking bastards." At any rate, it all became a blur for me as I passed through various neighborhoods; I couldn't discern one face from another, and I realized I have been listening to survivor testimony from around the world for close on ten years and I'm not sure I'm any better at it now than I was when I started.

The night of their telling, the women of the Fountain gave me small, delicate finger sandwiches, then, as I ate, generously encouraged me to have more. And I listened to them talk as the bread fell to pieces in my mouth and I swallowed the salty bits of ham and sweet butter, then sipped the tea with its creamy warmth. I lifted the "Blue Willow" teacup from the saucer resting on my knee and watched as they finished their talking and began some stage exercises.

Dennis wanted to warm up with exercises that focus an actor's attention on the present moment, the body and breath. This literal "return to the senses" was rejected by the women, and I felt an opportunity slip by everybody. But perhaps they have more wisdom than I do—peel away your thick skin, and it feels as if all you've got is a throbbing hurt.

᠅

"You went to the Fountain!" a man exclaimed later in the evening, "that's a good way to get yourself shot!"

"Look," I snapped, "you're kind enough to buy me a drink, but I'm not obligated to endure a lecture on safety as well."

I sipped my drink while he stepped back and took my measure. I looked over and realized that in trusting my hosts I had confronted *his* fear.

Chapter 10

History and Cosmology /
The Irish for "Mercy"

Telephone tapping is a long-established means of uncovering terrorist contacts. In the old Stormont Parliament there were regular questions about the alleged activities of monitoring agents based in Room 22 of the old Post Office Headquarters in Royal Avenue in Belfast.

—Flackes and Elliot, *Northern Ireland: A Political Directory*

We are also concerned about "other matters" which may be placed before you, including the use of evidence given by informers and possibly that obtained by telephone tapping.

It is important to remember that the whole criminal justice system in Northern Ireland was brought into international disrepute by the use of informer evidence in the "supergrass" trials of the 1980s. To revisit that era would be a disaster when we are now trying to establish justice mechanisms that will command the respect and confidence of the entire community.

We believe that the use of technical surveillance devices should be reviewed with the aim of providing a single regulatory system based on Article 8 of the European Convention on Human Rights which guarantees the right to privacy and which will soon be part of UK law.

—Briefing, Amnesty International, August 28, 1998

At about 9:00 A.M. the next morning, the phone rang.

"Edie . . ."

"Robbie?" I asked. His voice sounded as though he was calling me from the opening in a tin can.

"Edie, I'm at the foot of your street."

"You're at the foot of my street?" I could hear his car by now. The tires hit the gravel of my driveway.

"I'm now in yer driveway."

"Yeah . . ."

"Edie . . . ," he paused as I started to giggle. I could see him from my window, sitting behind the wheel talking into his cell phone.

"Edie, what are you doing today?"

"I take it you need a hand?"

"Well, Marie claims she's about to collapse with exhaustion."

"Can't imagine why."

"I was tryin' to figure it out myself. I'm in court this after, too."

"I'll be right down," I said.

"You're a hero, Edie."

"Yeah, yeah, yeah, you still owe me dinner at that French place downtown."

"That I do!" he said.

A Van Morrison song was on the radio as I climbed into the car.

> Precious time is slippin' away,
> you know you're only King for a day
> it doesn't matter to which God you pray
> precious time is slippin' away.

"Oh," I said, "this his new album?"

"Yeah."

"Yer man Kennedy's on this?"

"Aye."

Brian Kennedy was a rising pop star from West Belfast. He had performed to sellout crowds the previous summer at the Music Festival and was on tour with a new hit song. He was also a featured singer on Van Morrison's latest album, "Back on Top." Morrison is a native of East Belfast and performs once or twice a year in the city.

"I heard a story about Van the Man . . . " I started.

Robbie gave a laugh and rolled his eyes, "Oh, everyone does . . . "

We drove down the street onto University Avenue and then into the city center. I looked over toward West Belfast. An army helicopter hovered over the Shankill area. It didn't take me long to recognize the pattern of hover and arrest that the helicopters signaled. I would see them hovering one day over the north of the city and not long after would hear a news item about police arrests, whether for an arms cache or some other crime. At a certain point, I felt myself watching for the helicopters and predicting news stories, and this was unnerving.

"The eye in the sky," as people jokingly called the helicopters, was far less intrusive than it used to be—as if that indicated a lessening of the dysfunction. Depressingly, I realized that elsewhere, in particular England and the United States, this form of policing was *not* on the decline.

The Nobel Peace Prize was being awarded in Oslo, and in Ireland there was blanket coverage of the events. It was something to be proud of, but the Irish didn't quite embrace it. David Trimble had rather sourly accepted the award a few months previous with the statement, "It's a little premature." Irish citizens were sardonic about it, not hopeful. I had to admit that from the heart of the Troubles, the committee's reasoning struck me as embarrassingly uninformed.

"We thought it would be fair," a committee representative said, "to award one for the Catholic side and one for the Protestant side."

I cringed. The European Community had been trying to support the peace process through grant funding and various other incentives for the past few years. What was missing from a lot of the programs, however, was a true understanding of how things were working in reality. During the week of the award ceremony in Oslo, the adolescents at an integrated school in South Belfast held an all-day conference titled " *Which* Other Side?" in which they explored the increasing diversity of religions in northern Ireland. Their insight begs the question—what do they know that others don't?

We pulled up to the office.

"I see Marie's here good and early," Robbie said with a laugh.

We went inside. The air was already thick with cigarette smoke.

"Well, hello," Marie said, pleased she had an extra hand.

"Mornin'," I said with a smile, then got to work typing memos and notes.

Later in the morning, taking a break from my work, I began talking with Marie about the plethora of books revealing the maze of plots and goings on that were a part of the Troubles. In the mainstream media, much of the "inner workings" of both government and paramilitary institutions was described in books compiled by investigative journalists. Tony Geraghty, the author of *The Irish War: A Military History of the Northern Ireland Conflict*, had recently been jailed in Great Britain for revealing government secrets. His book was dismissed by Irish reviewers as "nothing new," but I was particularly intrigued by his description of the internal operations of Britain's security service, MI5, and the Special Air Services (SAS) and the paramilitary status of the police in northern Ireland. The scene was one that revealed the province as a live training ground for Britain's military and espionage services. Or, as Labour Party MP Kevin McNamara put it in the early 1990s, "an adventure playground for secret agents."

"Oh, of course," Marie said, with a dismissive wave for Geraghty's findings, "I could've told him all that."

I remembered how the place had seemed to live up to these conspiracy theories in winter 1998, when a woman driving a car one evening in North Belfast got involved in a high-speed chase with police, only to crash at a place called Carlisle Circus and come out of the car shooting. She wounded an RUC officer and left him in critical condition. Despite northern Ireland's reputation, I was sure this incident was unusual, but when I brought it up, people only shrugged. Media reports stated that the woman was an under-cover member of "the security forces" and unfamiliar with the lay of the land. In short, she panicked. The RUC and the Northern Ireland Office stated that "an investigation" would be set up to figure out what happened.

Nonetheless, spy training seemed par for the course to people in Belfast. In fact, Ireland had long been a training ground for Britain's civil servants. In the nineteenth century, it was the stepping stone to some of Britain's bigger, more exotic locales and a resource for its military. In 1839, government administrators, the East India Company, and the military settled on Trinity College and Colby's Ordnance Survey as a training ground for both engineers and sappers. First stop: Ireland, next stop: "Inja." Of course, in the twentieth century, the "exceptional circumstances" in northern Ireland created an environment neatly summed up in years previous by Margaret Thatcher's northern Ireland Secretary, Michael Mates: "There's no bloody democracy down there. That's why it works so well. I've never been happier." He was referring, of course, to his freedom to give a blank check to the police force at a whim—to move prisoners, to set up checkpoints, or to shut down operations. The mini-industry created by the Troubles was not simply in publishing. "Defense" is big business in Great Britain and the United States, and it spawned a world unto itself. Soldiers' testimony gathered in the late eighties captures the picture (and the attitude) neatly: "I totally, really enjoyed Northern Ireland," said one soldier. "I enjoyed everything that I did. . . . I've still got all my terrorist recognition leaflets, all my maps; I took a camera over there, I suppose I've got about four thousand photographs. I'm ready to go again."

Prior to Geraghty's work, *The Committee,* an investigative book by the British journalist Sean McPhilemey that uncovered a secret conspiracy to murder leading Republican political figures, was selling out all over the

Republic but was banned in the United Kingdom, thus was not for sale in Belfast. (I was reminded of Peter Matthiessen's struggle with the FBI over the publication of *In the Spirit of Crazy Horse,* a book about the American Indian movement of the 1970s.) Still, I had my suspicions about McPhilemey's work, relying as it did on only one source. Then again, truth is less believable than fiction—so he was probably right.

"Of course it's true!" Marie snapped at me as I questioned the veracity of *The Committee.* I shrank back. "The British Army isn't *really* the problem. They'd be happy to leave. It's the likes of Trimble who're the problem!"

"Oh," I said, not willing to add any more comments. I never warmed to David Trimble, but conspiracy theory didn't quite work for me, either. McPhilemey was reaching into territory explored as far back as the early eighties and the infamous, now ruined, Chief Constable John Stalker. Everything associated with the death of high-profile public figures in northern Ireland had a whiff of conspiracy and organization. From John Stalker on, corruption investigations started strong, then hung ragged and unfinished, like threads from discarded weavings. Examined over a fifteen-year span, these investigations had a bad smell. In fact, as Mother always said, "this stinks to high heaven."

In addition to those books, the journalist world was abuzz with the surreal findings in John Parker's *Death of a Hero,* an ironically titled book depicting the life of a British Army captain named Nairac, who—the writer contends—moved between reality and fantasy when talking about his service in northern Ireland. He boasted in Oxford pubs to "be underground in Northern Ireland" as an IRA "brigade commander." He also claimed to have assassinated a leading Republican gunman in North Armagh. But he wasn't alone in his delusions; other soldiers must have been indoctrinated with the same mind-set. A colleague who served with Nairac described him as "brilliant with the kids in West Belfast. *He just knew how criminality was in their blood*" (my emphasis). In the end, he was kidnapped, beaten, and shot, after singing Republican songs too enthusiastically in a South Armagh pub. In a conversation reported by the journalist Martin Dillon, Nairac apparently chatted with a local woman and claimed his Irish credentials came from a granny in Spiddal, County Galway, in the west of Ireland.

"Spiddal?" I said aloud, after reading excerpts. "Spiddal? That's where my grandmother's from." The story, apocryphal or otherwise, caught my imagination. Dillon wrote that Nairac was carefully crafting an identity. Carefully? Having driven through all of Spiddal East, Spiddal West, and Spiddal Middle in ten minutes, I was unconvinced. Nairac further bungled his connections, since the woman to whom he was talking was herself from that very area. Then there was the loud and obnoxious singing. If he *was* an SAS operative, he was a bad one. For all the talk about their talk, the Irish are unsurpassed at keeping quiet when they need to. (Not for mere effect did Republican broadsheets advise "Whatever you say, say nothing.") Nairac's story became the stuff of modern-day legend. Then, this being war in Ireland, his death became a rhyme with which children could chivvy patrolling soldiers: *Captain Nairac was a spy. / How did Captain Nairac die?*

Though he died twenty years ago, Nairac wasn't the only one fantasizing about a glorious fight for democracy in northern Ireland. From summer 1998 into the next winter, Loyalist rioters had been gathering in a nondescript little place called Portadown and fantasizing that they were in a battle for freedom. They stormed police ramparts set up to protect Nationalist streets and howled and heckled people across from them like hyenas gathering to move in for a kill. It was all done in the name of a parade celebrating the Battle of the Boyne, the 1690 victory of William of Orange over Catholic Ireland. It came to be known as the Drumcree Stand-off, since it was based outside Drumcree Parish Church.

"But do you think the Order should be allowed to march?" I asked a regular in the café one day.

It was a pointless question. Young people I knew from Protestant, or "Orange," communities had long since lost interest in the parades as anything other than a bitter point of debate among others. "I hate politics," they muttered over and over, "I don't pay any attention to those things."

Marie didn't demur. "Of course they shouldn't be allowed to march!" she yelled.

It was a brash dialogue at best, and I finished the workday without venturing into further discussion.

That very evening I arrived home, had my dinner, and turned on a British television documentary about the re-arming of a splinter Republican terrorist group. It opened at a fund-raiser in New York City with a reporter interviewing an American woman:

"No, I don't mind if our money goes to buy weapons for Continuity," she said, referring to the terrorist group. "As long as the British Army remains in Ireland they are"—and here she began jabbing the air with her cigarette and forefinger—"a le-gi-ti-mate tar-get." Then she took a drag and exhaled.

"What the hell is she talking about?" I said out loud, "has someone not told her the war's over?"

This was the bitter hypocrisy of my political inheritance: Allegheny International of New Jersey arms the RUC and British military with rubber bullets, and a deluded Republican fantasist fights the likes of Captain Robert Nairac and his Oxford pub boast. The film went downhill from there, moving between documentary and "mockumentary" as investigators met their Irish contacts, then were hooded and driven to a secret location to show the terrorists' cache of weapons. The whole thing seemed removed from reality. It was another version of white America filming Black and Latino gang bangers. While watching the film, you can't help but notice elements of performance that undermine the veracity of the whole scenario. A masked man "somewhere in Derry" displays a paltry collection of guns, then holds a grenade launcher like it's a hard-on while the reporter raises the alarm. It all seemed such playacting, and this in the neighborhood, where the Omagh bombers were said to have been held at gunpoint by the Provisional IRA and told to leave the island—or so people whispered, anyway.

Though the Troubles and their subsequent analyses became a mini-industry in both Great Britain and Ireland, and the plethora of investigative books were an informative and even engrossing read, they didn't reach me the way a story coming from casual conversation could. They didn't give me the details I could feel from a stranger's voice and gesture as they confessed their experience, anger, and bewilderment. Knowing the inner workings of a government maze, either in Communist Asia or in a so-called democratic nation like Great Britain or the United States, left me mute with indignation. The same could be said of the terrorist organizations and their hierarchical structure. For this reason those stories were unappealing to me; they were far removed from what I could understand.

For me, the postcards I collected and the stories casually told to me are the palimpsest over which the history text is written. These are not the words of either academic or informal historians, nor of a "commissioned report" or a front-line documentary, but they are the history the traveler encounters. They are the stories I like and will no doubt use in conversation to challenge the confines of some text somewhere with the infamous "word on the street."

✤ ✤

Sometime after my visit with the women's theater group, Rene told me that one of the women had stood up one day, walked herself across the city, and enrolled in a local college. I breathed a sigh of relief mingled with

admiration. I have great faith in the power of education to help people lib-
erate themselves from suffering and bring about change.

On the street this gesture is often referred to as "getting out," but more often than not it's about generating change in the environment around you.
People in the Fountain often referred to their lives as a "struggle" and a
"siege"—a reference to the city's original siege three centuries previous (and
if you're being assaulted on a regular basis, that's pretty apt), but in Belfast, Derry, and other places in Ireland there were hundreds of women
who didn't simply endure, but triumphed through sticking around and working for change.

During my time in Ireland there was a "siege" happening elsewhere as
well—and it wasn't just in Protestant communities. The Unionist politician
David Ervine referred to Portadown and the Drumcree Stand-off as "northern Ireland's Alabama." The Garvaghy Road, where the Orange Order wanted
to march, was what the analysis industry referred to as an "interface"—
street corners where two segregated communities bumped up against each
other. The route was a significant historical site for Orangism, but for residents, the parade was an invasion. Representatives of the Orange Order considered the government's decision *not* to allow them to march through the
Catholic neighborhood unfair and unjust. They concluded that the government had been bullied by Republican activists. And so the harangue began. From July 1998 through the winter and spring of the following year,
people camped out in the Drumcree area, and "'bad elements' walked to
the edge of Garvaghy Road each night and yelled threats across a police barricade. Dialogue was called for by everyone from ministers to politicians,
but the protesters refused. That Garvaghy Road was home to ex-prisoners
and current Republican activists was reason enough for them to refuse to
come to the table. In this line of thought, political affiliation with Republicanism was support for terrorism. As the debate continued to unfold on the
news, people outside the area simply shook their heads at the intractability
of the conflict and got on with their lives. By the end of winter, I knew better
than to try to figure out or imagine a solution. I simply watched the news for
as long as I could endure it, then, like others, I learned how to turn away
when the town was mentioned. But the courage of the Irish is that they don't
all turn away. It was a lousy job in the truest sense of the word, but someone
had to represent the Garvaghy Road Citizens Group in this mess.

Rosemary Nelson was a plain, serious-looking woman with auburn hair
and an unprepossessing demeanor. In fact, she looked like a lot of women

I know in both Ireland and the United States. She resembled those aunts you meet at family gatherings, the ones others often refer to as "one of my favorite people." Then people might politely whisper about the "tragedy" of Rosemary's botched plastic surgery—a lifelong burden, since it scarred the entire left side of her face, leaving her slightly disfigured and obviously marked as an "undesirable" woman. I can hear the sympathetic conversation make its way through her life: *Hasn't she made the most of it, though? A family, a legal career, quite a woman. Quite a woman.* Rosemary stays in my memory, first, as the woman who handled the sale of a friend's home. It's a simple thing, but that's what lawyering is—hundreds of little things being done for regular people. She could often be seen on the news as the legal representative for the Garvaghy Road Citizens Group. In one newsreel played over and over during my time there, she walked back and forth in front of a line of armored vehicles, trying to defuse a potential riot over the "right to march" and the "right to freedom from sectarian harassment." Struggling through law school, Nelson probably believed, like many I know in Ireland, that her future career would be centered on generating value and pulling justice up out of violence and tragedy, only to discover that, in the long run, injustice dressed itself in the mundane garb of paper pushing and regulation—and that's where the battle lay.

Lawyers' offices reveal the truth of their work: Rosemary's was a plain, shop-front firm, its door open for things as mundane but important as wills, the sale of property, divorces, and insurance claims. In addition, she was one of the few lawyers who spoke up regularly about the human rights of prisoners in northern Ireland referred to as "political" or "terrorist." In fact, she had done so in front of the United Nations and the U.S. Congress. She made a point of helping anyone who might have been labeled a terrorist sympathizer under British law. Naturally, this work also made her suspect under British law. In northern Ireland, it made her a target. On the Garvaghy Road case, her work became endless negotiation of a hundred thousand unwritten loopholes, handling a discourse of hatred ensconced in the finery of the government. Only at the end did it come to resemble that admirable thing the Irish call "the good fight." She would duck and weave around Lisburn, Belfast, and Portadown between bigoted cops, angry ex-prisoners, and scared mums. And each time a death threat came (as they had for Patrick Finucane before her), she stared it down.

In the event, she died in her sister's arms. A car bomb with a degree of sophistication only the well trained were capable of blew her legs off while she was pulling away from her house. The force of the blast was so loud that her sister came running from her own home, only to see Rosemary gasping and bleeding to death a couple hundred yards from her daughter Sarah's grammar school. The news media broadcast images of the car's charred remains for a week after the bombing, and each time I watched I could see Rosemary's hands straightening the little girl's collar as she left the house for school. Then I shuddered at the thought of the blast rattling the chain-link fence that surrounds the children's playground.

The day after Nelson's murder, Frankie Curry, a former Loyalist paramilitary prisoner, walked into the local Community Center on the Shankill Road, inquired about training programs, and then walked out. He was met by an execution squad in a nearby vacant lot. In the newspapers, the Provisional IRA were making promises about revealing the burial spots for Irish citizens they had murdered as British sympathizers. Some time just before Easter they reneged, so the daughter of Jean McConville, who had been looking for her mother's body for some twenty years, would have to keep on looking. When confronted with news such as this in the States, the proper response was always a heavy sigh and some muttering about tragedy. In Belfast, I was a bit more affected. The shock of experiencing these things up close didn't go away as days passed. On Monday afternoon, as I walked disconsolately around my neighborhood, I felt myself sinking into a depression.

The next day I hopped into a car and drove away from the city. I drove onto the M1, bypassing Portadown, heading into Tyrone and onto the A5 north. I took a right turn at a place called Ballygawley, where hedges and trees cast long lines across the road. The weather was warming up, the sun shining through on occasion before it was covered by passing clouds. I continued on through the town, then pulled into Omagh just as school was letting out. Passing Dunnes department store, I came to a stop at a set of lights and stared at the bitter and sorry remains of the summer blast. The area was boarded off like a construction site, and taped to a number of the walls were letters of condolence to the town leaders and citizens. I looked at the blue and brown of student uniforms against the white boards and listened to the flapping of torn paper as it disintegrated in the winter weather. I drove over the bridge spanning the Foyle River and past the bus station. I looked up the hill to the town center and lightened my foot on the gas pedal as pale-faced kids with sugar rings circling their lips swarmed around the streets.

"The bottom's a long way down for some people," a friend once told me, referring to addiction. If some people in Ireland were addicted to conflict and violence, then both Portadown and Omagh *had* to be the bottom. They just had to. The landscape in this addiction was made up of bomb blasts, vacant lots and executions, empty promises and missing bodies. "It's Easter," I said to myself, "could someone tell me the Irish for 'mercy'?"

Later, sitting in a coffee shop farther north, I looked through my travel guidebook for information on the county. Tyrone was an important part of England's aborted exit strategy from Ireland in the early part of the century. It was referred to by Lord Asquith in 1914 as "that most damnable creation of the perverted ingenuity of man." At that time, the province of Ulster was composed of nine counties, of which Tyrone proved to be a most difficult demographic mix for politicians. Gerrymandering a six-county Ulster would ensure political and economic stability for a majority of the pro-union and Protestant population. Heavy distribution of Republicans and Catholics in both Tyrone and neighboring Fermanagh presented a problem for Unionism. World War I and Republican dissent would ensure that competing political agendas would result in, at best, an imperfect creation called Ulster and, eventually, Northern Ireland. Where to draw the line separating this new province of Ulster seems to have been the difficult problem in the early part of the century. Here at the end of the century the problem was what to do with the line now?

Deidre Cartmill, a poet and native of Moy, County Tyrone, spoke to the world with her own vision. Perhaps it came to her on a ramble, perhaps it was inspired by the night sky in the countryside that falls like a dropcloth over the landscape and is pricked full of holes, letting light through in the shape of stars.

> Most days it's simpler
> to forget
> that I'm a carbon copy
> of that first exploding star
> an eternal flame
> born of an eternal flame
> the still burning cinder
> of a star-fire

I love that poem. Reading it out loud from a local newspaper, I smiled and nodded.

"Yeah," I said to myself, "that shattered star, that's where *I* come from, too."

What a relief, what a breaking of chains—a poem from young Ireland and it's not about a field or a wall or a gun, but about an explosion that *gives birth* to something. Here, on the lips of a poet, was John Hume's wish for Ireland to be free of its "mental border."

Swinging my car around in what felt like the hinterland, I headed toward Derry thinking of Deidre and "Cosmology" (the title of the poem). I later wrote in my diary of rambles in the countryside and being in Ireland:

From Boston, I can often imagine myself in Ireland. And when I imagine, I go back into myth and memory, as if I've found a bag loaded with antique trinkets. I see myself staring up at a sky filled to overflowing with stars, on nights when the country landscape is blackened. I feel my hands reach into thickets so strong as to be unbreakable, hedges so sharp they must have been split by lightning. I'm digging at this difficult, beautiful, dreary, undefeated landscape— walking its paths and feeling its sunken fire. And when I go back into the city, with its craic-filled sidewalks and painted walls, I am taken aback suddenly with the smell of Ireland's country towns, the salt air or the peat moving like dust on the wind and arriving at my doorstep, transporting me to that mystery-filled place.

I could have driven in rural Ireland for days without stopping. In fact, I often spent four and five hours moving around country roads drinking in all the details of the landscape. Perhaps I returned to the countryside so often in my memory because I still felt challenged to record it. I struggled and struggled to find words to capture its essence and then gasped in horror as I found myself detouring into sentimental phrases like "the wilds of Donegal."

Seamus Heaney recorded the narcotic effect of this landscape experienced while driving quite simply: "Useless to think you'll park and capture it." And it is true. The great seduction of driving in the countryside is the illusion that technology can trump the ancient. To stop and photograph the landscape— or even to pen a wee verse about it—is to come face to face with how insignificant you are under Ireland's big sky.

The other poet wandering occasionally through my consciousness, Belfast's Ciaran Carson, theorized that Ireland's roads were so intricate in their turns that if they were straightened, they'd run the length and breadth of the United States. (This explains why it takes so long to get from point A to point B in such a "wee place.") Walls of peat and grass rise up so high along the side of country roads that hedges grow up over your head. What lies around any given curve is unseen. Occasionally, I heard the roll of a tractor and saw a man's head floating across a nearby field. Winter storms had knocked down, and in some cases split, trees the size of buildings. Their roots stuck up into the air like torn flesh, and the remaining hole seemed to throb painfully, making me shudder. So grand did these trees suddenly appear to me that I was shocked into understanding their grace now that it had been ripped away so violently. I closed my eyes at the sight of the withering roots as if to avoid looking at a sucking wound.

Ireland, and particularly the northwest, had once been covered in trees. The image of the oak grove as a haven for Celtic druids and, later, Christian monks is one still repeated—as if in prayer—when talking about Ireland's ancient history. The country's deforestation is another crime laid at Great Britain's feet. Beginning in the sixteenth century, Irish trees provided ample material for the British shipbuilding industry, for barrelmaking, and for the production of charcoal. Another benefit to the British, of course, was that the destruction of the trees also exposed the hiding places of Irish bandits, Ireland's disunited resistance to a British invasion. Today, reforestation is a project the Irish government fulfills in rural areas with pine trees and all the inspiration of Christmas tree farmers.

Looking at what is now a relatively bare landscape, I thought often of the ancient Chinese meditative exercise T'ai Chi and its command to "hug a tree." It sounds absurd from the vantage point of the twenty-first century, but it is surprisingly consoling in practice. You could place both hand and ear close to the trunk of an oak and feel something akin to a pulse. I could lean easily against many of the bigger trees I saw in Irish gardens and parks and wonder whom they had shaded, on what conversations had they eaves-dropped? Sometimes I sat on a bench and indulged in the memory of hanging upside down from a maple back home, or imagined the giant arm of a neighbor's pine tree as a horse. I often came to a dead stop in Ireland when the sweet smell of pine sap mixed with the salty air of the coast. And some-times, when the wind ran quickly through leaf-filled branches, I imagined I could hear words. In garden-filled South Belfast, I could walk to work as birds flew from branches in groups, the sound bringing to mind the com-bined snap of a crowd of opening umbrellas. If the sky was clear, I could see the hills on the horizon. It wasn't the ocean, but it made me smile nonetheless, since another exercise in my on-off yoga regimen was imagining yourself a mountain. In Tandasana, you had to ground yourself to the earth in strength and harmony. When I did any of these physical/spiritual things in Ireland—

walking, standing, breathing, stretching—I was humbled by the power of the response from the land underneath me. Water runs deep in Ireland, everyone knows that, but the memory of trees runs deeper still. Stand anywhere, and you can feel the pulse of the roots left behind.

❧ ☙

Wondering and reasoning about these things, I drove slowly along the highway back to Derry. At one point I had to slow for a checkpoint. I had been wandering from Donegal to Leitrim, back across the border around Tyrone, and then had headed up toward Derry. Cars were being waved through past a police patrol and a set of army trucks. Perhaps it was due to my place in line, but instead of being waved on I was told to come to a full stop. I rolled down my window and said, "Yes?"

"May I see your license and registration, please?"

The policeman was less than two feet from my window, and he cradled an Uzi submachine gun that rested at exactly my eye level. I looked up at his face and saw no menacing intent as I handed over my Massachusetts license and the car papers. Looking at traffic and the soldiers behind him, the officer moved in such a way that his gun barrel swung back and forth with him. It pointed at me, it moved away; it pointed at me, it moved away. This was the infamous "gun in the face" experienced by so many in northern Ireland.

"So that's what an Uzi looks like from this side," I thought.

"Are you here on vacation?" he asked, handing back my papers.

" . . . uhm, well, yes." I answered, awkwardly.

"Well, we're not as bad as we're painted," he said, trying to be friendly.

Though I did not know to whom exactly he was referring, I answered, "Yes, I know," then drove away.

I continued to repeat *"So that's what an Uzi looks like from this side"* as my legs began shaking. Then, as my hands began trembling, my mind switched over to an observation that the highway signs had been graffitied, with the "London" of "Londonderry" deleted. Mental gymnastics dressed as detailed observation kept me in control of the car and fended off mild hysteria. A thought ran through my head, and I told myself to write it down: *"The British can never escape what they have done to Ireland and the Irish. The Irish can never escape what they have done to each other."* The steering wheel seemed to wobble in my hands, and my knees were banging together. As cars around me accelerated, I slowed to let them pass. I ran questions and comments back and forth in my mind, and they quickly spun into chaos:

"Edith, you don't have a problem with checkpoints. You've been through check-points before, no problem. What's the problem?"

"Sometimes you just break. Sometimes you just can't handle it. There was cause for fear."

"There was no cause for fear. It was standard procedure. What's the Irish for 'mercy'?"

"This standard procedure is not normal. Is that really what an Uzi looks like from this end? Oh, look, another sign's been painted over."

I pulled over outside an army barracks, came to a stop, and let myself shake uncontrollably. "It's not my fucking war," I said out loud. I wanted to cry but couldn't. Instead, I had this uncontrollable shaking and a terrible longing for the solace of trees. Cars around me accelerated further still. I thought of guns, walls, split trees, hawk-eyed women and men, and fleeing angels. I thought of the newspaper pictures of Sarah Nelson at her mother's funeral procession: her eyes clenched, her lips pressed tight against the truth of it.

Chapter 11

Scaraveen / Good Craic (reprise) / Homesick (reprise)

Ach, it's so much better than it was. You just don't know.

—One friend

I don't think it's better. I think it's different, but I don't think it's better.

—Another friend

Spring came. Then winter abruptly returned. Over hot brandy one evening Rene explained it as something the Irish called "scaraveen."

"That's how it sounds," she explained, "I'm not sure how it is spelled."

"A false spring," I said.

"Yes," Rene answered, "you'll notice there's no one working in gardens."

"Oh, right." I said.

Eventually they did, though. In my neighborhood people began poking around in their gardens some time after the sky told them spring had finally come. Tulips fell onto sidewalks outside flower shops. Branches of yellow forsythia stuck up over dull gray walls like cowlicks. Landscaping trucks parked in front of houses around the neighborhood, their beds full of shovels and peat and tools. Hedgerows brought forth blossoms, and trees let their buds slowly unfold. The smell of cut grass hung heavy and sweet in the air. Birds sang until after the dinner hour, and dogs sniffed around yards with loud, eager snorts. Outside my office window wood pigeons sat on empty branches for ages, their bellies large as pears. I thought they were meditating on the season's arrival. On the hillside underneath them, a black-and-white cat strolled casually, feigning disregard.

One afternoon, BBC radio ran a story about two British horticulturalists who had recently published an index to wildflowers and foliage plants of Belfast. It sounded strange, but to hear the ten-minute story of two friendly older men foraging through military rubble and uncovering untold numbers of gems was heartening. Gentian violet was peeking up through rubbish-covered riverbanks, alpine flowers blew sturdily in cold winds, and wild-flowers pushed their way up through broken pavement and sat like the memory of a previous incarnation come to remind us of our potential. I could relate to these men. I had arrived at this place "long wondered about," had felt it to be ordinary, had stayed a while, and had uncovered what was extraordinary about it.

A little over a year after the Good Friday Agreement was passed, I got ready to leave Ireland. In the North, people had been included, excluded, and then included again. Twelve Catholic men, along with a high-profile attorney, had been murdered execution-style; twenty-eight people had been killed and two hundred injured in a bomb attack by Republican terrorists; and three Catholic boys had been burned alive in an arson attack. The British and Irish governments continued to push for dialogue over deadlock. Women wept for the deaths of children and the broken bones of punishment beatings. Words got nasty, then became polite. Spite and slander made the headlines, but the slow, steady, painstaking progress of reconciliation continued.

On the first anniversary of the Agreement, political leaders continued to fight over the issue of weapons decommissioning, but they came up with something called the Hillsborough Declaration that included proposals for a "Day of Reconciliation." A noble gesture, I thought, but it was greeted with a resounding howl of mockery and dissent from leaders on what was still referred to as "all sides."

On Good Friday, 1999, the day after Unionist and Republican politicians had participated in "unprecedented" dialogue about decommissioning, a mixed community group carried a large wooden cross from a Catholic church on the Falls Road, down across the Westlink Motorway, into the city, and into the Church of Ireland Cathedral in the city center. Then they prayed together for peace. They had been doing it for six years. I thought the government's proposal for a day of reconciliation was enormous and visionary—the entire island would gather together, and events would possibly include an act of putting weapons "beyond use." But reconciliation was really found in the subtle gestures people made in daily life. They added up again and again until they generated enough strength to prompt holier, bigger gestures, like carrying a cross together. It was an act of community in a population outsiders commonly referred to as "deeply divided." I smiled at the news coverage. I knew I would miss the place. Many others do, too.

A twenty-first century postcard floating through cyberspace reveals the mild heartache at the center of Ireland's diaspora. A woman writes of her many years in America:

> The people are relatively friendly, but not like they are "back home." . . . My girlfriends and I would go dancing at the Floral Hall off the Antrim Road, as well as Albert White's Dance Studio downtown. I also remember the Crumlin Road movie theatres, and going to the chip shop afterwards for fish & chips, wrapped in the *Telegraph,* of course. My family attended church at St. Marks on the Ligoniel Rd. I also remember taking walks up the Horseshoe Road and the Ballysillan Road to meet all our friends. I also remember riding in the back of my sister's boyfriend's MG on the Seven Mile Straight, after the Belfast Grand Prix motorcycle races. I remember sitting on the steps of our home and watching Stanley Woods and other famous riders go past on their way to the track. My youngest sister still lives in the family home and my brother lives just down the road.

Of course, she can't go home again. Leaving the village is a gamble with a big payoff, but the same could be said of staying.

In spite of the horrors of the present and the past, no one I met who'd lived through the worst of times would ever consider leaving, would ever say anything other than "I love Northern Ireland." Home is always the loveliest place in the world. It is the mixture of pain, struggle, humor, compassion, exhilarating triumph, and seemingly inexhaustible despair. It is an inescapable hopelessness that one day turns around and changes ever so slightly for the better. The "home" I saw and heard about in Ireland was big-hearted, funny, generous, raucous, pious, superstitious, prim, sloppy, and enduring. It was full of people who handled my ignorance with kindness, rattled my cage to induct me into mettle-testing communities, sought understanding, and demanded respect.

❧ ☙

After Marie dropped me off from work one spring evening, I fixed a cup of tea, then, shaking off the memory of my mother's shoulder tap about sleeping in the living room, fell blissfully onto the couch for a nap. Around 9:00 P.M. the phone woke me. I rolled off the couch and stumbled toward the ringing.

"Hello?"

"Edie."

"Robbie? What's goin' on?"

"Edie . . . I'm at the foot of your street."

I could hear his car hit the stone driveway. We continued talking on the phone. I walked over to my front window and looked out.

"And here you are." I opened the window and sat casually on the ledge.

"Here I am," he said, stepping out of the car, still on the phone. "Here with some friends to drag you out into the night."

A woman and a man waved to me from inside the car. Robbie lifted his arm in gesture (going *just* over the line into dramatic excess), paused, and smiled. "It's good craic!"

"Give me a minute," I said, then went to change into some jeans and a fresh shirt. A minute later I was climbing into the back seat of the car.

"Edie, this is Catherine," he pointed to the woman sitting next to me, "and this is O'Neill."

The man in the front seat turned around and said hello.

Robbie continued, "Catherine is living here in Belfast, finishing her degree at Queen's. And O'Neill is up for the weekend from Dublin."

"Where we goin'?" I asked, inspired by the spontaneity of the excursion and what felt like the late hour (it was 9:30).

"First stop, the university club. We'll leave the car there, then taxi for the rest of the night."

When we walked into the university club, it was nearly empty. O'Neill went up to the bar to order beer.

"Edie," Robbie said, "Catherine's people come from Mayo."

"Oh," I said, with polite interest.

"Catherine, we don't yet know where Edie's people come from!" Robbie joked.

"Very funny," I said, "I'm rumored to be Irish," I said to Catherine, jokingly. As she was raised in England and I in the States, I knew we had different experiences being "Irish."

"What's your family name?" she asked.

"Shillue," I said with a smile.

"Oh," she responded.

O'Neill brought over two pints of lager, then walked back to the bar for two stouts.

I laughed at her slightly puzzled response.

"My great-grandmother was an O'Brien, my great-grandfather was from Clare."

"And your mother's side?" Robbie asked.

I remembered my mother's chilly replies to my questions about family history.

"Well," I said, "she was a Clifford."

"Anglo-Irish perhaps," O'Neill theorized.

"Oh, she'd love that," I said with a laugh, "there's a family story that says someone in the family once owned the title to the land Westminster Abbey sits on."

Catherine smiled.

"Lovely story, Edie." Robbie said (but I know he's just winding up).

"Yes, lovely," his co-conspirator, O'Neill, says.

"And not a bit of exaggeration," Robbie says.

"No, not a bit," O'Neill finishes, as I giggle.

We sat for a bit making small talk until politics reared its head.

"They're talking about decommissioning again, y'know," I said, looking at Robbie.

"Are they, Edie?"

"I have an idea, y'know. I think it could work."

"Well, if it makes the least bit of sense, it won't work here, Edie."

"It's completely absurd," I said.

"Excellent!" O'Neill said.

"I think we should find the grammar school English teachers of all the members of the IRA Army Council and get them to do the handover."

Robbie made a serious face and looked over at me. "You've found the answer, Edie. You've found the answer." Then he turned to the people behind us and said, "Send George Mitchell home! We've got the answer!"

He laughed loudly, then broke into an imitation of his own grammar school teacher, "Now Mr. O'Neill, Mr. P. O'Neill, I want you to put down that SAM and I want you to put it down now! Jimmy . . . I said now! And where's the Semtex? Give me the Semtex." He crooked his index finger, beckoning the man forward for a schoolmarm scolding.

Catherine and I were howling by this point.

"Y'know, before I came here, I thought Semtex was the name of a condom," I said with a laugh.

At this Robbie broke up.

"A condom?! All right now, Edie, I don't want to hear that talk out of a nice girl such as yerself."

I laughed again. "Robbie," I started.

"No, Edie, not a word!"

He laughed again, and by the time we prepared to move on, there was little that could spoil our mood. At around midnight we made our way to last call at the Terrace Bar, up the Lisburn Road.

"Robbie!" A young woman gasped with drunken surprise as we entered.

Catherine and I rolled our eyes and wandered off as Robbie indulged the girl and her friend. A few minutes later, a drunk man stumbled over to us and asked me if I was from America, as O'Neill had said.

"Yes, I'm from Boston," I answered.

"Boston! Well!" He opened his jacket and gestured to the lining. "I got some Semtex right here!" Catherine and I went into a fit over my earlier confession, and this prompted a raucous laugh from our new acquaintance, who continued his minstrelsy, "Perhaps you'd like to take a taxi up to the Felon's Club?" Then he fell against a pole laughing at himself. I caught my breath as he stumbled around. I was embarrassed for us both. What had America asked of Ireland's Irish? And why had they so often and so willingly complied?

We moved across to the end of the bar, and I started chatting with a man sitting alone at the end. He smiled at me as I headed toward him as if he was a safe harbor.

"Yes, yes," he said with a soft laugh as I gestured toward the empty seat beside him, "have a seat."

Catherine was over trying to coax Robbie and O'Neill away from the two ghastly drunk women.

"You here from Boston, did I hear?" he asked softly.

"Yeah, here for a spell," I answered.

"I was in America once," he said. "Didn't like it at all."

"Well," I said, "some don't. To each his own."

He swallowed his whiskey and gave me a sideways glance.

"Enough about me," I continued, "what about you? You're obviously here tonight waiting for someone."

His face dropped. "What makes you say that?"

"Ten years of waiting tables," I answered, "you've got that killin'-time look about you."

He smiled. "I'm waiting for my girlfriend. She's a nurse at the hospital up the road."

"Oh," I said, "and what do you do?"

He started, as if the question offended him. Caught off guard, he shrugged and answered honestly.

"I'm a police officer."

I laughed, then said, "No, really. What do you do?" I mean, he wouldn't really admit that, would he? I couldn't yet say I understood the place, and RUC officers were sort of bogeymen in my consciousness.

"Criminal investigations," he answered, after shaking his head over my naiveté.

I tried to rescue myself from increasing embarrassment with a joke: "Oh! I've heard of that—ordinary, decent crime, right?"

He smiled and nodded. Only in a police state like Northern Ireland could there be a category of crime like this. It included theft, fraud, assault, and other vaguely charming offenses in a place known for bombings, punishment beatings, and burnouts.

"Your girlfriend's a nurse?" I asked.

"Yes, we're together seventeen years now."

"Oh," I said, "you're sorta married by now."

"Oh, no," he said, "I'm married as well. We have an agreement."

I was surprised.

"She's a Catholic, my girlfriend," he confessed.

"Oh," I said. "That complicates things, right?"

He laughed softly. "Yeah, but not the way you think."

"How'd you meet?"

"I don't remember actually meetin'," he explained, "but apparently I got very drunk with her one night. The next morning I come to on a couch, and she's standin' over me. I asked where the hell I was," he wound up a bit as the story went on. "She says, 'Well, I didn't know what to do with you, so I brought you up here to Ma's house.'"

I put my hand to my forehead and laughed, "Only in Ireland!"

"Now, wait a minute," he continued, "I look out the window, then look at her and ask, 'Where the hell is this?' and she says, '*Andytown.*'"

I almost spat out my drink as he finished. In 1981, Andersonstown was a no-go area for the police. For him, it was a sure place to get killed.

"So I said to her, 'You find me a cab that'll come here and take me the hell out without getting me killed.'"

He sipped his drink, then shrugged.

"And you've been together ever since," I finished. He nodded. "Your wife?"

"She's quite sick. With MS. There's only so much I can do. We've got a comfortable arrangement."

A society that's ripped apart stitches itself together in odd ways. Relationships like this aren't really surprising and the number of them—that is,
"mixed" couples—seemed far more common than reported.

We sat in silence for a few minutes. Then I ventured forward with a beery
bravado, "Let me ask you something . . . "

He looked sideways at me—wary as ever.

"Patten," I began, "everyone's howling over the name change. What do
cops think?"

He smirked a bit and shook his head. "If it'll make things better, we don't
really mind," and he dismissed the subject.

The issue did seem rather superfluous for a guy who had to check his car
for bombs each day without looking as if he was checking his car for bombs.

I felt like pushing forward. I looked at him again and asked, "One more
thing?"

He waited.

"Do you think Robert Hamill was kicked to death in front of those cops in
Portadown?"

The question annoyed him, but he kept his temper.

"Look," he said quietly, "I'm a straight arrow. I'm very strict with the
rules and regs."

"C'mon," I said, ready for an argument.

He looked me in the eye. "Maybe. Now, do you think those police officers
in New York shot that Black man forty-one times because he had a gun?" He
asked referring to the Amadou Diallo case then being tried in New York
City.

I was stopped short. Such challenges are fair. Police departments in U.S.
cities are frequently investigated for corruption and violence. A single filthy
incident often reveals a web of deceit. The great irony, on the East Coast,
anyway, is that for a century departments have been replete with Irish
Catholics. What was similar in both contexts was that the higher up the corruption, the more the dead were local cops and civilians. People in the fancy
Unionist suburbs of Belfast might find the name change an insult, but they
couldn't fathom how dirty dealings at higher levels of decision making put
working stiffs in the line of fire. Patten was a highly regarded political figure
in Britain, but in uglier circles in Northern Ireland his Catholicism made him
suspect.

"Edie!" Robbie called out as he approached the bar, "let's go."

"Safe journey," the man said, then stood up and left.

The bar was emptying, and we were part of only a handful of people left in the building. O'Neill was trying to order a drink from the bartender. I looked around. One couple was arguing, another was locked in an embrace. At one table by the door a man was staring into the face of a large-breasted woman, begging with his eyes to be let into her bed.

"Robbie!" a doorman said, as he pushed two women out the door, "c'mon now, get your friends together and go!" O'Neill, who had no luck with the bartender, suggested we go to Magennis's. We headed out the door to wait at the taxi stand.

"Are you from Boston?" a stranger asked.

"Yes," I answered.

"I have some friends from Boston. Well, they're not from Boston, they're from Scituate."

"Scituate?" That's my hometown."

I was standing on a sidewalk in Belfast, it was one-thirty in the morning, and this connection seemed perfectly normal.

In the shift generated by such conversation, I was looking with a stranger through the pinhole that is a view of the world from Belfast.

"Pretty town," she said.

"You've been?" I asked.

"Yeah, lovely."

Thus it was that, standing on the sidewalk with a crowd waiting for a taxi, I suddenly saw my family home. And looking out over the water, the echo of people's names came back: Sweeney, O'Neill, O'Brien, Carney, Flaherty, Geraghty, Sheehan, McCarthy, Crowley—the Irish Riviera, that. Our house rose into view: the chimney struck by lightning one winter, a baby that died, another one that lived and took her name, a small flood, French glass doors and hands going through them, slammin' screen doors and ones that stuck, rusting summer furniture and discarded couches lingering on our front porch.

I could see my mother, too. She was alone, performing her secret ritual— the one that brings her peace amid the eight children. She sits up after waking, puts her feet on the floor, expresses gratitude for being able to have another day; she gets up, walks around the end of her bed and out onto the front porch, where it's cold and creaky and, we claim, a banshee howls in the winter. Mother leans on the windowsill and searches the horizon. She moves her head just so, focusing her lenses, and then settles for a moment.

"Still there," she says of the ocean. She stands straight and lets another slow breath out, and then the day begins.

Then, there was our last year in the house. My mother and I were trying to sell the big old thing after Daddy died, and mockin' the buyers as they went through. No nibbles until the spring, and mother finally sold it to a couple named Cullen who had snatched it from the shaky hands of a young couple named Brown, and when the winter came, she and I laughed over missing the groany old thing and how the banshee howls when the wind comes in off the water. We joked about how all ten rooms manage to lean to one corner, making everything slide toward the left.

All in a minute this rushes through my head, waiting for a cabbie who'll take us to Magennis's for after-hours music. We were up on the Lisburn Road, and Union Jacks snapped in the wind at the top of telephone poles. We wanted to go down to the waterfront. It was late and taxi drivers were nervous.

"You really didn't know," one man told me, referring to the recent past, "you didn't know if you'd live to the end of your shift."

People seemed nervous in places where a mixed community gathered; but in places like that people got along. I called those folks "peacemakers," since they could talk to each other easily enough (whereas, in contrast, politicians couldn't even sit at a table together). There were loads of these small pubs and clubs tucked into little corners in out-of-the-way places.

Robbie had everyone in stitches waiting at the taxi stand. I could hear people laughing and calling his name all night, like they were laugh junkies and he a dealer. I was quite an absurd sight myself, standing on the sidewalk waving each time an empty cab went by and muttering, "What's wrong with these guys?" I'd see the car from a block or so away, then wave casually, increasing my urgency as they got closer but didn't slow.

"Can you not wave down cabs here?" I asked, waving at another empty one as it passed.

"Aye," said Dublin Jack, "they'll only come if you call 'em," then laughed at his inadvertent joke. His white hair often fell forward over his brow, and he occasionally muttered that he couldn't "understand this place."

"Yeah," I answered, "neither can I. And I live here!" Then I reignited the taxi joke by whistling at one coming down the road and singing out: "Here, cabbie, heeeeere, cabbie."

I stopped gesturing as it passed. "I suppose it's no different than in the States," I grumbled, referring to cabs that wouldn't pick up or drop off in certain city neighborhoods.

Catherine was surprised to hear someone had been in my hometown.

"Has she?" she said, opening the door of a cab Robbie had phoned, "small world isn't it?" We climbed in, three in the back and Dublin Jack up front.

"I suppose," I said, thinking about the people from Scituate and their family name—"you become oddly obsessed with names in Belfast—'Scollins' she had said." It wasn't anyone I knew, but I didn't know much of the town anymore. Robbie muttered again about did Catherine know that I really was Irish, he had found my name in the book of Irish surnames.

"He had his doubts," I said laughing.

"You go to America," he added, launching into a story about encountering Americans in the States. "They ask you where you're from" (in Ireland the obsession is with names, in the States it is with place).

"I'd tell people I'm Irish and they'd say . . ." he pauses to laugh and bring O'Neill's attention to the incident, "O'Neill, they'd say," and he turns on the American accent, "Ah'm part Ahrish, a kwarter Scawttish, some French and German, and one-tenth Oglala Sioux," he breaks down laughing again. "I mean, how many passports do these people have?!"

The taxi takes a turn into Shaftsbury Square, me fallin' sideways against Robbie.

"Have I told you about home, Edie?" he murmurs in my ear. It is not flirtation, but a wave he wants to both make and ride.

"A number of times," I answer, referring to his Warrenpoint upbringing. "The hare soup?"

"It's rising!" Catherine says from my left, "Here it comes!" she laughs, referring to the tide of his story.

"By this point there were probably twelve or fifteen of us, Edie."

"Fifteen hunter-gatherers," I add, feeding the tale, a mere teaspoon added to a flood.

"Oh, we'd come home through the fields, y'know, making our way to the house for the dinner of hare soup, y'know."

"God help the late one," O'Neill quips from the front seat.

Robbie turned to talk directly into my ear and said, with the right touch of dramatic sigh, "My mother's not even skinnin' the things by this point, Edie."

"They're sucking the meat through their teeth," O'Neill said solemnly.

Catherine and I were stiff with laughter. Robbie sighs, perhaps at the memory of his mother.

"Oh, the difficulty of it. . . . I'd come home in the evenin', 'n' the big pointy ears were stickin' up out of the pot there," he put his hands up to his head in imitation of a rabbit.

The taxi slowed to let an RUC truck pass. A crowd of twenty-somethings was milling about Bradbury Place, after the close of a disco. We stopped again. They pushed their way across the street to Bishop's for take-away fish and chips, lickin' their lips in anticipation of the smack of salt and vinegar.

Robbie continued, "I'd come in of a cold winter day and make my way through the crowd, and you'd hear Ma—God rest her soul—you'd hear Ma say," and here O'Neill chirps in and they're a vaudeville act:

"OK, WHO'S FOR THE LIVE ONE?!"

I laugh and smile at the last line, but it's tinged with a sadness, because the story is over, and I don't want it to be. My family home makes one last appearance in my memory—we're all reaching for rolls at a holiday dinner and the basket's empty in a blink.

We were still making our way across town to Magennis's bar, which, for some reason, had an after-hours license. There was a salsa band playing, and we knew it would be full of a whole mix of people. The taxi driver edges along down Ormeau Avenue, through an alley to the back side of the pub. He slows down and insists we get out quickly.

"There's not a chance!" the doorman is yelling to people lingering outside, then he slams the door. Robbie edges forward, diplomatically knocking on the door and inquiring again.

"No, Robbie, not a fuckin' chance!" SLAM.

Robbie knocks again.

"No! Not even with that American jerk!" SLAM.

"He knows you're here," O'Neill said to me.

"Wow, man," I answered, "I've arrived."

I looked around at the neighborhood. Across the street St. George's market was being refurbished, down the road the gasworks was being transformed. ("Y'know, it's only just recently," people said, "that we've stopped smelling the sulfur rising up from the ground of that place.") In the Bar Wars, the mods were fighting it out with the traditional pubs. Magennis's had entered the fray by buying the Whiskey Café next door and knocking down the wall between them, so that what came out was half pub, half bar, with high stools and round tables jostling with the low enclosure of snugs. (They, however, had not yet succumbed to the fetish for cappuccino machines sweeping the city.) I leave Robbie to negotiate with the doorman, then move to the side of the building and dance to the salsa music. I admire the windows of the pub and watch a young couple suss out the workings of the side door. Watching them and listening to the music inside, I could feel myself sliding back to where I started from when I arrived in Ireland not too long ago. I was slipping down into the timelessness and mystery of "good craic." Inside, I know, is warm, dark wood, a few old snugs, conversation that buzzes like background music, lowering sometimes, rising at others, and then crashing into laughter.

I often theorized that the pauses in conversation in Northern Ireland were broken, and more words generated, by the whispered input of the missing. If I could move around among the people, like a ghost or a memory, the sounds would begin to take on form, then get even clearer and become something like words in my American ear. The barkeep floats back and forth in relation to the crowd, like a net catching the sea's bounty. A pretty blond man stands at the bar alone, his chin resting in his hand, his blue eyes watching everything through the mirror. Chairs, benches, and snugs lay like small clearings amid a grove of trees. Hands cup pint classes while words float across their rims like breezes, stories circling around as accompaniment to the music, landing only occasionally. The wooden floor is sticky to the shoe, a mess of spilled liquor turned to sugar trailing dirt brought in from the pavement and brought back out again via the rubber-soled work shoe, the high-heeled pump, the flat black loafer. A pair of Dexters scuff back and forth below the hum of conversation, flirtation, argument, and innuendo.

"Did she?" "He never!" "Goodonya, girl," echo and rise from the buzz as I pace back and forth outside.

"Really," says Catherine, returning to our earlier conversation on the nature of craic in Belfast, "people here are just what they are, and they accept you for what you are." This is both true and contradictory in a city renowned for its sectarianism.

Five minutes pass. I stand a while longer on the side street, but am taken with the music from inside the pub. The couple is still tryin' to sneak in, and I forget the urge to get inside. While the negotiations for entry went on, I continued dancing a salsa to the background music.

"Small world," echoed in my head. "Can you imagine! Meeting someone who'd been to your hometown!"

My mother eventually sold the family home. It was after Father died. We moved one spring day, with the appropriate amount of melodrama, but a few sighs of relief, too.

"No, Ede," Mom said, "I'm not sad. In order to really honor the past, you have to move on from it."

A cab pulls up and someone gets out. Robbie says we should take this one. We climb dutifully inside, remarking that the driver is the same one we started with early in the evening—isn't that lucky?—and O'Neill complains that he's actually gotten into Magennis's when there was an even bigger crowd outside and we should have given it a bit longer.

"No," Robbie says, with a touch of resignation, "we shouldn't linger."

"Must make you feel at home," someone said of meeting the stranger who'd been to Scituate.

"Not really," I answered, but couldn't say why.

I went home and slept. I slept so deeply during my time in Ireland that when I woke it was as if I were breaking the surface of water. My sleep was filled with wordy, thick dreams that helped me grab hold of my own connection to the island, as if it were first a thread of polite phrases, then became a thick rope that I could use to pull myself back to shore.

If travel is a journey toward understanding—and I believe it is—then I went away from Ireland with an understanding of it as a land of sweat and cut and fight. Ireland was planted and stolen and worked and built. The roads are curved around the granite heart of the Mourne Mountains; they dip along the Antrim coast and the ledges along Lough Foyle; across from Donegal are cliffs of dramatic, frightening proportion. The place is a wonder to me because all these things—land, history, politics, and something called "tradition"—jostle with each other for our attention and allegiance.

I came to feel the topography intimately, but in truth, I was always on the outside of Ireland looking in. It didn't matter that I lodged with families (I can still see Aisling in my dreams, walking across a landscape like a warrior princess), that I took a lover (in my memory I trace the calloused interior of his hand; I listen to his compliments given only sotto voce, his teasing paraded aloud), that I eavesdropped on the quivering conversations of the elderly, that I came from a line of women who clawed their way out of poverty and isolation by leaving the island for America. My coming back, Irish "credentials" in hand, was no matter. It would always be that I was outside the debate and couldn't understand. I was outside the discrete and dysfunctional gestures that made up public and private life both.

But a stranger sees places in a way that the native has forgotten. The Irish are very fragile. Don't let their razor tongues, gnashing teeth, or sharp wit fool you. Don't be tricked into shrinking back at their bluster and saber rattling. The ancient howl and the wicked laugh are metal cages built to safeguard tender hearts.

⤙ ⤚

"How was it?" people asked me upon my return to a Boston summer. This is a frequent but unanswerable question made to the traveler.

"It's a place. People live there; they have lives," I answered.

All these things are sacred—places, people, and their lives. They all have infinite potential and disarming creativity and humor. But these kinds of insights about the Northern Irish are hidden under offhand phrases like "The place grows on you," or the shrug of embarrassed enjoyment and the sheepish laughter that accompanies the phrase "It was nice. I like it there." Or it is part of the echo of shock in the phrase "You'd be surprised! It's quite lovely."

A Boston friend with northern roots began digging around at the inevitable:

"How was your flight?"

I looked at her with suspicion.

"Fine." I answered, curtly.

"Did you . . . "

" . . . yes . . . ," I sighed.

" . . . cry?"

"I don't even know why," I said with a shrug, "I kept playing Van Morrison on the headset and wiping my eyes. It was awful."

"Ah," she explained, "we've got one foot in each place."

We sipped coffee and stared at Boston harbor.

"So, who do you suppose your minder was?"

"I didn't have one," I answered with a groan.

"Sure everyone goes there like you's got a minder. Maybe you didn't know it."

"Gimme a break, would you? If I did," I laughed, "it was the most boring assignment in the history of the practice."

Ireland of the Imaginations. What did she imagine? A conspiracy of followers? Well, he—one of "the lads" to be sure—could not have been the only one. There are more surveillance cameras per square foot in Ireland than in all of Great Britain, more strange electronic devices, listening posts, and patrolmen than in some of Europe's biggest cities. In such a wee place, there's so much waiting for trouble, so much expecting the worst of people.

But assuming I did have some followers, real or imagined, alive or dead, spirit, flesh, or technology, did they see the world as I did when I wandered through it? And if they did, did they learn something? I must have appeared comical on sunny winter days as I took pictures at the gates of the Belfast courthouse, hidden behind barricades and metal sheeting like something under construction. As a cop edged about across the street trying to figure out what I was up to, did he get nervous? Then I wandered around, took a picture of Magennis's and someone inside got annoyed and slammed the door shut on me.

I ambled into the Castle Court area, through shopping streets and malls. I walked up Royal Avenue and spent a dog's age in Waterstone's before I made my way into Linenhall Library, where I could curl up on a bench and read some travel books about Africa or India while the sky threatens rain. Clouds will pass, sweeping wind down the narrow alleyway between Marshall's bakery and the shops that lead to Queen Street. The wind threads its way through crowds that gather in the late afternoon outside Thornton's candy shop on Royal Avenue, before it whips around through shopping districts, zigzagging its way past taxis that go up the Shankill to the lot of puttering taxis that go up the Falls.

Didn't the minder get bored walking the streets to the Ulster Museum and then watching me stare at the looms and machines and textiles that I found endlessly interesting? Did they sit, bored and annoyed, as I worked my way through piles of photographs at the Linenhall Library, along with all the other bookish folk and university students digging through papers and "source documents" trying to find another theory, another way to explain, understand, or speak of the source of hatred and conflict coexisting with such liveliness, richness, even value—could any of us accept and understand such painful contradiction? Did any of them—the minder, the electronic surveillance expert, the soldier (reader of "terrorist spotting leaflets"), the revolutionary—did any of them wince with regret when they saw the flicker I often saw in women's eyes?

One sunny day I am standing in a shopping mall watching a woman with a group of children. The "wains" stare into windows, they fiddle with merchandise, the woman scolds them, and they sass back. She is large, with a voice like gravel and a shape like an apple. Her face is haggard, her hair faded to a mousy brown, and her clothing has seen better days. Solid girl, I know. She is one you can depend on, but she is tired and worn down. *Did they see her eye exits with an escape plan in mind?* She wears no makeup but some fading lipstick, which, I am certain, stains the filters of her cigarettes—for I know she smokes. I admire her hands. She wears rings on every finger, and they give her, if only for a moment, a carefree look. These are the echo of her earlier hope to wander like a gypsy through the world, bumping into adventure, bringing back to the village her stories of faraway places, but gladly coming home to "the craic."

I can see, in the reflection of a nearby window, all the faces that make up this world she secretly longed to leave and then return to: an old man wearing a cap waits patiently for his wife outside a clothing store, a woman named Marie has thick red hair and a face with so many freckles you'd think she walked through a rain of them. Beside her, a handsome doctor straightens his tie, a young husband succumbs to his wife's reasoning over new furniture, a pair of teenagers ogle each other. My friend Pauline is running through the crowd, staying with the lengthy, eager strides of her daughters. A gang of boys egg each other on to acts of daring. And in the middle of this group I can see—like they are living toys in a ballet—three girls practicing Irish dance. They move up and down like springs, steady and solid, their curls bouncing around their shoulders. Another little girl balances upside down, like a monkey, at the edge of a bench. I want to jump forward, afraid she will fall. There's another who gets there before me. A toddler falls and cries with the shock of it, "Ach, you're all right, now," says his dad, picking him up, "you're all right." I see a white-haired window washer, a truck driver wearing a silver stud earring, students, and solicitors. I listen to the clack and drag of metal crutches, the slow healing of tender bones, the brutal scolding that veils fear of loss. It all seems to merge in the window, wiggling, like heat in a desert.

Could my minder notice? Did the camera catch what I did when the crowds got too thick and the overweary mom lost track of the kids? She is startled from a daydream and notices the crowd. Only in a place where the rug has been pulled out from under you so many times can an alarm bell be triggered by memory alone. Doing a quick head count, she tries to remember who she brought with her and wonders if anyone has wandered away. A little girl who knows too much too soon puts her hand inside the woman's and reassures her:

"It's okay, Mum, we're all still here."

The reflections wobble and shift once again. She wakes.

"So we are," she answers. In repetition it becomes resolution: "We're all still here."

Coda—Prelude

With a phrase that would define political upheaval the world over, William Butler Yeats described changes in twentieth-century Ireland by writing the line, "Things fall apart, the center cannot hold."

Such upheavals generate a diaspora—a scattering of peoples. It is such a pretty word, with such a simple definition. Diaspora almost appears to be a natural occurrence, the inevitable outcome of collapse. It suggests sad but necessary departure and dispersal. My family is part of the Irish diaspora. Our happiness and success say much about Ireland's capacities.

But contemporary northern Ireland has a different dispersal to overcome. Rather than a diaspora, northern Ireland and its political history have generated a community of exile. In the words of the Palestinian intellectual Edward Said, "Exile is strangely compelling to think about but terrible to experience. It is the unhealable rift forced between a human being and a native place. . . ." It is a form of banishment, a cutting of ties. It is painful. It is lonely. It is profoundly bitter. Communities of exile, Said notes, become accustomed to not belonging. If a diaspora has a celebratory return and reunion, exiles slip back into the landscape quietly.

Today, the "legacy of profound regret" expressed in the Good Friday Agreement is captured in the slumped shoulders of those exiled by legal and illegal means—pushed out by lawyers or racketeering, bombs or warrants. As political drama decreases, words like "over" and "end" deceive us into thinking that the 2001 and 2002 decommissioning of weapons is a coda to the dramatic excess of the Troubles. Such events are more a prelude to the quieter offering made by voices long suppressed—vocal chords warming to new tunes. Northern Ireland's new challenge, then, is a twist on that confronting the Republic. The diaspora's return helped rejuvenate the Irish Republic. Survivors and exiles have a tougher challenge, and optimism in such humbled circles appears too luxurious to embrace.

Lawyers, politicians, and gunmen have defined northern Ireland for much of its history. Removing the pretense of their cultural authority means there is much to gain in listening to the quieter voices hidden within the landscape.

Like the wildflowers springing up through rusty fences at old army bases, voices in the North may be less guarded now, conversations less coded, more true to people's earlier dreams. Survivors and exiles living together produce just such a rattling, discordant image as the flower and the barbed wire—it is the prickly, jagged experience of continuing after all.

Acknowledgments

It is difficult for writers of nonfiction and memoir to remember all their debts. We often find ourselves inspired by the most mundane daily experiences and conversations. The Irish are particularly interesting to listen to—so, to them all I owe thanks. In Belfast, I found numerous friends who were less concerned with my creative ambition than my all-round well-being and happiness. Among the many I thank are Theresa Burke, Joe McPartland, Noelle Houston, Jane Irving, Colin Spence, Marie McCallin, Trish O'Kane, and the many others who make up Northern Ireland's small but growing Buddhist community. Thanks also to another friend who gave me a place to sleep when I first arrived. Thanks to Mary Maw and Radha Patterson of Cargoes Café on the Lisburn Road, Annie, Gillian, and all the other girls there. Dennis and Rene Greig were a wonderful, informative resource for me and among the very first who welcomed me in Belfast. I thank them for their guidance and permission to use their words. Robert Crawford is a good employer but a better friend and a wonderful example of Northern generosity and kindness. Alison Henderson is a true friend and wonderful traveling companion. Thanks also to Eoin and Eva Bourke, generous hosts in Galway.

In Boston, Paul Wright was a trusted editor and stalwart campaigner in bringing this book to fruition. My aunt Clare Higgins was an important source of family history and stories and is a great example of the strength and beauty of Ireland's American diaspora. My parents and siblings are a never-ending source of humor and enthusiasm for my work. Kathy Harkin is a great friend who has "been there, done that" in Ireland and was always ready to talk to me about my own troubles. I am happy I bumped into Toshimi Hisamura in Belfast; we've been friends ever since. Esther Iwanaga paid my rent one cold winter month; all writers should have such kind friends. For listening to excerpts, thanks to Susan, Betsy, Kathy, Joanne, and Kevin, among others; also, thanks to Ellie Kutz, Marie Coleman, and the first-year students of University of Massachusetts Boston for listening in on "the craic."